THE ESSENTIAL
PAGEMAKER 5
FOR MACINTOSH AND WINDOWS

Robert Smyth

WYSiWYG

*What You See in the book
Is What You Get on screen*

Published by
WYSiWYG Books
Galway Technology Centre
Mervue Galway Ireland

Fax +353 (0)91–755635
Internet: wysiwyg@iol.ie

First published in July 1994

Copyright © Robert Smyth 1994

ISBN 1–898046–01–8

The moral rights of the author have been asserted under
the Copyright, Designs and Patents Act 1988.

British Library Cataloguing-in-Publication Data.
A catalogue record for this book is available from the British Library.

Designed and produced by the author.

Printed in Ireland by MICROPRINT.

*Dedicated to my
brothers, Pete and Tom.*

All rights reserved

No part of this publication
may be reproduced, recorded
or transmitted in any form or
by any means electronic or
mechanical, including
photocopying, without prior
permission in writing from the
publisher.

If you need to use Aldus PageMaker® but you don't have time to read the manuals or to study the program in detail, this book is for you. It explains, in an easy-to-follow format, all you need to know to begin using PageMaker 5 effectively.

Learning. When you need to use a new piece of software you can't always afford the luxury of spending time wading through manuals or wordy user guides. With more and more demands on your time, you need to master software quickly and efficiently.

This book is based on the assumption that, although you are busy and have other things to do, you would like to learn how to use PageMaker and that you need to do so in the quickest and easiest way possible.

It assumes that you are already familiar with the basics of using your computer (how to save and how to print, for example).

A WYSiWYG book. The Essential PageMaker is a concise, easy-to-follow, self-teaching guide that is organised specifically to allow you to get the most from this popular desktop publishing program with a minimum of effort. The book presents PageMaker as a series of topics, each of which explains how to use a particular feature of the program—how to rotate text and graphics, for example.

Each feature is explained on a single page so that you can learn quickly by not having too much to read—there are only a few hundred words on each page.

Turn it sideways! You do not have to be sitting at your computer to use this book. If you are, you will find the book very easy to follow. If you are not, it has been designed so that you can use the book itself as though it is the computer.

The book opens like a laptop computer—the upper page shows what you will see on the computer screen, and displays, visually, the steps you need to take. The supporting detailed explanation is on the lower page.

You don't need to have the computer in front of you as you learn.

Macintosh and Windows. Although the screen graphics throughout the book are taken from a Macintosh computer, they could just as easily have been taken from Windows—the program is now almost identical on both types of computer.

The main difference to watch out for in everyday use is that for the Macintosh COMMAND key you should use CONTROL under Windows and for the OPTION key use ALT.

Once you are familiar with PageMaker you will be able to use it both on Macintosh computers and on PCs under Windows.

While every care has been taken to ensure the accuracy of the information in this book, no liability for loss occasioned by any person acting or refraining from acting as a result of any statement in it can be accepted by the author or publisher.

Aldus and Aldus PageMaker are registered trademarks of Aldus Corporation. Apple and Macintosh are registered trademarks of Apple Computer Inc. Windows is a trademark of Microsoft Corporation.

Other products are referenced for identification purposes and are trademarks of their respective owners.

Contents

An introduction to the book and an overview of desktop publishing.

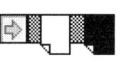

- i. About this book
- ii. Successful publications

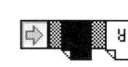

PageMaker fundamentals

The features of the program that everyone needs to know.

1. Starting up
2. A new publication
3. The publication window
4. Master pages
5. Putting text on a page
6. Viewing a page
7. Selecting objects
8. Modifying text blocks
9. Placing graphics
10. Page numbers
11. Saving and printing
12. Ruler guides
13. Changing settings
14. Help

Text in PageMaker

All you need to know to manage text on a page successfully.

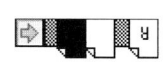

15. Formatting text
16. Basic text editing
17. Placing text efficiently
18. Formatting paragraphs
19. Leading
20. Text under control
21. Defining styles
22. Using styles
23. Style spin-offs
24. Text editing tools
25. Indents and tabs
26. Word spacing
27. Fonts

Graphics in PageMaker

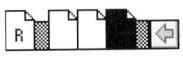

How to manipulate and control graphics to best effect.

28. Lines and fills
29. Graphics under control
30. Rotating and skewing
31. Using a scanner
32. Improving images
33. Graphics in text
34. Text around graphics
35. Building a library
36. Managing graphics

PageMaker in production

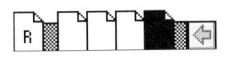

How to make PageMaker do most of the work for you.

37. Spot colour
38. Colour separation
39. Multiple publications
40. Managing pages
41. Text additions
42. Layout additions
43. Printing additions
44. Producing booklets
45. Longer publications
46. Preparing for print
47. Using an imagesetter
48. Working faster
49. Gaining in confidence
50. Where next?

A1. What's what?
A2. Function index

Index

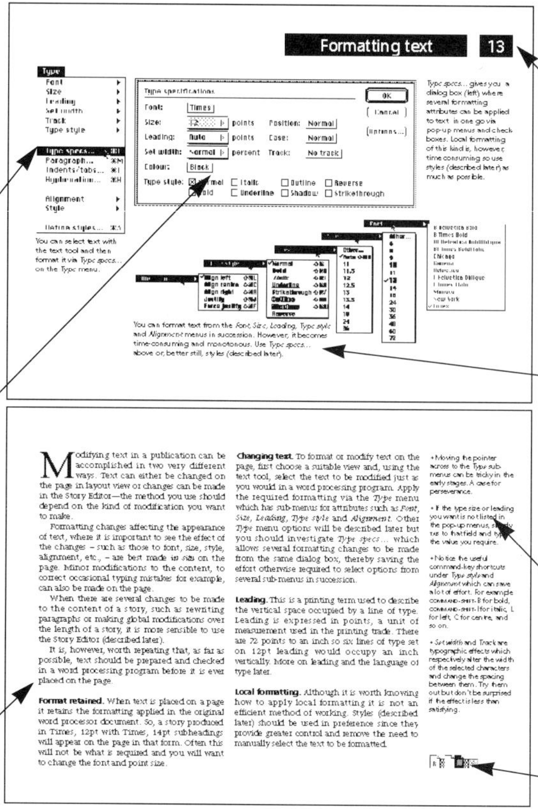

About this book

i

Formatting text | 13

Type specs... gives you a dialog box (left) where several formatting attributes can be applied to text in one go via pop-up menus and check boxes. Local formatting of the kind is, however, time-consuming so use styles (described later) as much as possible.

The number and title of the topic under discussion.

The relevant menu item is highlighted and is accompanied by a brief caption explaining what you should do.

The resulting dialog box where you choose the options you require.

Illustrations are supported by a brief explanation.

Efficiency techniques and hints are provided in this column.

The topic is explained in detail on the lower page.

The section icon with topic number repeated.

You will notice that each pair of facing pages in the book is devoted to a particular topic. To guide you visually through the program, the upper page shows pictures of what you will see on your computer screen, together with a brief explanation. The lower page explains the topic in detail. This format is designed for ease of use and to allow you to learn the program as quickly as possible.

To benefit from this format, scan the top page to get a visual appreciation of what is involved. Then, read the detailed description on the lower page. Finally, return to the top page again to consolidate what you have learned.

Structure. Topics are grouped into sections in a logical sequence. If you have the time, read the book from the beginning—you will develop a better understanding of the program. However, if you want to dip into the book or you are only an occasional user, the topic headings will help you to find information quickly.

The first section deals with PageMaker basics and is the foundation on which the remainder of the book is built—everyone should read this section. Section two explains how text is handled, and section three is concerned with graphics. The remainder of the book deals with PageMaker production issues and describes how you can get the most from the program.

Use the contents page to find topics quickly. An index to the features of the program is provided in an appendix, to help you find program options quickly.

Maximum benefit. Although there are different routes through the book, to get the most from it you should read the fundamentals section first and become familiar with its contents. Once you are comfortable with the basics, feel free to dip into the book as your needs dictate.

Assumptions. This book is written with the assumption that you need to use PageMaker to get something done. It assumes that you are new to PageMaker 5 but that you have used at least one other program and that you are familiar with the basics of your own computer (how to save and print your work, for example).

Version. The examples in the book are from PageMaker 5 for the Macintosh® running under System 7. However, because it deals with the essentials of the program, you can also use the book if you are using PageMaker 5 on an earlier version of the Macintosh system or on a PC under Windows.

• This column is used throughout the book to provide supplementary information outlining particular hints and techniques which will save you time and effort.

• To keep the book to its manageable size, obvious aspects (such as the keyboard shortcuts shown on menus) are not explained. Repetition, too, is avoided except when it is necessary to stress efficient use of the program.

• Manual layout methods are explained first to give you a chance to become familiar with the concepts involved. More powerful techniques are introduced gradually so that you can take control and get the program to work for you.

• Menu names and menu items are highlighted in *italic* type throughout.

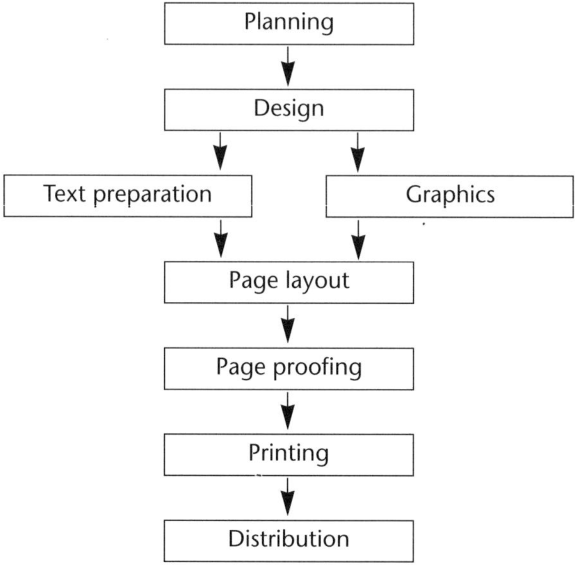

Successful publications ii

```
┌─────────────────┐
│    Planning     │
└─────────────────┘
         │
         ▼
┌─────────────────┐
│     Design      │
└─────────────────┘
    │         │
    ▼         ▼
┌──────────┐ ┌──────────┐
│   Text   │ │ Graphics │
│preparation│ │          │
└──────────┘ └──────────┘
    │         │
    ▼         ▼
┌─────────────────┐
│   Page layout   │
└─────────────────┘
         │
         ▼
┌─────────────────┐
│  Page proofing  │
└─────────────────┘
         │
         ▼
┌─────────────────┐
│    Printing     │
└─────────────────┘
         │
         ▼
┌─────────────────┐
│  Distribution   │
└─────────────────┘
```

The sequence of stages involved in producing a publication from start to finish. Note that steps are required before page layout begins and that there is also work to be done afterwards.

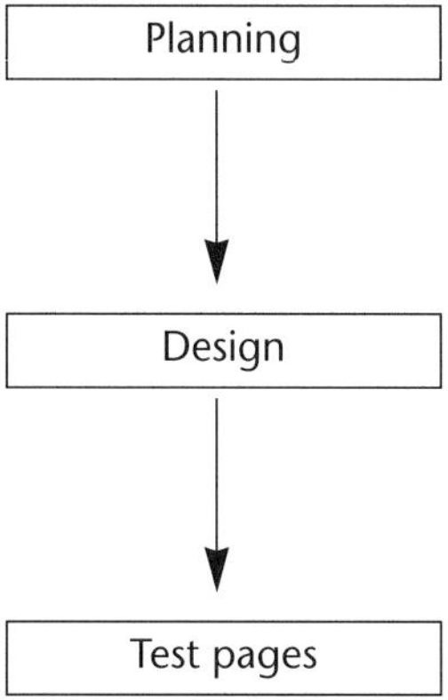

```
┌─────────────────┐
│    Planning     │
└─────────────────┘
         │
         ▼
┌─────────────────┐
│     Design      │
└─────────────────┘
         │
         ▼
┌─────────────────┐
│   Test pages    │
└─────────────────┘
```

To guard against complications and expensive mistakes, run some test pages through the process at an early stage (and show them to your printers).

When you have to produce large and complicated publications, you know instinctively that you need to spend time planning to get them right. But, even small and simple publications benefit from forward planning.

Although your main focus in using this book will be on learning how to use the tools provided in PageMaker 5, you will be encouraged to plan ahead, too, and to spend time getting some of the fine detail right. Time spent on these aspects of production are what separate successful publications from the mediocre.

Making decisions. To succeed with a publication you will first need to have a clear idea of its purpose and of its intended readership. Without that knowledge, how can you succeed? But, once you have clear objectives, you will find it easier to decide on the appropriate format and tone to use for the publication.

You will also need to be aware of budget constraints, of course, and of any technical considerations that might be involved which dictate, for example, choice of paper or typefaces to use.

You will need the same answers even if you decide to use a designer to plan or produce your publication for you—these are likely to be the first questions you will be asked.

The production process. Each stage in the production process is itself a process. For example, the production of text involves writing it in the first place, then editing and proof reading it until it suits its purpose, and finally preparing it in a form suitable for PageMaker (in a word processor).

There are usually many people involved in the production of larger publications, each with clear responsibilities at particular stages. You need to be aware of these stages, particularly if you are responsible for production or if you are producing a publication yourself.

It is important, for example, to edit and proof-read text at the word processing stage rather than wait until it reaches its final form on the page. Changes at that late stage can cause unnecessary delay or, even worse, can force you to reconstruct pages all over again.

Your printers. It is important to discuss design and production decisions with your printers. Good printers will discuss your requirements with you and be willing to suggest ways in which you might be able to cut costs. Such discussions can also be helpful in identifying potentially costly mistakes.

Above all, take some sample pages all the way through the production process at an early stage. By doing so you can often highlight production problems (software or font incompatibilities, for example) before it is too late.

• Don't be afraid to discuss the design and format of your publications at various stages during production—you might get a few adverse comments, but you will be surprised at how many helpful suggestions you get for improvement.

• Similarly with writing. The more important a publication is, the more others should be given the opportunity to comment on it. If you let people see early drafts you will find it easier to accept criticism. Besides, the last thing you want is to let mistakes slip through.

• Pay particular attention to the advice given at various stages in this book about using PageMaker efficiently—it makes more sense to learn how to make the program work for you rather than to develop laborious and time-consuming habits.

Starting up　　1

About This Macintosh...

Suitcase	⌘K
.Programs	▶
ClickPaste	
HomeLetter	
Monitors	
Scrapbook	
Super Boomerang	▶
SystemFolders	▶

About This Macintosh

Macintosh II

System Software Z-7.0 ●
© Apple Computer, Inc. 1983-1991

Total Memory :　8,192K　　Largest Unused Block :　2,733K

ClarisWorks	900K	
Microsoft Word	2,048K	
System Software	2,468K	

— System software version.

— Total RAM installed and amount currently free.

— Amount of memory each active program is using.

Before you start PageMaker, choose *About this Macintosh...* (System 7) or *About the Finder...* (System 6) from the *Apple* menu if you need to find out what System software versions you are using.

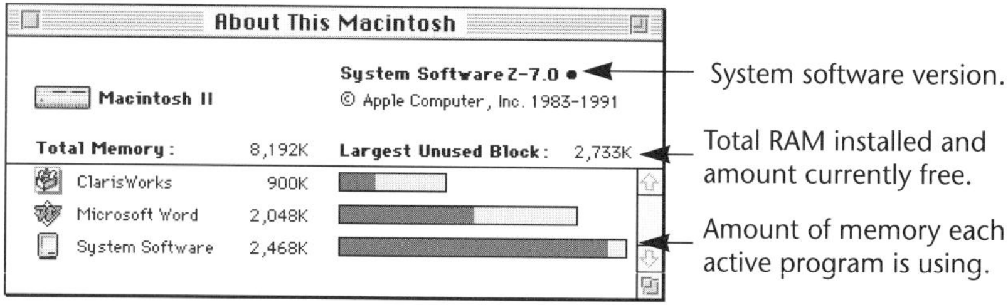

Aldus PageMaker 5.0

Double-click the PageMaker icon (above) to start the program.

OK

Robert Smyth
WYSIWYG Books
00-0000-000000000

MPM5000000000000
1
623284 bytes free
System version 7.00

ALDUS. PAGEMAKER. 5.0

When the program is running, choose *About PageMaker®...* on the *Apple* menu (below) if you need to confirm the version of PageMaker you are using or the serial number of your copy of the program.

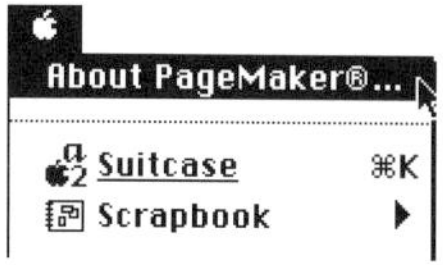

About PageMaker®...

Suitcase	⌘K
Scrapbook	▶

As the program starts up, a banner screen is displayed which shows the version number of the program and its serial number, and the name of the person to whom the copy is registered. A similar screen (above) is displayed when you choose *About PageMaker...* once the program is running.

Although it is possible to use PageMaker to write, edit, design and produce your publications, it is more usual to use a suite of programs and to take advantage of the strengths of each program at different stages. Typically, you will use a word processor to produce text and an illustration program for graphics, in addition to using PageMaker for design and production.

It makes sense, therefore, to prepare text and graphics in other programs and to check them for accuracy before you capitalise on PageMaker's strengths for layout work.

Strengths. If you are new to publishing you will find that PageMaker is easy to learn and that it works in a way that is not difficult to understand. It becomes more intuitive as you use it—each new feature works in the way you would expect and is, therefore, easier to assimilate.

If you already have a background in publishing you will find that PageMaker offers features to meet the most exacting of standards.

Before you begin. This book makes reference to particular versions of the System software from time to time. Since you might not be using your own computer (and even if you are!) you will find it worthwhile to know what version of PageMaker you are using and to know something about the System environment in which you are working.

Software versions. Choose *About this Macintosh…* or *About the Finder…* on the *Apple* menu to find the version number of the System software you are using and the amount of internal memory (RAM) you have available. With a window open, choose *View by Icon* from the *View* menu to display the size of the hard disk and the free space available.

If the version of PageMaker you are using is unclear, select the PageMaker icon by clicking on it once and choose *Get Info* from the *File* menu. The program version is also shown as it starts up or can be found by selecting *About PageMaker…* from the *Apple* menu while it is running (this also shows the serial number).

Installation. This book assumes that you have already installed PageMaker, or that you are using a computer on which it is available—at college or at work, for example. If it has not been installed, follow the straightforward instructions explained in the manual. Appendix 1 shows a summary of PageMaker's components so that you can check that the program has been installed correctly if you encounter problems.

Launch. Locate the PageMaker icon and double-click it to start the program.

• The recommended configuration for PageMaker 5 is 5 to 8Mb RAM with 13Mb hard disk space, preferably running under System 7. Windows 3.1 is required to run PageMaker 5 on a PC.

• It is best to leave items where they have been installed to avoid possible confusion later.

• It is also be possible to start the program from the *Apple* menu on System 7 by putting an alias to PageMaker in the Apple Menu Items folder.

• If you need to contact Technical Support to discuss a problem, you will be asked for the registered serial number of the program. You will find it in the *About PageMaker…* box under the *Apple* menu.

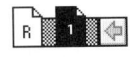

A new publication

2

File
New... ⌘N
Open... ⌘O
Close
Save ⌘S
Save as...
Revert
Export...
Place... ⌘D
Links... ⌘=
Book...
Preferences...
Page setup...
Print... ⌘P
Quit ⌘Q

Page setup

Page: [A4]

Page dimensions: [210] by [297] mm

Orientation: ◉ Tall   ○ Wide

Start page #: [1]   Number of pages: [1]

Options: ☒ Double-sided   ☒ Facing pages
☐ Restart page numbering

Margin in mm: Inside [25]   Outside [20]
Top [20]   Bottom [20]

Target printer resolution: [300] ▷ dpi

[OK]
[Cancel]
[Numbers...]

The values you type and the options you choose can be changed later, if necessary—you can choose *Page setup...* from the *File* menu to return to the Page setup box, at any time, to make changes.

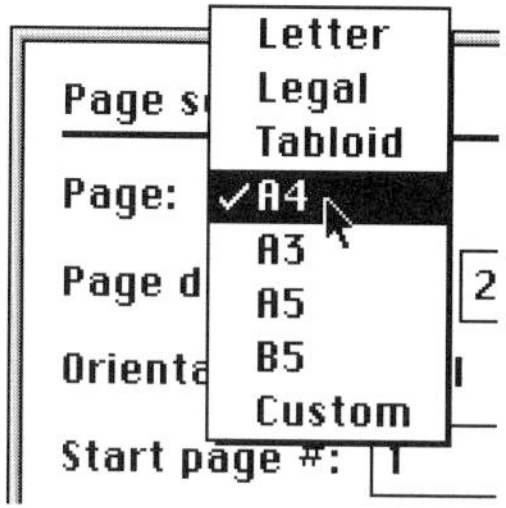

Choose *New...* from the *File* menu to start on a new publication. You are presented with the Page setup box where you can define the page structure you require.

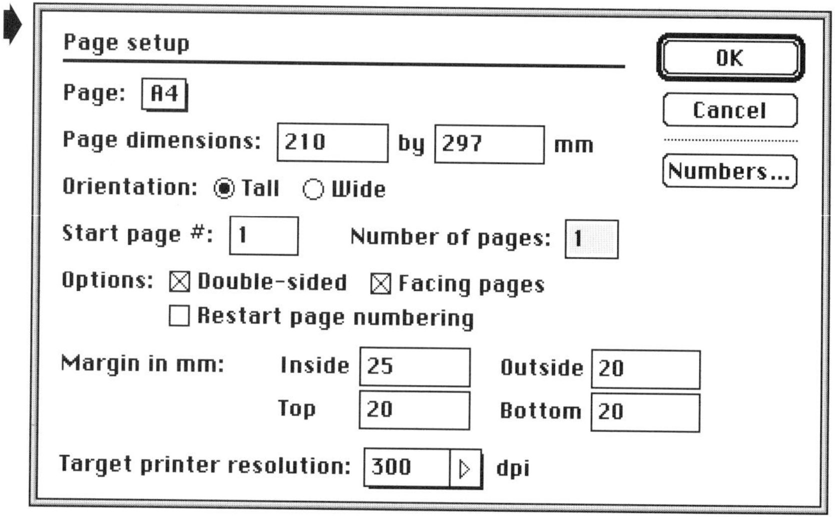

The Page setup dialog box. Type the values and select the options you require for your publication. Choose Tall for a portrait-shaped publication or Wide for landscape orientation. To ensure that bit-mapped images (paint-type) are resized correctly if you alter them, you should choose the resolution at which your document will finally be printed from the Target printer resolution pop-up menu. The additional Compose to printer option under Windows ensures that the correct fonts are available.

Page s...
Page: ✓A4
Letter
Legal
Tabloid
A3
A5
B5
Custom
Page d... [2]
Orienta...
Start page #: [1]

You can select a standard page size from the Page: pop-up menu (left). Or, type specific values (width by height) into these fields yourself. If you are not familiar with these page sizes, choose one at a time and its size will be shown in the Page dimensions fields.

S‍tart PageMaker by double-clicking its icon. After the credit banner is displayed, the program's menu bar appears and you can begin working on a new document.

New document. To create a document, choose *New...* from the *File* menu and the Page setup dialog box appears. It is here that you specify the overall structure of your publication—page size, number of pages, margins, etc.

What you specify can be changed later: for example, you can add or delete pages when you have started work on the publication. However, time spent thinking about the purpose and overall structure of your document before you begin to construct it is time well spent and will save you effort later.

Page structure. You can use the page setup values automatically provided by the program or, if you feel confident enough and have a particular publication in mind, you can change them to suit your needs. Change them by typing the values you want into the relevant boxes (fields) and by changing button and check-box settings. Click with the mouse to position the insertion cursor within the field you want to change or click the appropriate buttons and check boxes.

Note that the page size can be selected from a pop-up menu which gives you access to a set of standard page sizes. If you need a non-standard size, simply type the values you need (width by height) in the Page dimensions fields.

Measurement units. You can use different units of measurement within the program—inches, millimetres, picas, etc. If the unit of measurement in use does not suit you, change it by choosing *Preferences...* from the *File* menu. The subject of preferences, and program and document settings, will be discussed in detail later.

Double-sided. Check the Double-sided option if your document is eventually going to be printed back-to-back. The Left and Right margin fields change to Inside and Outside to ensure consistency.

The Facing pages option allows you to view side-by-side pages (called a spread) together on screen, for example pages 2 and 3, and is only relevant in double-sided publications.

Page number format. The Numbers... button gives you access to a dialog box which allows you to set the kind of page numbers you want within the document—arabic, roman, etc. This is described in more detail later under page numbering.

OK. When you click OK in the page setup box, the PageMaker window appears.

• To help prevent unauthorised use of the program, PageMaker checks the network to see if the number of copies of the program in use exceeds the number licensed. If so, then this Network Copy Detection will deny you access.

• Use the TAB key to move from field to field when you want to change values—it's quicker than going from keyboard to mouse and back again. The contents of the field are also selected for you so you do not even need to use the DELETE key before typing new values.

• The target printer resolution should be that of the printer on which you intend eventually to produce masters for volume printing. The resolution specified can help to ensure that you resize bit-mapped graphics appropriately for a specific printer.

The publication window 3

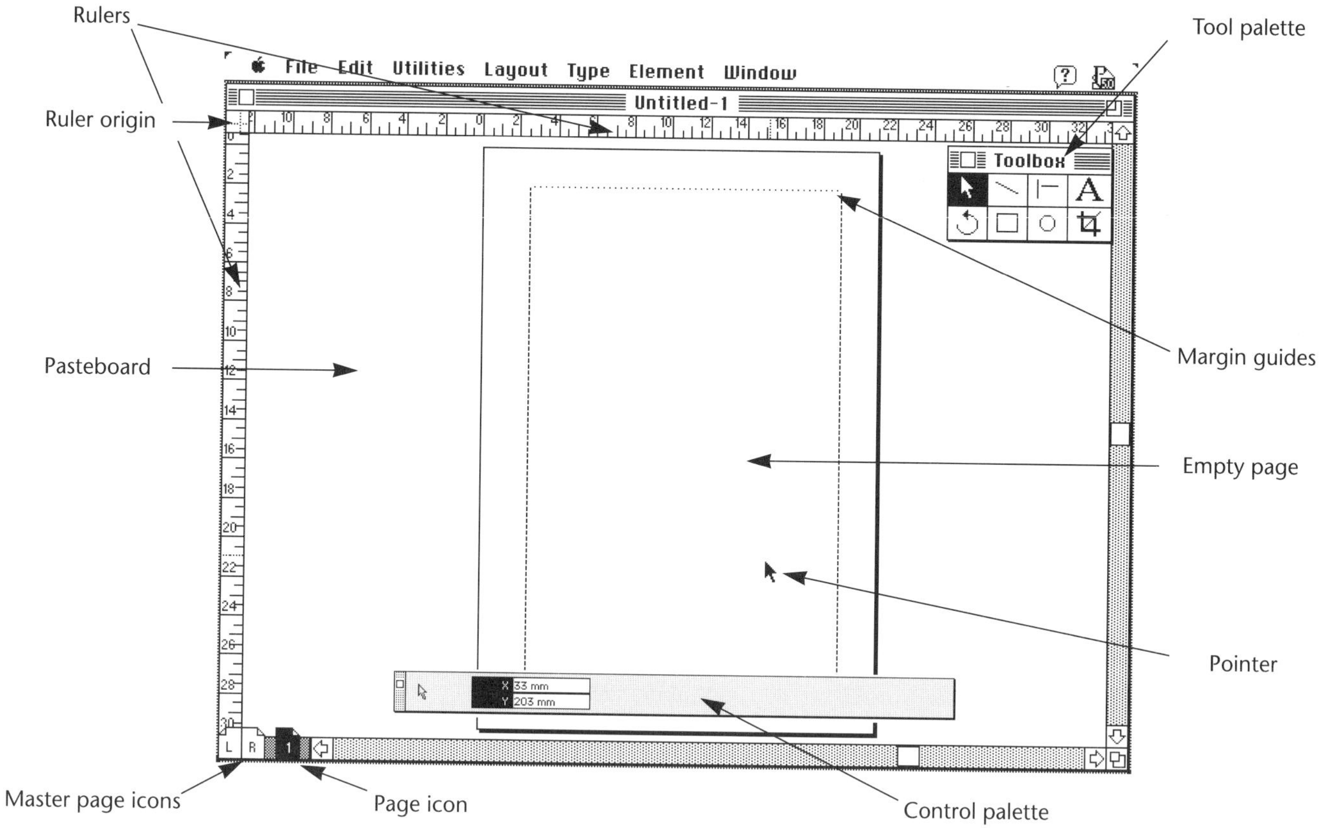

Rulers

Ruler origin

Pasteboard

Master page icons

Page icon

Tool palette

Margin guides

Empty page

Pointer

Control palette

File Edit Utilities Layout Type Element Window

Untitled-1

Toolbox

L R 1

X 33 mm
Y 203 mm

Once you click OK in the page setup box, the PageMaker window appears. The window shows an empty page with the margins and structure you defined in the page setup box. Margin guides are shown to assist you with your layout work and are not printed.

The page is positioned on a pasteboard—an area you can use for rough work and to position items temporarily while you are constructing pages. Items on the pasteboard are not printed.

Horizontal and vertical rulers are provided along the top and to the left of the window. To the top left is the ruler origin—you can drag it from there to any location on the page for measurement or alignment. Scroll bars are in the usual place.

Page icons. Note in particular the page icons at the bottom left corner of the window. Clicking on a particular page icon is the easiest way of moving from one page to another in the early stages.

The 'L' and 'R' icons (the 'R' icon only is visible in single-sided publications) represent what are called the master pages. Anything which is to appear on all pages of the publication – page numbers, headers, footers, number of columns, etc. – should be placed on these notional pages (think of them as a separate background layer for each page). If you don't use master pages, you will have to manually position repeating items on each page individually.

Tools. The Toolbox shows the tools provided within PageMaker. Left to right they are:

▶ **Pointer**
(to select text blocks and graphics)

◸ **Diagonal line**
(to draw lines at ANY angle)

⊢ **Perpendicular line**
(to draw vertical, horizontal and 45° lines)

A **Text tool**
(to add, edit and format text)

↻ **Rotation tool**
(to select and rotate text blocks and graphics)

▢ **Rectangle tool**
(to draw rectangles and squares)

◯ **Oval tool**
(to draw ovals and circles)

⌗ **Cropping tool**
(to trim graphics)

Choosing a tool. You select the tool you need by clicking on its icon within the toolbox. So, for example, to draw a vertical line (also called a rule) on a page you first select the perpendicular line tool and then proceed to draw the line (in the usual way by clicking on the start position and dragging to the end position).

• Additional palettes may be visible in the window— these are explained later.

• If the Toolbox is not visible, or you close it by accident, choose *Tool palette* from the *Window* menu to make it visible.

• Note that the outside edges of the page have a shadow—this can be a useful clue to your location on the page when you work in a close-up view.

• To draw squares and circles, hold down the SHIFT key when you use the rectangle and oval drawing tools.

• You can drag a cross-hair cursor from the ruler origin box (top left of window) to zero the ruler origins on a particular part of a page. To reset the origins back to their normal place (top left corner on single pages and centre top on spreads), double-click on the ruler origin box.

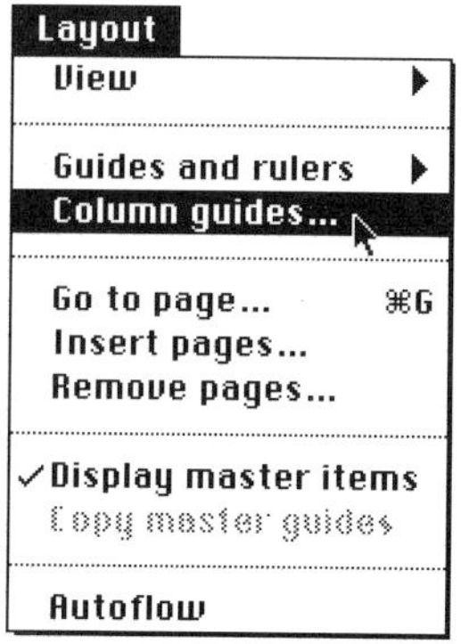

Master pages

4

Layout

View ▶

Guides and rulers ▶
Column guides...

Go to page... ⌘G
Insert pages...
Remove pages...

✓Display master items
Copy master guides

Autoflow

Column guides

OK

Cancel

Both

Number of columns: 3

Space between columns: 5 mm

☐ Set left and right pages separately

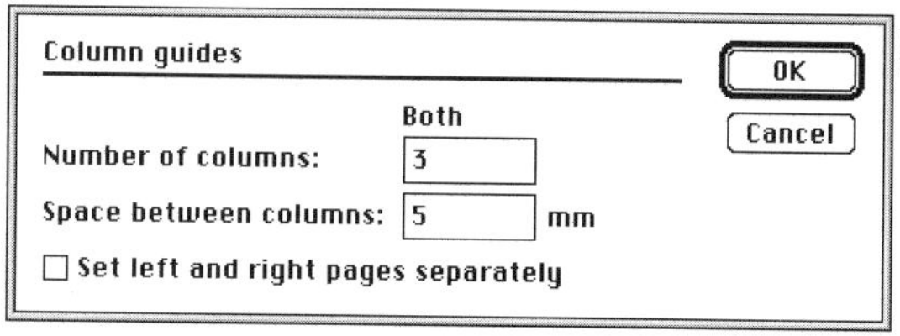

Type the number of columns you require (above). With facing pages open on screen, click on the 'set left and right' check box if you want to vary the column settings on opposite pages: separate fields then appear for left and right pages.

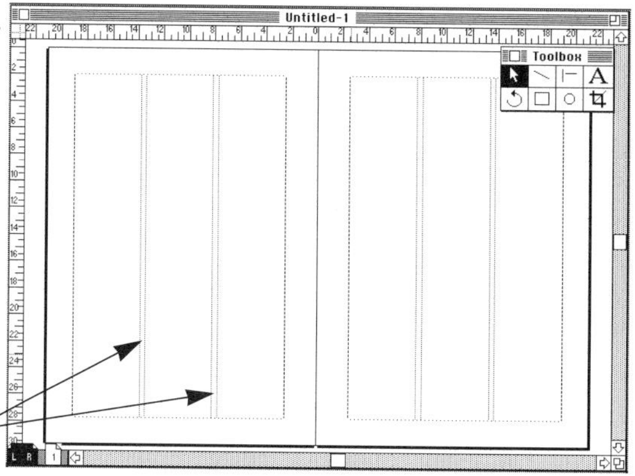

To construct columns for text, move to the master pages and choose *Column guides...* from the *Layout* menu (above) to display the Column guides box.

Column guides

Facing master pages (above) showing guides for three columns on each page.

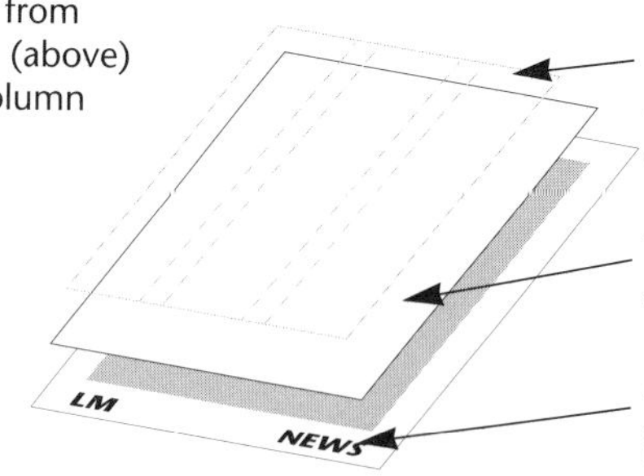

Column guide layer. Guides are not fixed and can be moved manually.

The page you are constructing.

'Pre-printed' master page layer underneath.

Master pages (above) are like a pre-printed background layer on which you construct your page. Column guides are on a separate layer.

Single-sided publications have one master page icon (right); double-sided documents have two. The page icon is highlighted when you move to a page. On double-sided and facing master pages, both icons are highlighted. To move to another page, click its icon (bottom right).

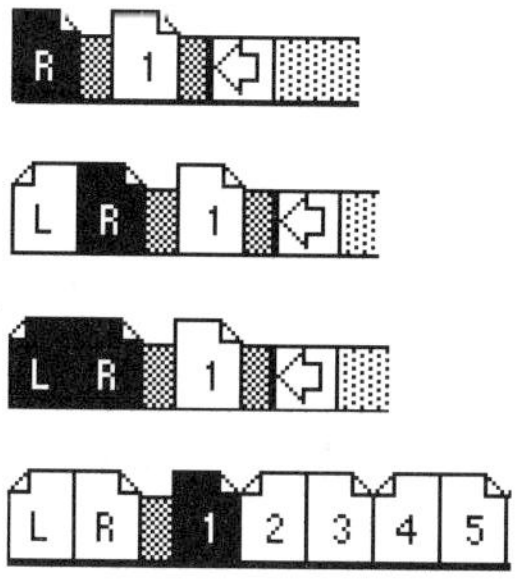

Since they are not 'real' pages, the concept of master pages can be confusing. Think of them as something like headers and footers in word processing documents, except that elements can be positioned on any part of the page – not just the top and bottom – as a separate background layer.

Click on the master page icon (mini pages with 'L' or 'R' for Left and Right) at the bottom left corner of the publication window. When you do so you move to the master pages—empty pages on which you put the items (text and graphics) you want to appear on every page in your document. The master page icons are highlighted to show you that you are currently working on those pages.

Don't forget! One of the early hurdles for beginners is remembering to make use of the master pages to save effort and then to return to the publication proper before starting on a page. Don't be surprised to find yourself re-doing master pages because you put master items like page numbers or lines on page '1' by mistake, or rebuilding a page because you forgot to move from the master page (we have all done it!).

Creating columns. Along with page numbers (which will be discussed later), one of the most common requirements in a publication is for text to flow in columns. While it is possible to construct columns on individual pages, it would be wasteful of your effort. It is far more efficient to position column guides once on the master pages—they are then available on every page.

Apart from saving effort, columns on the master pages aid consistency throughout the publication – an important design consideration – since they are set up only once and will not, therefore, vary from page to page.

For example, to construct three columns into which you will later flow text, choose *Column guides...* from the *Layout* menu and type 3 in the Number of columns box and click OK. If you make a mistake choose *Column guides* ... again.

Once you are satisfied with the master pages, return to the publication proper by clicking on the page '1' icon.

Save regularly. Get into the habit of saving the document once you have completed the master pages. Do this by using *Save* from the *File* menu. Saving will be discussed in more detail later.

Preparation. You are now ready to bring text onto the page. You will normally have produced and corrected the text in a word processor. PageMaker has its own story editor (discussed later) which can also be used.

- To move to a particular page, click on its icon.

- Putting column guides on the master pages does not necessarily lock you in to that arrangement on every page. You can use *Column guides...* again to override master settings on individual pages.

- You can remove master page items from particular pages (title pages, for example) by unchecking *Display master items* on the *Layout* menu.

- If you specify a double-sided publication in the page setup box, two master page icons will be visible—one for left-hand pages and one for right-hand pages. If you choose not to have Facing pages you can click on the icons individually to construct left and right master pages. For single-sided publications there is only one master page.

Putting text on a page — 5

File

New...	⌘N
Open...	⌘O
Close	
Save	⌘S
Save as...	
Revert	
Export...	
Place...	**⌘D**
Links...	⌘=
Book...	
Preferences...	
Page setup...	
Print...	⌘P
Quit	⌘Q

To bring text onto the page, choose *Place...* from the *File* menu.

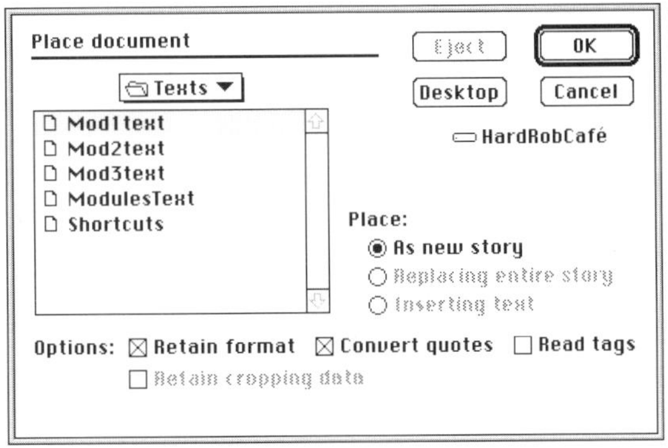

Place document

[Eject] [OK]

🗀 Texts ▼   [Desktop] [Cancel]

▢ Mod1text
▢ Mod2text
▢ Mod3text
▢ ModulesText
▢ Shortcuts

▱ HardRobCafé

Place:
◉ As new story
○ *Replacing entire story*
○ *Inserting text*

Options: ☒ Retain format   ☒ Convert quotes   ☐ Read tags
☐ *Retain cropping data*

The text is 'loaded' into the pointer so you can manually position it on the page.

For now, switch off *Autoflow* on the *Layout* menu if this icon appears.

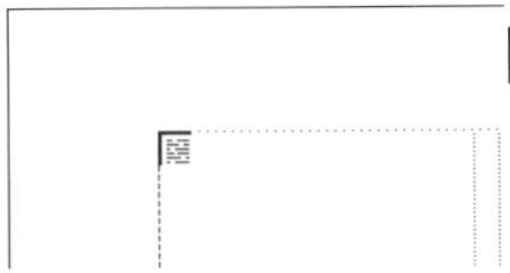

In the dialog box, select the file containing text to be placed (left).

Click with the loaded-text pointer in the top-left corner of the first column to position text within that column. Make sure that you click between the column guides (i.e. not outside).

Then load the next portion of text by clicking on the arrow at the bottom of the text block and click this text into position in the next column.

Continue until all the text has been placed (i.e. the last windowshade handle is empty).

When you have prepared the master pages you can start to construct your publication. You will usually begin by bringing in text that you have produced and saved in a word processor, and then add graphics from an illustration program.

Move to page. First, make sure you are not still on the master pages. If you are, move to the first page by clicking on the icon for page one in the bottom left-hand corner of the window.

See if *Autoflow* is ticked (i.e. switched on) in the *Layout* menu. If it is, switch it off for now by selecting it again.

Placing text. To bring text into a publication choose *Place…* from the *File* menu and select the document containing the text from the dialog box that follows.

PageMaker then imports the text and the pointer changes to a 'loaded-text' icon. Position the loaded pointer at the top left corner of the first column (or at any other position on the page where you want to place the text) and click—text flows between the column guides.

To load the next portion of text, click on the downward-pointing arrow at the bottom of the column of text (which indicates that there is more text to place). The pointer again changes to the loaded icon which you can then click at the top of the next column to place the next part of the story (text within PageMaker is referred to as a story). If there is more text to place, click again on the downward pointing arrow at the bottom of the second column to load it and continue until all of the story has been placed.

If you have more text to place when you reach the end of the page, click to pick up the text in the loaded pointer and then move to the next page by clicking on its icon (when you move over the page icons the arrow pointer temporarily appears; the loaded-text pointer returns again when you move back). If there is no page following, add one by choosing *Insert pages…* from the *Layout* menu (this will be discussed again later).

Text blocks. As you place text, notice the way PageMaker differentiates between text blocks. The handles at the beginning and end of a story are empty. Intermediate handles show a plus (+) sign to indicate, at the top of a text block, that there is preceding text and, at the bottom of a text block, to show that there is text following.

Titles and captions. You can also type text directly onto a page by selecting the text tool and clicking in a column to position the text insertion cursor. You can then begin typing. This method should only be used for headings or small portions of text and will be discussed in more detail later.

• Accurately clicking on the downward arrow can be tricky at first. Persevere!

• If you need to unload the text cursor, click it on any tool in the toolbox.

• It is much easier to place text accurately when *Snap to guides* on the *Guides and rulers* submenu of the *Layout* menu is checked.

• Ensure the Retain format option in the *Place…* box is checked so that text formatting applied in a word processor (such as font, size and type style) is retained on transfer.

• Proof text before you *Place…* it or you will waste time readjusting text and layouts on the page.

• To place text from a word processor, a filter for that WP must be installed in the Aldus folder.

• Click SHIFT-OK in the *Place…* box to see specific filter options (if any).

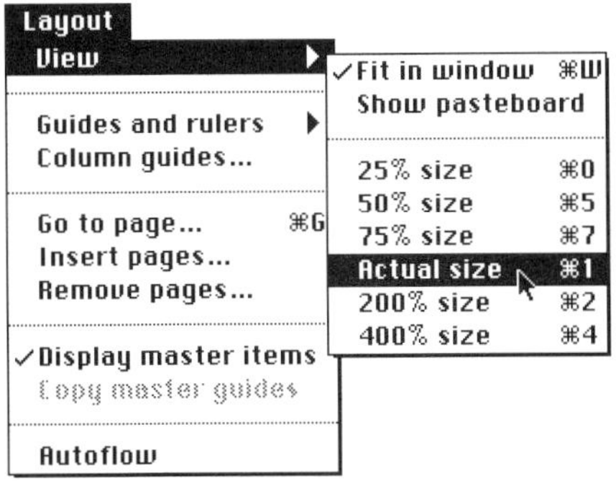

Viewing a page 6

Layout
View ▶
- ✓ **Fit in window** ⌘W
- **Show pasteboard**

- **Guides and rulers** ▶
- **Column guides...**

- **Go to page...** ⌘G
- **Insert pages...**
- **Remove pages...**

- ✓ **Display master items**
- **Copy master guides**

- **Autoflow**

- **25% size** ⌘0
- **50% size** ⌘5
- **75% size** ⌘7
- **Actual size** ⌘1
- **200% size** ⌘2
- **400% size** ⌘4

When you view the page in actual size you can read the text. A flashing vertical bar shows the insertion point. |

To view the page at different magnifications, choose the size you want from the *View* submenu of the *Layout* menu.

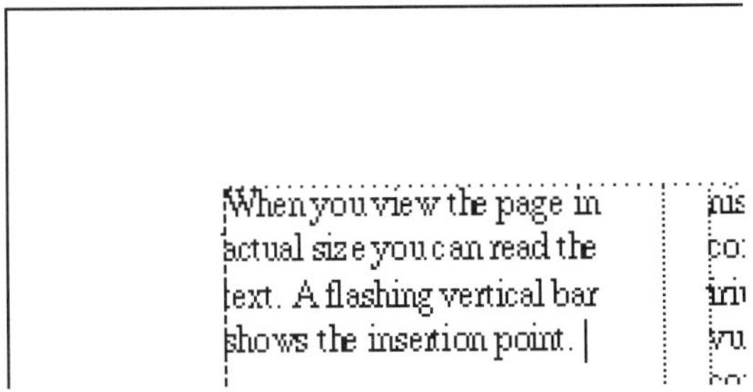

Two views of the same page. The top-left corner shown in *Actual size* (above) and *Fit in window* (right) showing the whole page. Notice that the text is greyed-out (called greeking) in the *Fit in window* view.

Zoom to an 800% view (right) not on the *View* menu by holding down COMMAND (CTRL under Windows) and SPACE (in that order). The pointer changes to a magnifying glass with which you can drag-zoom on the area you want to view. Hold down COMMAND-SPACE-OPTION (CTRL-SPACE-ALT under Windows) to zoom out again.

When you need the highest magnification, if you hold down the COMMAND key and then the SPACE key a magnifying glass pointer appears with which you can click or drag on the location you want.

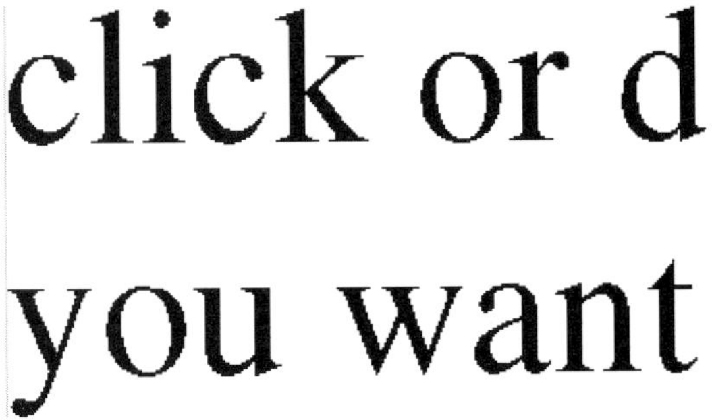

click or d
you want

New publications open at the *Fit in window* view, showing the whole page or facing pages. From this viewpoint you can clearly see the overall structure of the page (number of columns, margins, etc.). With a little practice, you can place text and graphics fairly accurately in this view. However, unless you are working on a large monitor, text in the *Fit in window* view is greyed out (called greeking) so that the page can be displayed faster on screen.

Page views. To read text on a page you will need to change to a more suitable view by selecting one from the *View* submenu of the *Layout* menu. Once you have placed some text on a page, try out the different views to become familiar with them – their names are self-explanatory. You will find that you need to scroll the window using the scroll-bars to get to particular parts of the page when you use the close-up views.

Keyboard shortcuts are provided for each view and these are shown on the *View* submenu.

View shortcuts. Other useful keyboard shortcuts are available, besides those on the *View* submenu.

If you hold down the OPTION key as you choose a view from the *View* submenu, you change all pages to that view.

SHIFT-click on the page icon as another shortcut to the *Fit in window* view.

Zoom with accuracy. You can save scrolling effort on a Macintosh if you use COMMAND-OPTION-click to move around a page. This keyboard shortcut takes you from the *Fit in window* view to *Actual size* or from *Actual size* back to *Fit in window*. The right mouse button does the same under Windows.

The advantage of using this method is that you zoom in on the page at the point where you click the cursor.

It takes a bit of practice to get it right—press and hold down the COMMAND key, then do the same with the OPTION key and (while you have both keys pressed down) click the mouse button.

In the same way, COMMAND-OPTION-SHIFT-click will allow you to get to the 200% view and back to *Actual size*. Press SHIFT while clicking the right mouse button to do the same under Windows.

Close-up zoom. For close-up magnification, hold down first the COMMAND key (CTRL under Windows) and then the SPACE key, and click on the area you want to view. You can keep repeating this shortcut until you reach 800% magnification (not shown on the *View* submenu).

Pasteboard. Sometimes you will want to view the whole pasteboard (usually because you have mislaid something!). You can do so by choosing the *Show pasteboard* view.

• *Place...* text on the page before experimenting with the different page views, otherwise you will have difficulty knowing where you are on the page.

• As an alternative to scroll bars, if you hold down the OPTION key as you click the mouse you can slide the page with a grabber hand.

• You can place text in views other than *Fit in window* but you might then need to navigate the page to find the handles at the bottom of text blocks.

• On complex pages it is often quicker to zoom out and then in again than to scroll around the page.

• Although you can edit text on the page, the story editor is often more appropriate.

• You can use the zoom shortcuts with any tool selected.

Selecting objects   7

Edit

Cannot undo	⌘Z
Cut	⌘X
Copy	⌘C
Paste	⌘V
Clear	
Multiple paste...	
Select all	⌘A
Editions	▶
Paste link	
Paste special...	
Insert object...	
Edit story	⌘E
Edit original	

When you use *Select all* from the *Edit* menu it is important to select the correct tool first.

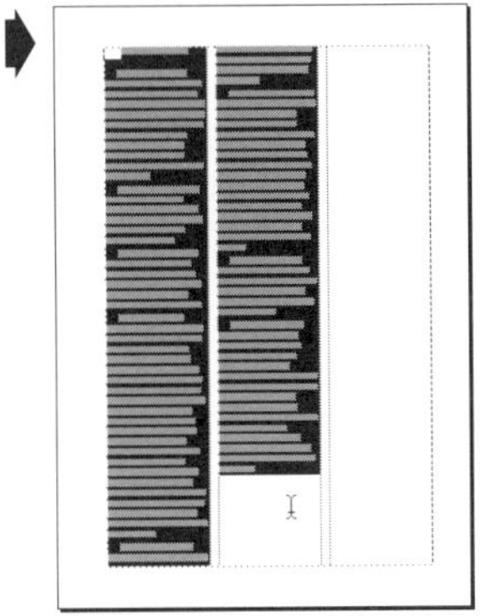

To apply a typographic change to a complete story (above), click with the text tool to position the text cursor within the story first.

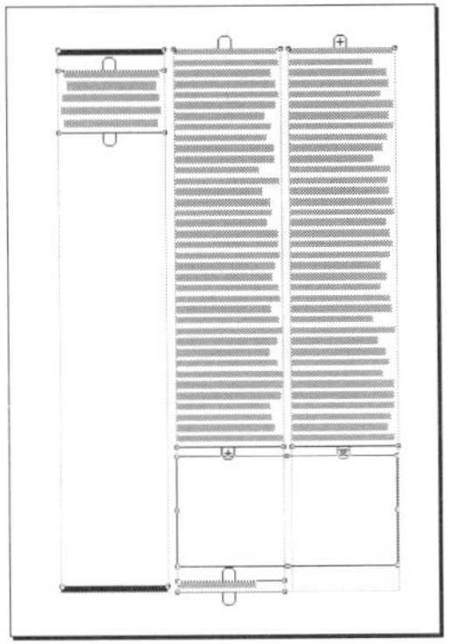

Use the pointer tool to select everything (above) on a page (and on the pasteboard).

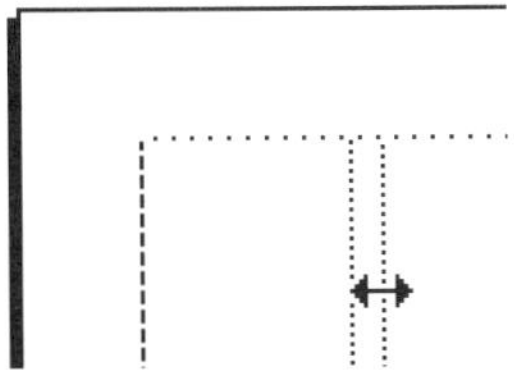

Text is selected, using the text tool, by dragging across it or by using a selection shortcut such as two clicks to select a **word** or three clicks to select a paragraph.

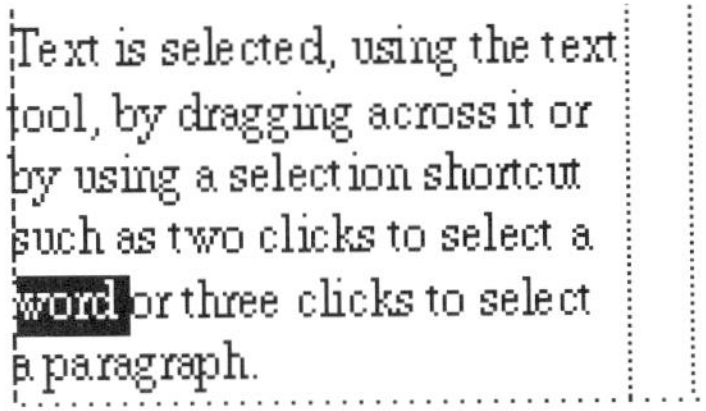

You must use the text tool to modify text on a page. Select text (with the I-beam text cursor) as you would in a word processor (above).

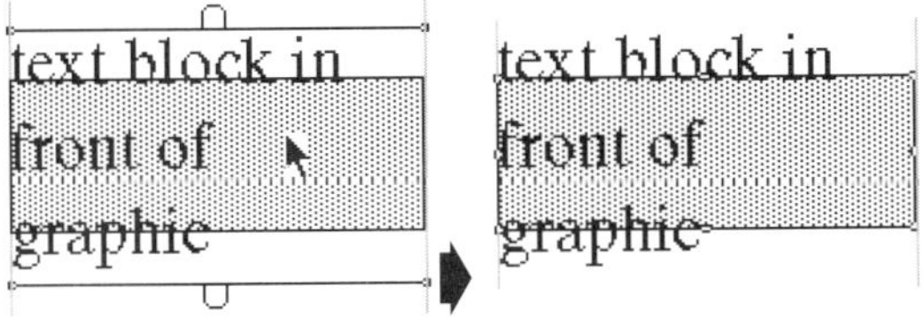

text block in front of graphic   text block in front of graphic

Hold down the COMMAND key (Macintosh) or CTRL key (Windows) and click with the pointer to select an object obscured by another (above) or to move down through layers of objects.

You can also select an object and change its stacking order using *Bring to front* or *Send to back* on the *Element* menu.

Move a column guide by clicking and dragging it (right). You might need to zoom in for accuracy.

To modify or move a text block or graphic, you must first select it. This you usually do by clicking on it with the pointer tool. Once you have selected the object, you can drag it to a new location or modify it using the appropriate menu item—you can also use the Control palette. To select the text inside a text block, you must use the text tool.

If you are going to rotate a text block or graphic, you can save time by clicking on it with the rotating tool to select it instead.

Selection. PageMaker allows the usual selection methods: click to select and SHIFT-click to select multiple items. You can select multiple objects by clicking just outside them in one corner and dragging to the opposite corner. Objects contained within the defined area are selected. *Select all* is also provided on the *Edit* menu.

To deselect objects that are selected, click on an empty space on the page (or pasteboard) or click to select something else.

Layers. Sometimes objects on a page overlap—a text block might be obscuring a graphic that you are trying to select, for example. If you hold down the COMMAND key (the CTRL key under Windows) before you click on an object, you can move through the individual layers to select an object underneath.

Modifying text. To edit and format text you need to choose a view that allows you to see and read the text comfortably.

To make changes you must first select the text tool by clicking on it (the letter A in the toolbox). The pointer changes to the text cursor (an I-beam) which you can then use to select individual words. Selected text is highlighted and can be formatted as in a word processor.

To select a word (and the space after it), double-click on the word. To select a complete paragraph, triple-click within it.

Click to position the cursor within a story and choose *Select all* from the *Edit* menu to select a complete story, parts of which may even be on other pages or not yet placed.

Columns. You can create asymmetric column guides on a page by clicking on individual guides and dragging them to a particular location. It is sensible then to *Lock guides* (on the *Guides and rulers* submenu of the *Layout* menu).

Cropping. Select the cropping tool in the Toolbox and then click with it to select a picture or graphic whose size or shape you want to trim.

• If you are unable to select all of the text in a story, make sure that you have clicked first with the text tool to position the text cursor in that story.

• Although you can use the text tool to make minor corrections on the page, it is better to use the story editor to edit text.

• *Bring to front* on the *Element* menu and *Send to back* can be used to move objects to the front or back layer.

• Occasionally guides get in the way (you move them accidentally when trying to select something else). If this happens you can lock them into position using *Lock guides* on the *Guides and rulers* submenu of the *Layout* menu, or send them to the back layer using *Preferences…* on the *File* menu.

Modifying text blocks | 8

The windowshade handle at the beginning of a story is empty.

Text blocks with preceding or following text show a plus (+) sign in the handle.

A downward-pointing arrow shows that there is more of the story still to be placed.

The windowshade handle at the end of a story is empty.

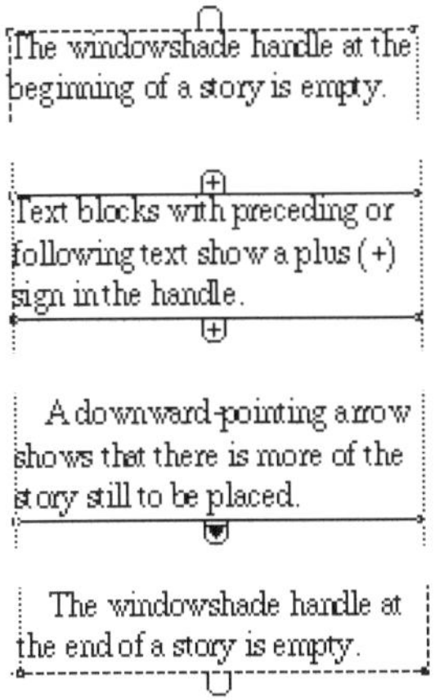

The anatomy of connected text blocks (i.e. parts of the same story) showing the detail of the different windowshade handles (left).

Click with the pointer tool to select a text block (left). You can move text blocks by first selecting and then dragging them (right).

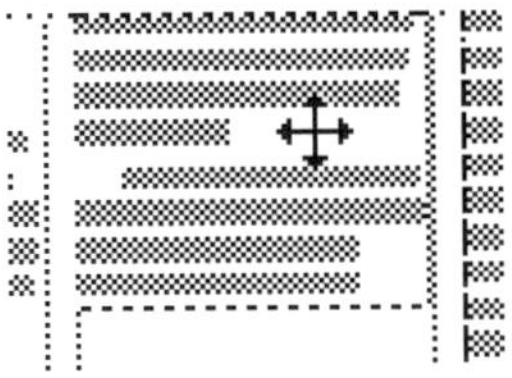

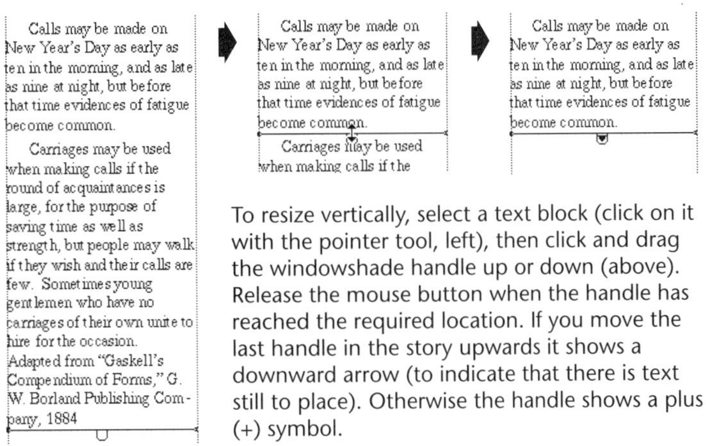

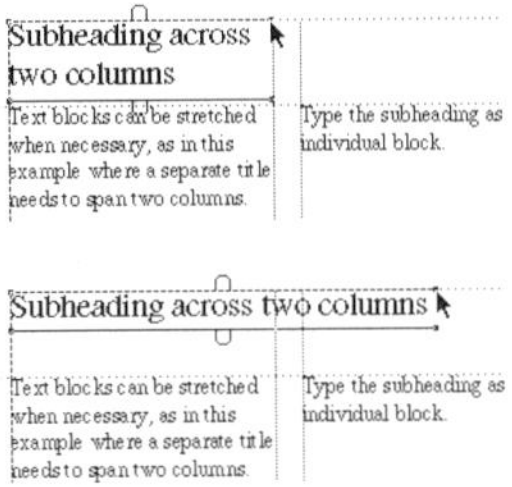

Calls may be made on New Year's Day as early as ten in the morning, and as late as nine at night, but before that time evidences of fatigue become common.

Carriages may be used when making calls if the round of acquaintances is large, for the purpose of saving time as well as strength, but people may walk if they wish and their calls are few. Sometimes young gentlemen who have no carriages of their own unite to hire for the occasion. Adapted from "Gaskell's Compendium of Forms," G. W. Borland Publishing Company, 1884

Calls may be made on New Year's Day as early as ten in the morning, and as late as nine at night, but before that time evidences of fatigue become common.
Carriages may be used when making calls if the

Calls may be made on New Year's Day as early as ten in the morning, and as late as nine at night, but before that time evidences of fatigue become common.

To resize vertically, select a text block (click on it with the pointer tool, left), then click and drag the windowshade handle up or down (above). Release the mouse button when the handle has reached the required location. If you move the last handle in the story upwards it shows a downward arrow (to indicate that there is text still to place). Otherwise the handle shows a plus (+) symbol.

Subheading across two columns

Text blocks can be stretched when necessary, as in this example where a separate title needs to span two columns.

Type the subheading as individual block.

Subheading across two columns

Text blocks can be stretched when necessary, as in this example where a separate title needs to span two columns.

Type the subheading as individual block.

To resize horizontally (above), select the text block with the pointer tool and drag one of the corner handles to the left or to the right.

Text can be manipulated in different ways depending on how you select it. If you use the pointer tool (arrow), text is selected as a block which can be moved around the page, resized and deleted as a single entity without any regard to its contents.

To format text at the character level (i.e. to change font, size, type style, etc.) select the text tool and modify the text using the I-beam cursor as in a word processing program. Choose the tool you need by clicking on its icon in the toolbox.

Resizing text blocks. When you select a text block using the pointer tool, windowshade handles appear. You can use the loop on a handle to resize a text block up or down a column by dragging on it (a double-headed arrow shows the direction in which you can move). Drag the small rectangular handles at either corner to the left or to the right if you want to change the width of a text block.

Moving text blocks. To move a text block, select it using the pointer tool and drag—the pointer changes to a cross with arrows.

When moving a text block stay well clear of the handles, otherwise you might end up resizing it accidentally. Click squarely in the middle of the block to select it and stay there as you move it.

Similarly, when changing the depth of a text block, click in the centre of the windowshade handle and hold the mouse button down as you drag the handle up or down.

Text flow. PageMaker preserves the flow of a story for you by reflowing the text to accommodate any changes you make to the width or depth of connected (threaded) blocks. If you make a block smaller it moves text into the next block; if you make a block larger it takes text from the blocks that follow.

Practise! Try deleting, moving and resizing text blocks. For example, if you accidentally place a story on the master pages and wish to delete it before moving to the correct page to place it again, you have two options open.

Select each text block by clicking on it with the pointer tool (you can also SHIFT-click to select several at once) and use the DELETE key to remove it (or *Cut* and then *Paste* on the right page).

Or, click on the text tool in the toolbox and position the text cursor (I-beam) in the story by clicking somewhere inside it. Choose *Select all* from the *Edit* menu to highlight the text and then use DELETE to erase it. Note that this method selects all of the text in a story, not just the text in a single text block or, necessarily, on a single page.

• If you make a mistake resizing or moving, use *Undo* from the *Edit* menu to recover.

• Don't worry about stretching a text block across column guides— they are there to help with placement and are not sacred. However, you might need to consider the design implications of varying column widths on the same page.

• The Control palette can also be used to move and resize text blocks.

• If you accidentally click on a windowshade loop you will load the text cursor (or be told there is no more to place). Click on the pointer tool in the Toolbox to unload the cursor.

Placing graphics 9

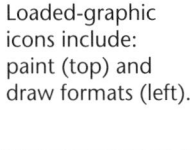

File

New... ⌘N
Open... ⌘O
Close

Save ⌘S
Save as...
Revert
Export...

Place... ⌘D

Links... ⌘=
Book...
Preferences...

Page setup...
Print... ⌘P

Quit ⌘Q

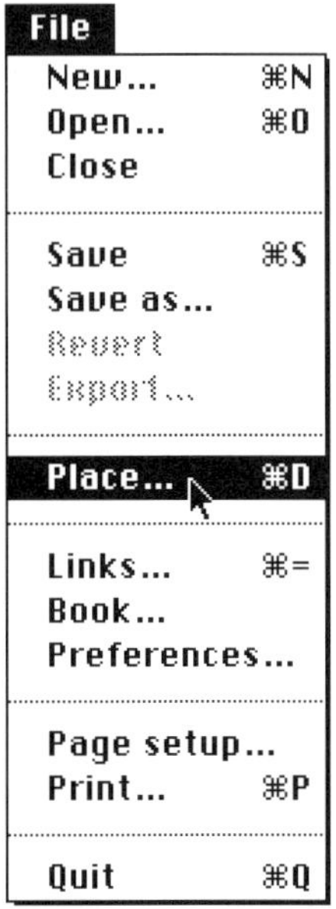

To import a graphic, use *Place...* from the *File* menu and select the graphic from the Place document box.

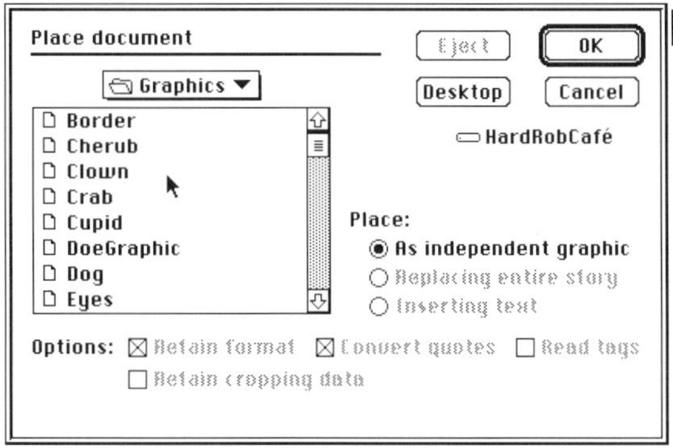

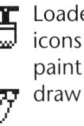

Place document

Graphics ▼

Eject
Desktop
OK
Cancel

▫ Border
▫ Cherub
▫ Clown
▫ Crab
▫ Cupid
▫ DoeGraphic
▫ Dog
▫ Eyes

⊂ HardRobCafé

Place:
● As independent graphic
○ Replacing entire story
○ Inserting text

Options: ☒ Retain format ☒ Convert quotes ☐ Read tags
☐ Retain cropping data

Place the graphic independent of any story for now (by selecting the pointer tool before you *Place...*).

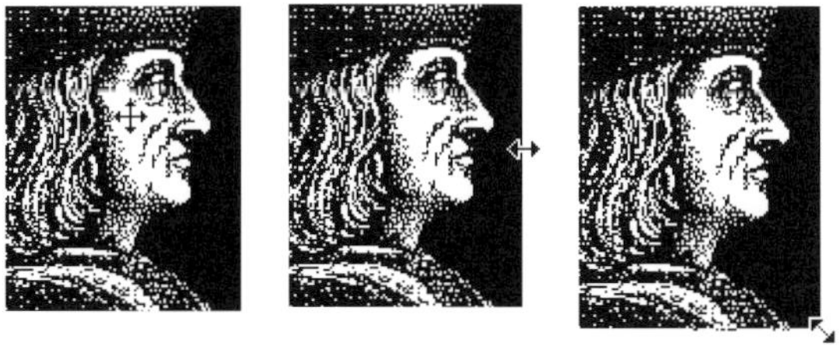

Once you select a graphic (with the pointer tool) you can move it (left), or resize it by dragging a handle (centre and right). Hold down the SHIFT key to retain proportions and prevent distortion while you drag to resize—corner handle is easiest to use.

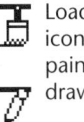

Loaded-graphic icons include: paint (top) and draw formats (left).

Click the loaded-graphic icon at the required location on the page, to drop the graphic into place (below).

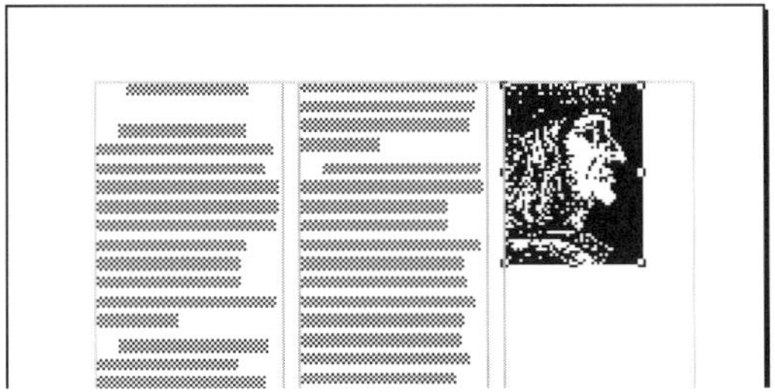

Trim a graphic to size by centering the cropping tool over a handle and dragging (above). Move the graphic within the cropped area by clicking in the centre of the graphic with the cropping tool (a grabber hand appears which lets you move it freely).

Graphics which have been scanned or prepared in an illustration program can also be brought onto a page using *Place…* from the *File* menu. The method is very similar to that previously described for placing text.

Select the pointer tool from the toolbox (to keep things simple for now) and choose *Place…* from the *File* menu. Select the document containing the graphic in the box that follows. PageMaker then imports the graphic and the pointer becomes a 'loaded-graphic' icon. Position this icon where you want the graphic's top left corner to be located and click the mouse button.

Moving graphics. You can move a graphic if you click on it first with the pointer tool (to select it) and then drag it to a new position on the page. Take care not to drag too close to the handles or you might reshape the graphic instead.

If you begin dragging immediately on clicking, you will see the graphic in outline only. However, if you hold down the mouse button and wait for a few seconds before dragging, you will see the complete graphic as you move it.

Don't forget *Undo* on the *Edit* menu if you accidentally pull on one of the handles, or you decide that the new location is not suitable—the graphic will be put back to its original shape or its original position on the page. You can also make use of *Undo* to try things out.

Resizing graphics. To resize a graphic, select it (by clicking on it with the pointer tool) and pull on one of the small peripheral handles. The pointer changes to a double-headed arrow indicating the direction in which you can resize (depending on the handle you choose). You can see the shape of the graphic change as you drag.

To resize proportionally (i.e. maintain the ratio between width and height), hold down the SHIFT key while you drag on a handle. Otherwise you will distort the graphic.

Cropping graphics. Often you will want to trim the edges of a graphic (called cropping) to remove unwanted detail or to adjust the shape. To do this first select the cropping tool and with it click on the graphic to select it. Position the centre of the cropping cursor over the handle on the edge you want to trim and drag to crop the graphic.

Once trimmed, you can move a graphic inside the cropped area by clicking on it with the cropping tool and dragging the image around within its boundary.

Once cropped, a graphic can be resized using the pointer tool as described above.

Practise! Place a graphic and try moving, resizing and cropping it to get a feel for what's possible.

The control palette (described later) can also be used to position, move and resize graphics.

• Graphics need to be in a format which PageMaker can handle. Illustration and scanning programs provide a variety of *Save as…* or *Export…* formats such as PICT, TIFF and EPS, which are suitable.

• If you accidentally place a graphic within a story (by placing with the text tool and not the pointer tool) choose *Undo* from the *Edit* menu for now. In-line graphics (those embedded in text) will be described later.

• To delete a graphic, select it and press the DELETE key (or *Cut* it).

• To deselect a graphic simply select something else or click on an empty part of the page.

• Don't overuse the cropping tool to eliminate detail. Produce a more precise graphic in the original illustration program instead.

Page numbers 10

On the master page:

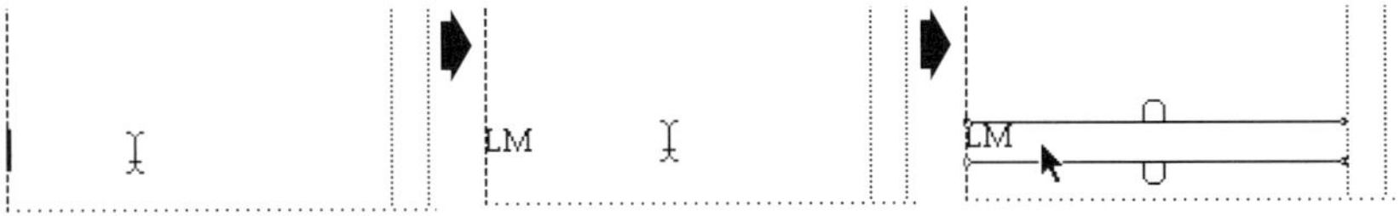

Using the text tool, click to position the text insertion cursor (above).

Holding down both the COMMAND and the OPTION keys, type 'p' for the page number marker.

Click with the pointer tool to select the text block and move it to the desired location.

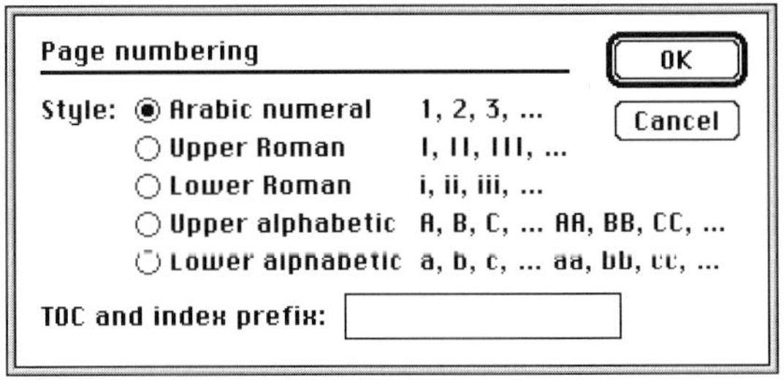

Page numbering

Style:	⦿ **Arabic numeral**	1, 2, 3, ...
	○ **Upper Roman**	I, II, III, ...
	○ **Lower Roman**	i, ii, iii, ...
	○ **Upper alphabetic**	A, B, C, ... AA, BB, CC, ...
	○ **Lower alphabetic**	a, b, c, ... aa, bb, cc, ...

TOC and index prefix: [   ]

OK

Cancel

Choose *Page setup...* from the *File* menu and click the Numbers... button in the Page setup box to reach the Page numbering dialog box (above). You can then set the page numbering style you require.

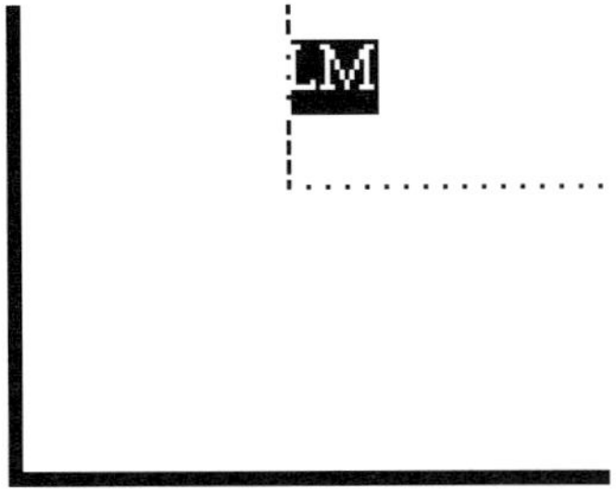

You can select the page number marker with the text tool to format your page numbers as you would any text (above).

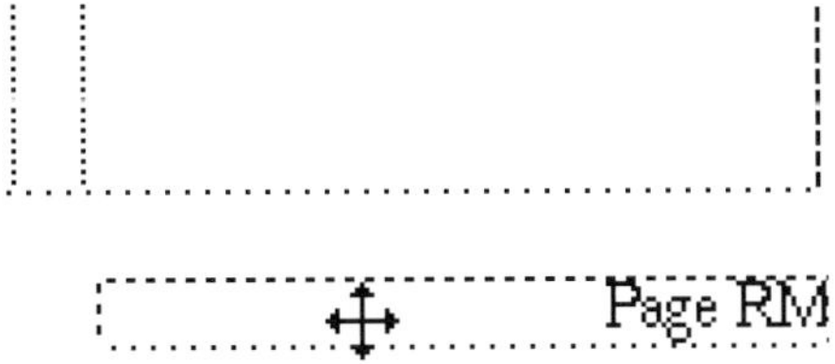

Page RM

The text block with the page number marker can also contain additional text (just type it as normal) and can be moved, like any text block, to the place on the page where you want page numbers to appear.

Layout work can be labour-intensive and time-consuming. Fortunately, PageMaker provides features which allow you to develop efficient methods of working, but they require a degree of discipline on your part. You can, after all, ignore them and do things the hard way.

Page number marker. As explained earlier, if you place items which are to appear on every page on the master pages you save yourself the effort of generating them repeatedly. If you put the marker for page numbers on the master pages, PageMaker will automatically handle page numbering for you throughout the publication.

To do so, first open the master pages (by clicking on their icon at the lower-left corner of the window) and select the text tool. Then click once to position the insertion point and type:

    COMMAND-OPTION-P   (Macintosh)
    CTRL-SHIFT-3   (Windows)

the marker for page numbers. Depending on which master page contains the cursor, PageMaker will then display either the characters 'LM' (on a left master page) or 'RM' (on a right master page). These markers will display as real page numbers on the pages of your publication.

If the marker does not appear, try again (hold down first the COMMAND key, then the OPTION key). Also ensure that CAPS LOCK is not on.

Formatting page numbers. Using the text tool, you can select the page number marker and format it just as you would any other piece of text to specify the font, size, type style and alignment you want for your page numbers.

Saving effort. When you have positioned the marker on one master page you can repeat the procedure on the opposite page, or use *Copy* and *Paste* from the *Edit* menu to duplicate the marker—it will change automatically to the appropriate marker (LM or RM) for that page.

It is best to type the marker for page numbers after you have positioned column guides. This will allow you to position the insertion point between column guides close to where you eventually want the marker to be (you can move it to the correct location afterwards). The advantage of this technique is that you get a text block that is manageable (i.e. not too wide). If you click in the margin area, where the page number will eventually sit, the text block will extend across the width of the text area and might involve you in unnecessary scrolling later.

Headers and footers are positioned in a similar way. Simply type the text you require into text blocks on the master page and position them where you want to on the page.

• You can accurately position items such as page numbers, header and footer text, etc., by making use of ruler guides, or by using the Control palette.

• If when you type the page number marker you get a real page number instead of the marker, you are not on the master page.

• By using the page number marker you ensure that pages are correctly numbered even when pages are moved around, inserted or deleted.

• You can also drag with the text tool (described later) to define the boundaries of a text block before you start typing on the page or before you use *Paste*.

• SHIFT-3 (Windows) on American keyboards produces the hash (#) sign used in the US to mean a number.

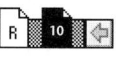

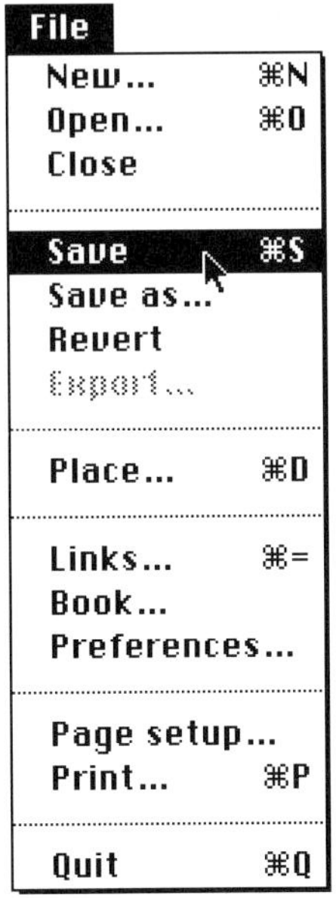

Saving and printing 11

File

New... ⌘N
Open... ⌘O
Close

Save ⌘S
Save as...
Revert
Export...

Place... ⌘D

Links... ⌘=
Book...
Preferences...

Page setup...
Print... ⌘P

Quit ⌘Q

Use *Save* from the *File* menu (above) to store your publication on disk. When you first use *Save* you are presented with the *Save as...* box so that you can give the untitled document a name.

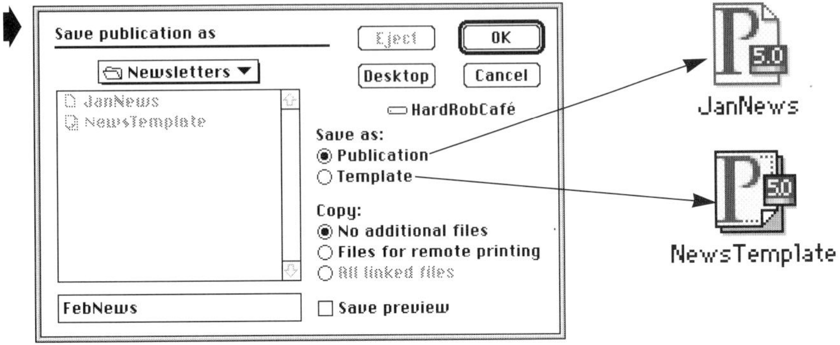

Save publication as

Eject | OK
🗁 Newsletters ▼
Desktop | Cancel
☐ HardRobCafé

JanNews
NewsTemplate

Save as:
◉ Publication
○ Template

Copy:
◉ No additional files
○ Files for remote printing
○ All linked files

FebNews

☐ Save preview

Give your publication a name and specify its disk location in the *Save as...* box (above).

You can save your document as a normal PageMaker publication...

JanNews

...or as a template (stationery) from which to generate other publications.

NewsTemplate

Choose *Print...* from the *File* menu to reach the Print document box (right). Note the standard options provided—number of Copies and Ranges of pages to print (which need not be consecutive). You should select the type of printer you are using from the Type: pop-up menu. Other print options are described in detail later.

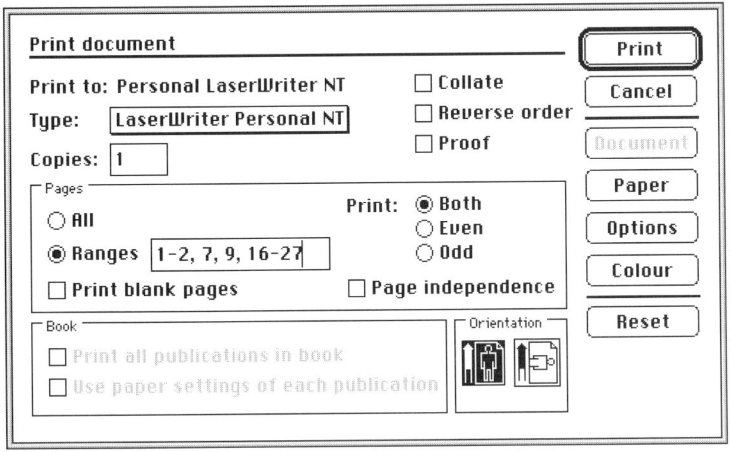

Print document

Print | Cancel | Document | Paper | Options | Colour | Reset

Print to: Personal LaserWriter NT

Type: LaserWriter Personal NT

Copies: 1

☐ Collate
☐ Reverse order
☐ Proof

Pages
○ All
◉ Ranges 1-2, 7, 9, 16-27
☐ Print blank pages

Print: ◉ Both
○ Even
○ Odd
☐ Page independence

Book
☐ Print all publications in book
☐ Use paper settings of each publication

Orientation

As you would expect from a publishing program, the options provided to control printing are many and varied, but straightforward printing is possible and does not require in-depth knowledge of the program.

Use the fact that you want to print your publication as a cue to saving it first—saving before printing is sensible (in case something goes wrong) and is a habit worth developing.

Saving. Save in the usual way by choosing *Save* from the *File* menu. If the publication has not previously been saved you will be presented with the *Save as...* dialog box so that you can give it a name. If it already has a name (other than Untitled), *Save* updates the existing copy on disk.

The Copy: options in the *Save as...* box will be described later.

Templates. If you are producing a series of publications you should save your publication as a template for future use, once you have done the groundwork and are satisfied with its design.

You can save a publication as a template by clicking the Template button in the *Save as...* box. Similar in concept to stationery under System 7, when you *Open...* a template you open a copy of the document. The original is left untouched for you to use again.

If, for example, you are producing a series of monthly newsletters, save the document as a template with the elements common to each publication in the series (title, logo, editorial address, etc.) in place.

The easiest way to do this might be to complete the first publication and make a copy of it using *Save as...* from the *File* menu. Then remove what you don't want in subsequent issues – specific articles and graphics, for example – and save the document as a template which you can use as a starting point for subsequent titles in the series.

Printing. Choose *Print...* from the *File* menu when you are ready to print and you will find that the first-level options are fairly straightforward—number of Copies, page Ranges, Orientation, etc.

Check that the printer type you are using is specified towards the top of the box. If not, choose it from the Type: pop-up menu.

Note that the Ranges of pages to be printed need not be contiguous and that you can also print all odd or even pages separately—useful if you want to produce double-sided publications on your own printer.

The more complex printing options (provided under the Paper, Options and Colour buttons) will be described later.

• Get into the habit of giving your publications sensible names – ones that provide you with some information on their contents – you will save yourself a lot of effort later.

• Templates also retain styles (discussed later) and make it easier for others, with a little instruction, to produce publications in your absence (holidays, illness, etc.).

• You should, of course, make backup copies of publications and of templates (which become more valuable with time).

• If you make changes to a particular publication, which will apply to others in the series, remember to modify the template too.

• You can turn printing in the background on and off in the *Chooser*.

Ruler guides   12

Layout

View	▶
Guides and rulers ▶	**Rulers** ⌘R
Column guides...	Snap to rulers ⌘[
	Zero lock
Go to page... ⌘G	
Insert pages...	✓Guides ⌘J
Remove pages...	✓Snap to guides ⌘U
	Lock guides
✓Display master items	
Copy master guides	✓Scroll bars
Autoflow	

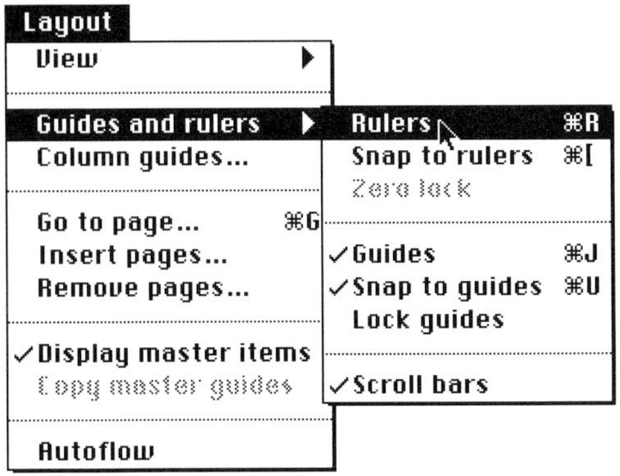

If the rulers are not displayed (or if you want to switch them off), choose *Rulers* from the *Guides and rulers* submenu of the *Layout* menu.

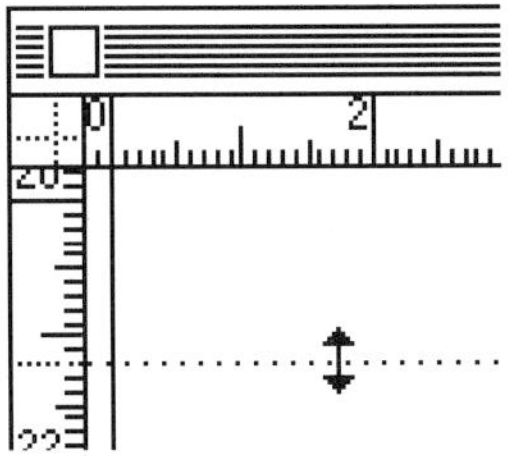

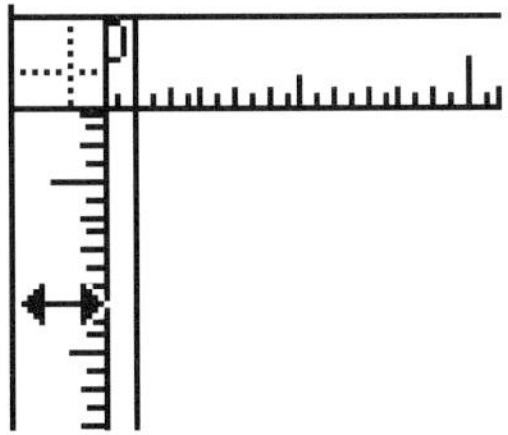

To position a ruler guide on the page, click in the ruler (the cursor changes to a double-headed arrow) and drag a guide down (above, left) to the location required. The cursor position is shown in the corresponding ruler (and in the control palette) so that you can position the ruler guide with accuracy. *Snap to rulers* forces movement to follow the increments on the ruler. Ruler guides can also be dragged from the vertical ruler (below, left).

Ruler and column guides together form a layout grid (below). Grids are a useful aid to producing consistent layouts.

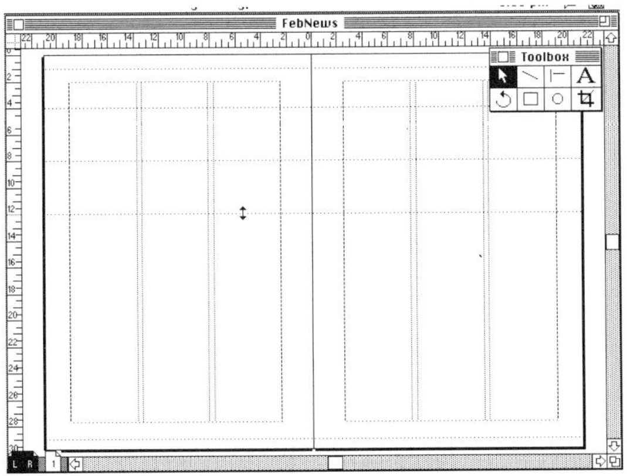

To change the position of the ruler origin (0,0), drag the cross-hair from the ruler origin box at the top left. From top of page (right) to top of text area, for example.

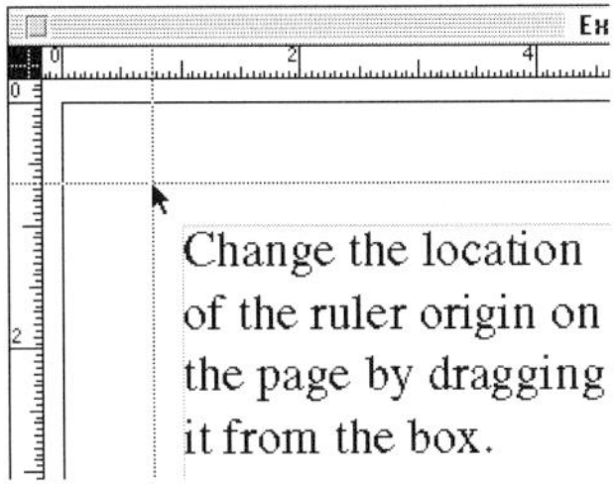

Change the location of the ruler origin on the page by dragging it from the box.

After content, attention to detail in design and layout is what sets a good publication apart from a bad one. Even if you do not have a design background, awareness of the key elements involved in successful layout work will give you a better chance of success. One important consideration in any publication is alignment—how various items relate to one another on the same page, on opposite pages and throughout the pages of a publication.

For example, if your page numbers move about from page to page, or your margins are constantly changing, you will annoy your readers. By using master pages these particular traps can be avoided since page numbers, headers and footers, etc., are fixed for the publication as a whole.

Just as important, however, is alignment across pages. How do you ensure that your page numbers are in the correct place relative to one another so that they print properly back-to-back? Or that lines of text in adjacent columns continue to align horizontally after the introduction of a graphic?

Ruler guides. A ruler guide is a non-printing guide (similar to column and margin guides) which you can position on the page as a reference point to help you align elements consistently.

Design considerations. Before you position ruler guides you will need to consider the appearance of the finished page. Where are page numbers to be located? Are there pages which need text or graphics at particular locations? Would ruler guides on the master pages help you to position these elements consistently and with accuracy? Try to make these design decisions before you start doing the layout work.

Positioning guides. To position a horizontal ruler guide, click squarely inside the top ruler and drag downwards. A double-headed arrow appears. As you move away from the ruler, a dotted line shows the position of the ruler guide. Release the mouse button when the guide reaches the location you want on the page (a dotted line in the vertical ruler highlights the position of the cursor so that you can position it accurately). You can drag vertical ruler guides from the ruler at the left edge of the window.

If you set *Snap to rulers* on the *Guides and rulers* submenu of the *Layout* menu, cursor movement follows ruler increments—so you can accurately and easily position guides.

You can move a ruler guide later by clicking on it and dragging it to a new location (or back to the ruler itself to remove it). If you later find that you are moving guides accidentally, set *Lock guides* on the *Guides and rulers* submenu.

Ruler guides set on the master pages appear on every page but can be moved on individual pages.

• The control palette can also be used to align items on a page, and to track the location of the cursor when positioning ruler guides.

• Ruler guides do not appear on printed publications. They are provided to ease layout work on the screen.

• Turn the display of *Guides* on and off from the *Layout* submenu. If ruler guides disappear immediately after you have positioned them turn this option on.

• You can position ruler guides with any toolbox tool selected.

• It is easy to click in the title bar by mistake at first and to move the window. If this happens, click in the title bar again and move the window back.

• Double-click in the ruler origin box to reset the origin (0,0).

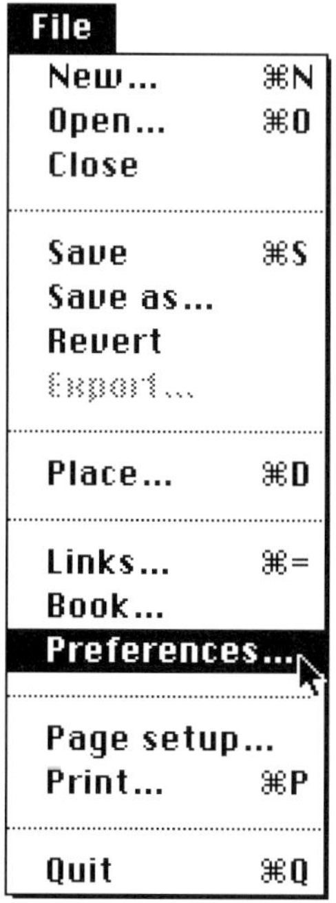

Changing settings 13

File

New...	⌘N
Open...	⌘O
Close	
Save	⌘S
Save as...	
Revert	
Export...	
Place...	⌘D
Links...	⌘=
Book...	
Preferences...	
Page setup...	
Print...	⌘P
Quit	⌘Q

Preferences

OK Cancel Other... Map fonts...

Layout
Measurement system: Millimetres
Vertical ruler: Millimetres [   ] points

Layout problems
☐ Show loose/tight lines
☐ Show "keeps" violations

Graphics
○ Grey out
◉ Normal
○ High resolution

Guides
○ Front
◉ Back

Save option
◉ Faster
○ Smaller

Control palette
Horizontal nudge: 0.01 Inches
Vertical nudge: 0.01 Inches
☐ Use "Snap to" constraints

You can customise program settings for individual documents by choosing *Preferences...* on the *File* menu.

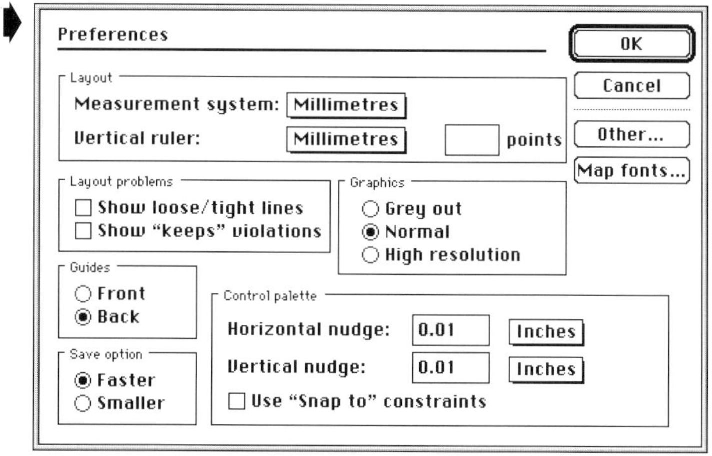

In the Preferences box, you can choose the measurement system you want to use. You can also choose to have graphics replaced by a grey box to speed up screen redrawing, and can specify nudge values and units to use in the control palette.

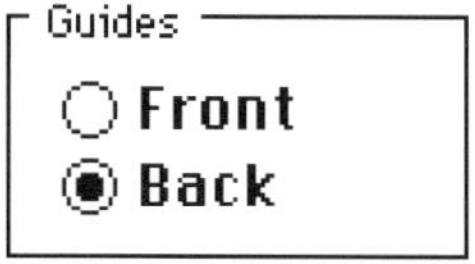

Guides
○ **Front**
◉ **Back**

If guides start to get in your way – you move them accidentally when you are trying to select something else – send them to the back layer in the *Preferences...* box.

Preferences

Layout
Measurement system: | Inches / Inches decimal / ✓Millimetres / Picas / Ciceros
Vertical ruler: [   ] points

Select the measurement system you prefer to use from the pop-up menu (above). Note that the vertical ruler, too, can be set via its own pop-up menu—it can even be customised so that its divisions match lines of text (by typing the leading value used in text into the box).

You can change many of the preset values in PageMaker to suit the way you work. This customisation can be achieved on two levels—at the level of an individual publication and at the program level.

Each time you open a new publication the menu options and the values set for you in dialog boxes will be the same—these preset values are supplied by PageMaker and are called defaults. They are provided as suitable values to save you having to work them out and set them each time.

You can override the settings supplied. For example, when you open a new publication the page size might be set to A4 but you can change it to A5 in the *Page setup…* dialog box. The new setting will apply to that publication only. If you *Save* it and *Open* it again later it will still be A5. However, if you open another new document it will again be preset to A4.

Changing defaults. Changes you make within a publication apply to that publication only and have no effect on already existing publications or on new documents subsequently created.

However, you can customise the program itself by changing settings when the menu bar is visible but you have not yet opened a document—start up the program but don't use use either *New* or *Open*. Changes made at the program level apply to every new publication thereafter (but have no effect on existing publications). In effect, you are changing the program's preset values.

For example, if you consistently alter the page size or the margins settings each time you open a new document, you can save yourself effort by changing to those settings in the Page setup box, *before* you open any publication. They are changed at the program level and apply to every new publication that you open from then on.

Available options. Menu settings can also be changed at the program level. When you do not have a document open, some menu options are not appropriate and are greyed out. These you cannot change at the program level. However, in general, any menu item shown in black can be set so you don't need to remember what can and can't be changed. Simply alter whatever is available if it will save you having to type or change values repeatedly.

For example, if you find that in your new documents you are choosing *Column guides…* from the *Layout* menu and constantly setting the same value, why not set it once? That column guide setting will then be automatically provided in each new publication, even on the master pages. You can always override it when necessary!

• Don't change the presets at the program level if the computer you use is not your own or if you share it with other people—it could lead to confusion.

• You can also change some menu preset options by setting them without a document open.

• Although the *Type* menu is available when you don't have a document open, attributes set apply only to text typed directly onto the page or pasted as a separate text block. Text imported from a word processing program retains the formatting applied in the originating program (unless you uncheck the Retain format option in the *Place…* box).

• Additional preferences can be set via the Other… and Map fonts… buttons.

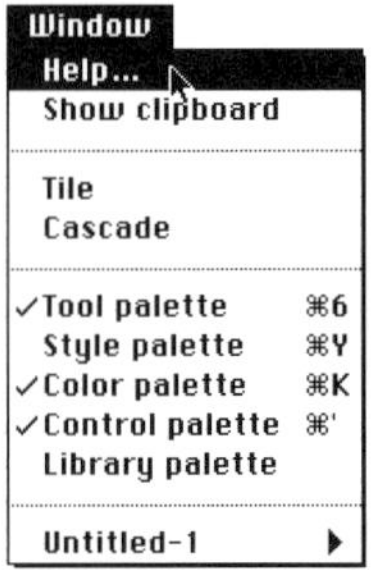

Help   14

Window
Help...
Show clipboard

Tile
Cascade

✓Tool palette   ⌘6
Style palette   ⌘Y
✓Color palette   ⌘K
✓Control palette   ⌘'
Library palette

Untitled-1   ▶

To reach the internal help information, choose *Help...* from the *Window* menu (above) or use COMMAND-? (SHIFT-F1 on Windows) to go direct to help on a particular command (below).

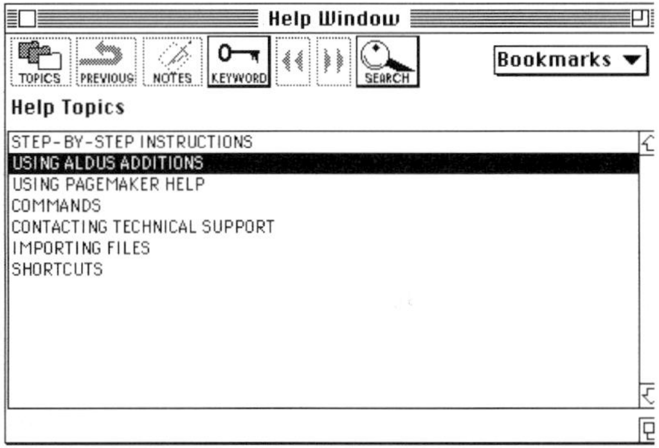

Help Window

TOPICS   PREVIOUS   NOTES   KEYWORD   SEARCH   **Bookmarks ▼**

Help Topics

STEP-BY-STEP INSTRUCTIONS
USING ALDUS ADDITIONS
USING PAGEMAKER HELP
COMMANDS
CONTACTING TECHNICAL SUPPORT
IMPORTING FILES
SHORTCUTS

In the Help window, click on the topic you want information about (above) and then on the specific topic in the window that follows (above right).

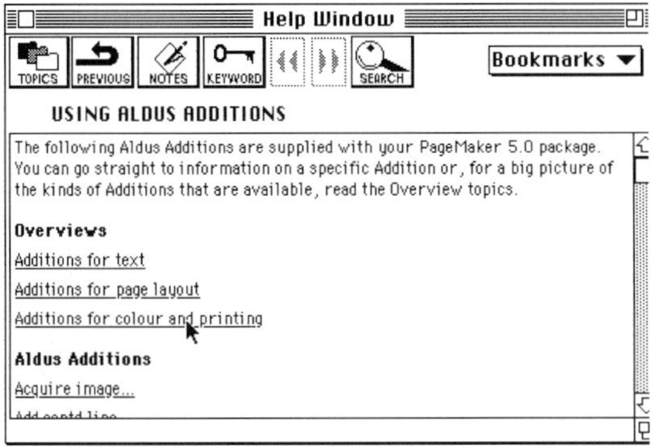

Help Window

TOPICS   PREVIOUS   NOTES   KEYWORD   SEARCH   **Bookmarks ▼**

USING ALDUS ADDITIONS

The following Aldus Additions are supplied with your PageMaker 5.0 package. You can go straight to information on a specific Addition or, for a big picture of the kinds of Additions that are available, read the Overview topics.

Overviews

Additions for text

Additions for page layout

Additions for colour and printing

Aldus Additions

Acquire image...

Add contd line

Element
Line   ▶
Fill   ▶
Fill and line...   ⌘]

Bring to front   ⌘F
Send to back   ⌘B
Remove transformation

Text wrap...
Image control...
Rounded corners...

Define colors...
Restore original color

Link info...
Link options...

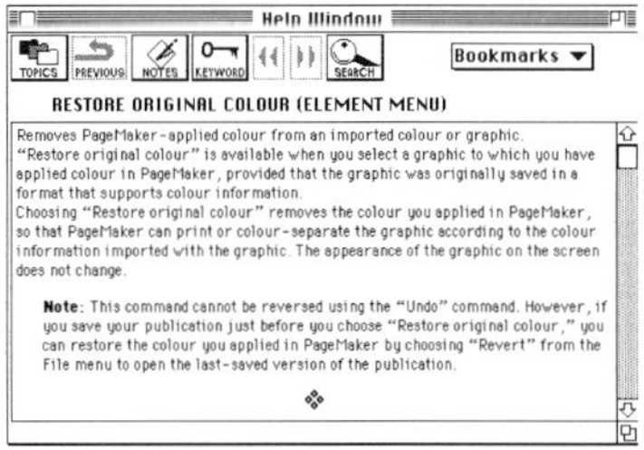

Help Window

TOPICS   PREVIOUS   NOTES   KEYWORD   SEARCH   **Bookmarks ▼**

RESTORE ORIGINAL COLOUR (ELEMENT MENU)

Removes PageMaker-applied colour from an imported colour or graphic. "Restore original colour" is available when you select a graphic to which you have applied colour in PageMaker, provided that the graphic was originally saved in a format that supports colour information.

Choosing "Restore original colour" removes the colour you applied in PageMaker, so that PageMaker can print or colour-separate the graphic according to the colour information imported with the graphic. The appearance of the graphic on the screen does not change.

Note: This command cannot be reversed using the "Undo" command. However, if you save your publication just before you choose "Restore original colour," you can restore the colour you applied in PageMaker by choosing "Revert" from the File menu to open the last-saved version of the publication.

With the ? cursor, select the menu command you want help with.

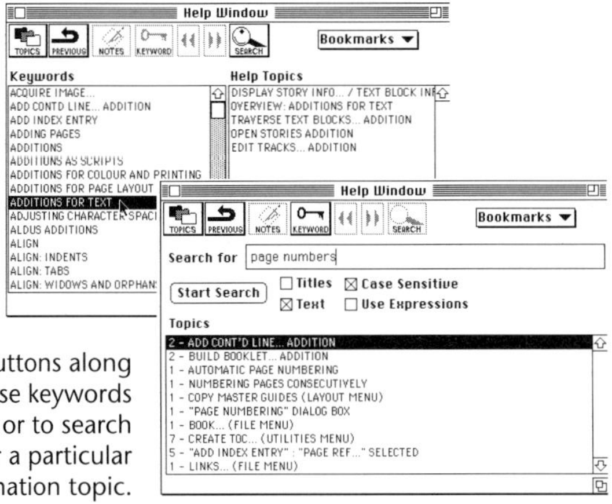

Help Window

TOPICS   PREVIOUS   NOTES   KEYWORD   SEARCH   **Bookmarks ▼**

Keywords   **Help Topics**

ACQUIRE IMAGE...   DISPLAY STORY INFO... / TEXT BLOCK INFO...
ADD CONTD LINE... ADDITION   OVERVIEW: ADDITIONS FOR TEXT
ADD INDEX ENTRY   TRAVERSE TEXT BLOCKS... ADDITION
ADDING PAGES   OPEN STORIES ADDITION
ADDITIONS   EDIT TRACKS... ADDITION
ADDITIONS AS SCRIPTS
ADDITIONS FOR COLOUR AND PRINTING
ADDITIONS FOR PAGE LAYOUT
ADDITIONS FOR TEXT
ADJUSTING CHARACTER SPACING
ALDUS ADDITIONS
ALIGN
ALIGN: INDENTS
ALIGN: TABS
ALIGN: WIDOWS AND ORPHANS

Click the buttons along the top to use keywords (above) or to search (right) for a particular information topic.

Help Window

TOPICS   PREVIOUS   NOTES   KEYWORD   SEARCH   **Bookmarks ▼**

Search for   page numbers

Start Search   ☐ Titles   ☒ Case Sensitive   ☒ Text   ☐ Use Expressions

Topics

2 - ADD CONT'D LINE... ADDITION
2 - BUILD BOOKLET... ADDITION
1 - AUTOMATIC PAGE NUMBERING
1 - NUMBERING PAGES CONSECUTIVELY
1 - COPY MASTER GUIDES (LAYOUT MENU)
1 - "PAGE NUMBERING" DIALOG BOX
1 - BOOK... (FILE MENU)
7 - CREATE TOC... (UTILITIES MENU)
5 - "ADD INDEX ENTRY" "PAGE REF..." SELECTED
1 - LINKS... (FILE MENU)

Don't overlook the help information provided within PageMaker—it is a useful resource which is too often forgotten. Besides using it to find information quickly, you can also use it to learn more about a particular aspect of the program in some detail.

The information is organised so that you can search through it in different ways. You can either select a topic and move down through subsequent windows until you find the information you want, or you can use a keyword to go straight to the information on a specific topic.

If you do not know where a particular piece of information might be located, you can also specify a subject and have the program search for the information for you.

You can move from one help window to another by using a 'hot-spot'—highlighted text which, if you click on it, will take you to further information on that topic. Thus, it is possible to follow a thread through the text and to learn about a topic in detail.

Help. Select *Help...* from the *Window* menu to use the internal help information. A help window appears showing topic headings which you can click on to reach sub-topics of more specific information. Click on these to see the information you require. The commands topic, for example, leads to a list of sub-topics organised by menu.

Buttons are provided across the top of the help window to allow you to choose a Keyword or to Search for a particular topic of your choice. There are also buttons which allow you to go back to the Previous window of information or to go back to the top-level list of Topics.

Keywords. Click on the Keyword button and scroll through the list if you want to select information by keyword (you can also type the first few letters to locate a particular keyword quickly).

Search. If you click the Search button you will be presented with a field into which you can type the subject you want help with. You can then choose from the list of topics which match your search criteria.

Shortcuts. This topic leads to a goldmine of information on keyboard shortcuts organised by function. You will find it overwhelming as a beginner but it becomes especially useful once you have gained some experience of the program.

Help in context. As an alternative, you can use COMMAND-? (SHIFT-F1 under Windows) to go direct to the information on a particular command. The cursor changes to a question mark (?) which you then use to select the command on its menu.

- If PageMaker cannot find the help information you will have to install it from the PageMaker disks.

- Although topics in some of the help windows have icons, you need to click on the highlighted text itself to reach the next window.

- The step-by-step instructions in the first help window follow the chapter headings in the User Manual.

- Using the Bookmarks drop-down menu you can *Define...* a bookmark to find the current window of information more easily again later.

- Use the Notes button if you want to associate some comments with a particular window. To read a note, click the icon which then appears next to the window title.

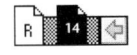

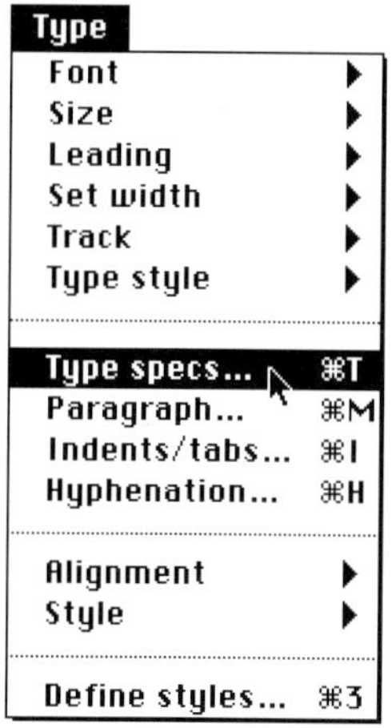

Formatting text   15

Type
- Font ▶
- Size ▶
- Leading ▶
- Set width ▶
- Track ▶
- Type style ▶

- **Type specs...** ⌘T
- Paragraph... ⌘M
- Indents/tabs... ⌘I
- Hyphenation... ⌘H

- Alignment ▶
- Style ▶

- Define styles... ⌘3

You can select text with the text tool and then format it in the type specifications box by choosing *Type specs...* on the *Type* menu.

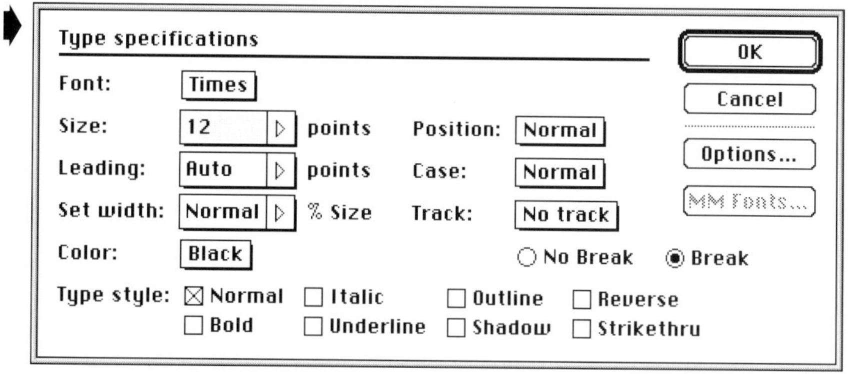

Type specifications

Font:	Times	
Size:	12 ▷ points	Position: Normal
Leading:	Auto ▷ points	Case: Normal
Set width:	Normal ▷ % Size	Track: No track
Color:	Black	

○ No Break   ● Break

Type style:
☒ Normal   ☐ Italic   ☐ Outline   ☐ Reverse
☐ Bold   ☐ Underline   ☐ Shadow   ☐ Strikethru

[OK]
[Cancel]
[Options...]
[MM fonts...]

Type specs... gives you a dialog box where several formatting attributes can be applied to text simultaneously via pop-up menus and check boxes.

Set width alters the width of selected characters; *Track* alters the space between them. Try them out but don't overuse.

Position is a submenu for sub- and super-scripting.

Use the Case submenu to convert text to capitals or small capital letters.

Control the position/size of sub/super-scripts and small caps via Options...

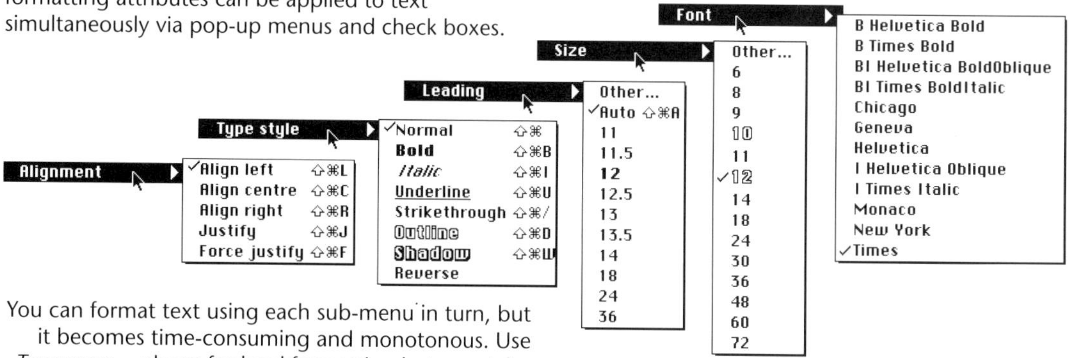

Font
- B Helvetica Bold
- B Times Bold
- BI Helvetica BoldOblique
- BI Times BoldItalic
- Chicago
- Geneva
- Helvetica
- I Helvetica Oblique
- I Times Italic
- Monaco
- New York
- ✓Times

Size
- Other...
- 6
- 8
- 9
- 10
- 11
- ✓12
- 14
- 18
- 24
- 30
- 36
- 48
- 60
- 72

Leading
- Other...
- ✓Auto ⇧⌘A
- 11
- 11.5
- 12
- 12.5
- 13
- 13.5
- 14
- 18
- 24
- 36

Type style
- ✓Normal ⇧⌘
- **Bold** ⇧⌘B
- *Italic* ⇧⌘I
- Underline ⇧⌘U
- Strikethrough ⇧⌘/
- Outline ⇧⌘D
- Shadow ⇧⌘W
- Reverse

Alignment
- ✓Align left ⇧⌘L
- Align centre ⇧⌘C
- Align right ⇧⌘R
- Justify ⇧⌘J
- Force justify ⇧⌘F

You can format text using each sub-menu in turn, but it becomes time-consuming and monotonous. Use *Type specs...* above for local formatting but use styles (described later) whenever possible.

Modifying text can be accomplished in two very different environments. Text can either be changed on the page in layout view, or in the separate Story Editor—the choice will depend on the kind of changes you want to make.

Formatting changes affecting the appearance of text, where it is important to see the effect of the changes – such as those to font, size, style, alignment, etc., – are best made on the page itself. Minor modifications to the content, to correct occasional typing mistakes for example, can also be made on the page.

When there are several changes to be made to the content of a story, such as rewriting paragraphs or making global modifications over the length of a story, it is more sensible to use the Story Editor (described later).

It is, however, worth repeating that, as far as possible, text should be prepared and checked in a word processing program before it is ever placed on the page.

Format retained. When text is placed on a page it retains the formatting applied in the original word processor document. So, a story produced in Times 12pt with Times Bold 14pt subheadings appears on the page in that form. Often this will not be what you require and you will want to change the font and point size within PageMaker.

Changing text. To format or modify text on the page, first choose a suitable view and, using the text tool, select the text to be modified just as you would in a word processing program. Apply the required formatting via the *Type* menu which has sub-menus for attributes such as *Font*, *Size*, *Leading*, *Type style* and *Alignment*. Other *Type* menu options will be described later but you should investigate *Type specs...* which allows several formatting changes to be made from the same dialog box, thereby saving the effort otherwise required to select options from several sub-menus in succession.

Leading. This is the term used for the vertical space occupied by a line of type, and is expressed in points, a measurement unit used in the printing trade. There are 72 points to an inch so six lines of type set on 12pt leading would occupy an inch vertically. More on leading and the language of type later.

Local formatting. Although it is worth knowing how to apply local formatting, it is not an efficient method of working. Styles (described later) should be used instead—they provide greater control and remove the need to manually select the text to be formatted.

• Moving the pointer across to the *Type* sub-menus can be tricky at first. Persevere!

• If the type size or leading you want is not listed in the *Type specs...* box, simply TAB to that field and type the value you require. Type can be specified from 4pt up to 650 pt in 0.1pt increments.

• Click the No Break button if you do not want the selected text to separate at the end of a line—to keep a first and last name together, for example

• Notice the useful command-key shortcuts under *Type style* and *Alignment* which can save you a lot of effort.

• You can also format text using the Control palette.

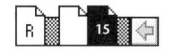

Basic text editing

16

Edit

Undo edit	⌘Z
Cut	⌘X
Copy	⌘C
Paste	⌘V
Clear	
Multiple paste...	
Select all	⌘A
Editions	▶
Paste link	
Paste special...	
Insert object...	
Edit story	⌘E
Edit original	

For extensive text editing, select a story and choose *Edit story* from the *Edit* menu.

 File   Edit   Utilities   Story   Type   Window   4:37 pm

testdoc

testdoc:It is best to prepa:1

TextDrop   It is best to prepare and proofread your text in a word
            processing program well before you reach the layout stage.
            However, there are occasions when you have to modify text
            on the page. At a suitable page view you can make changes on
            the page using the text tool (as described earlier) but you
            can waste a lot of time trying to locate the text to be
            modified and in waiting for the screen to catch up every time
            you make a change (particularly when there are complex
            graphics on the page which need to be redrawn each time).
            Neither is it sensible to type large volumes of text directly
            on the page. It is more efficient, and easier, to edit text
            using the built-in Story Editor.

Text

Text   Story Editor. To use the Story Editor on a story which has
            already been placed in a publication, select a text block of
            the story using the pointer tool or click with the text tool to
            position the insertion point somewhere within the story.
            Then choose *Edit story* from the *Edit* menu.

TextIndent   A new window appears over the page and *Story* is added to
            the menu bar. The story you selected on the page is displayed

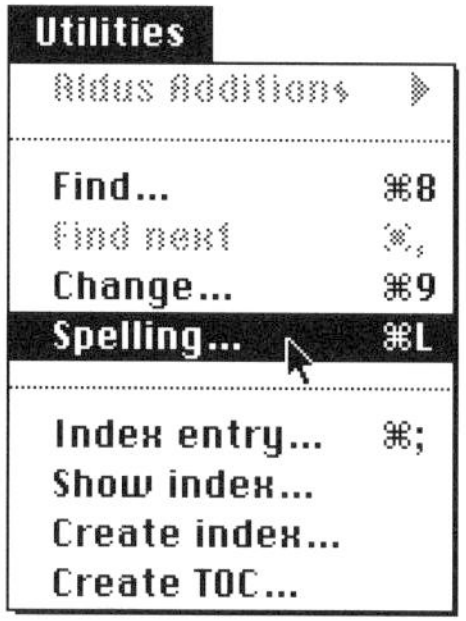

L R 1 2 3 4 5 6 7 8 9 **10**

Utilities

Aldus Additions	▶
Find...	⌘8
Find next	⌘,
Change...	⌘9
Spelling...	⌘L
Index entry...	⌘;
Show index...	
Create index...	
Create TOC...	

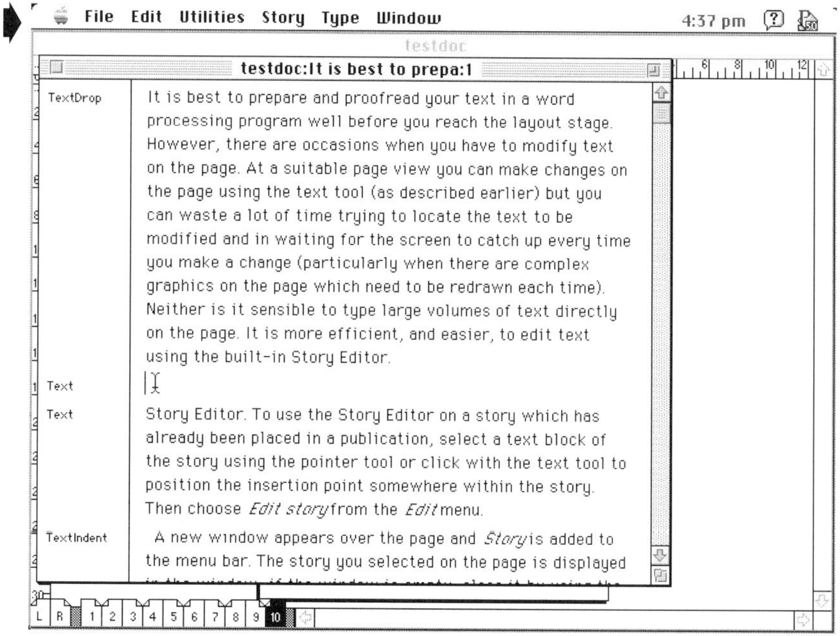

Within the Story Editor, editing tools such as the spelling checker selected above (described later) become available on the *Utilities* menu. A separate *Story* menu is also provided (below).

You can open Story Editor windows, as required, to edit existing text, compose new text or *Place...* text from other programs (provided the appropriate filter is installed). Move between windows by selecting their titles from the *Window* menu.

From the *Story* menu (right) you can open a new (empty) story window and close a window. You can also choose what to display.

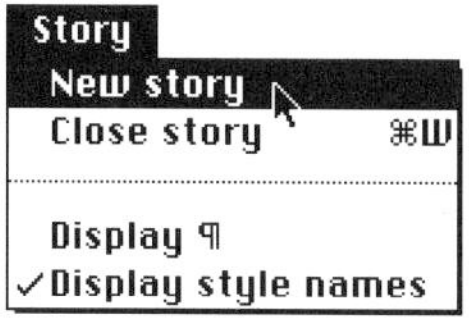

Story

New story	
Close story	⌘W
Display ¶	
✓Display style names	

It is best to prepare and proofread your text in a word processing program well before you reach the layout stage. However, there are occasions when you have no choice but to modify text on the page. At a suitable page view you can make changes on the page using the text tool (as described earlier) but you can waste a lot of time trying to locate the text to be modified and in waiting for the screen to catch up every time you make a change (particularly when there are complex graphics on the page which need to be redrawn each time). Neither is it sensible to type large volumes of text directly on the page. It is more efficient, and easier, to edit text using the built-in Story Editor.

Story Editor. To use the Story Editor on a story which has already been placed in a publication, select a text block of the story using the pointer tool or click with the text tool to position the insertion point somewhere within the story. Then choose *Edit story* from the *Edit* menu.

A new window appears over the page and *Story* replaces *Layout* on the menu bar. The story you selected on the page is displayed in the window—if the window is empty, close it by using the close box and select the story on the page before choosing *Edit story* again.

You will notice that the window contains only text and that it is probably not even displayed in the font you are using on the page. This is as it should be. When you are editing a story (as opposed to formatting its appearance) your main concern is readability—being able to see the text clearly enough to edit it with ease. Text is, therefore, displayed in a font suitable for this purpose and usually in a large size.

The left-hand margin of the window displays the style name (described later) for each paragraph if *Display style names* is set on the *Story* menu.

Editing tools. Additional options become available on the *Utilities* menu which allow you to locate particular words or phrases (*Find...* and *Find next*), to change some or all instances of one word to another (*Change...*) and to check for spelling or typing mistakes (*Spelling...*). These work in a very similar way to the tools found in most word processors and you should have no trouble with them—but remember that they are there should you ever need them!

Layout view. When you have finished making corrections, close the Story Editor by clicking in the close box or by choosing *Close story* from the *Story* menu—this changes to *Close all stories* if you hold down the OPTION key (SHIFT on Windows). The text is reflowed automatically onto the page.

Don't use *Close* from the *File* menu unless you want to close the publication itself.

- It is not sensible to use the Story Editor for text formatting (changing the appearance of text) since bold and italic are the only attributes displayed in this window. Use the layout view as described earlier.

- You can change the font used in the Story Editor in *Preferences...* (*File* menu).

- If you want to use the Story Editor to compose text, simply choose *Edit story* without having selected a story. You can then type into the untitled window. When you close it you will be given the option to place the text on the page (using a loaded-text icon) or to discard it.

- You can import previously prepared text into a story editor window by using *Place...* from the *File* menu.

- Use the *Open stories* addition on the *Utilities* menu to open all stories in a publication at once.

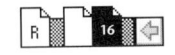

Placing text efficiently   17

Manual flow icon

Semi-automatic flow

Autoflow icon

Remember!

Use the COMMAND key on a Macintosh, or the CTRL key under Windows, to move temporarily between manual and autoflow.

Use the SHIFT key for semi-automatic flow.

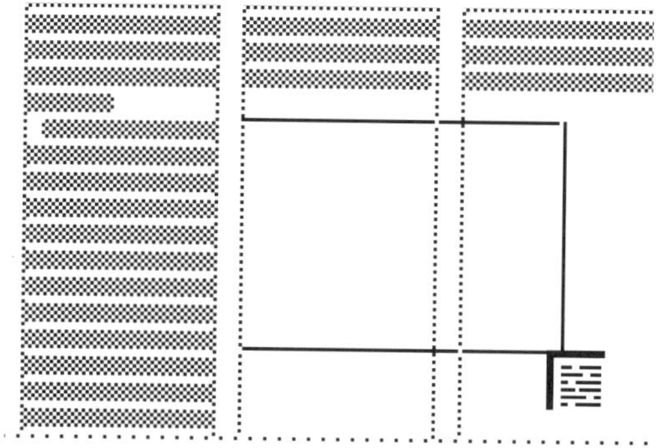

If every column is used for text in a simple grid (above), then autoflow saves effort.

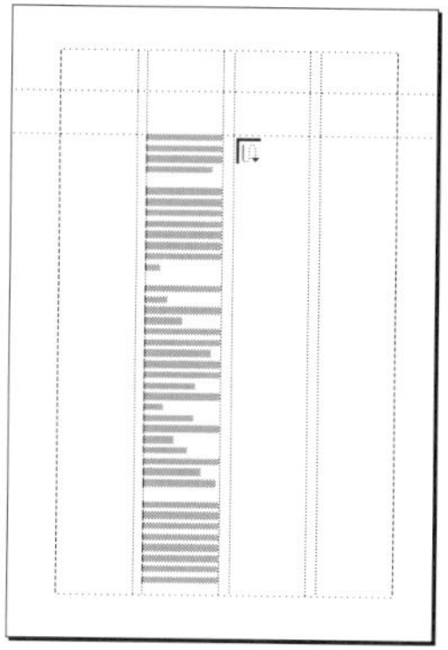

When text is not to flow into each column, do not use autoflow.

If you want text to flow into a particular location (across two columns, for example), click and drag the loaded text cursor across the area to be filled (above).

Semi-automatic flow is ideal in a publication such as the one shown above. Not only do you save effort but you retain complete control over placement of each text block.

Placing text on the page by flowing it into each column in turn and then clicking on the downward arrow is straightforward but gets very monotonous. Fortunately, PageMaker provides more efficient mechanisms. Text can also be placed automatically to save time and semi-automatically when more control is required.

Automatic flow. Use *Place...* from the *File* menu, but for automatic flow turn on *Autoflow* from the *Layout* menu—you can do this either before you choose *Place...* or when the text is loaded and you are about to flow the story on to the page.

You will notice that the loaded-text cursor changes to one indicating text flowing into columns. This tells you that *Autoflow* is active.

Now when you click to position the cursor in the first column, PageMaker continues to flow the text automatically into successive columns for you—you don't need to click at the bottom of the text blocks. In fact, you don't even need to hold the mouse anymore. Just sit back and let PageMaker do the work for you.

Not only will it flow text into each column but it will also add pages to the publication, as required, and continue to flow the complete story. New pages are added with the structure you have specified on the master pages (another good reason for setting master pages!).

Autoflow can also be switched on and off temporarily by holding down the COMMAND key (Macintosh) or CTRL key (Windows) before you click the loaded-text cursor into place. If *Autoflow* is not set, holding down the COMMAND or CTRL key temporarily gives you the loaded-text icon for automatic flow; if *Autoflow* is set, the COMMAND key temporarily gives you the manual flow icon.

Automatic flow is a real time saver in straightforward publications where text flows into each and every column. However, in publications where some columns are set aside for special purposes (such as subheadings or side panels) it can involve a lot of extra reworking.

Semi-automatic flow. This gives you the control of manual flow but removes the need for you to click at the bottom of each story block to load the next part of the story.

To flow text semi-automatically, use *Place...* and hold down the SHIFT key when the loaded-text icon appears. It does not matter if *Autoflow* is set or not—the SHIFT key temporarily changes both manual and automatic flow to semi-automatic flow. The icon is similar to the autoflow icon but with dotted lines to indicate the flow of text.

Click to place the first column of the story. The next part of the text is then automatically loaded for you to click into place, and so on in subsequent columns. Keep the SHIFT key pressed.

• Semi-automatic flow gives you control over the placement of text blocks and also saves effort.

• With *Autoflow* set, text is flowed into the next column with free space. This can be unpredictable on complex pages.

• To stop autoflow in its tracks, simply click the Cancel button.

• If the font size of the text being placed is to be reduced when it is on the page it is best not to place the complete story using *Autoflow*. If you do you will end up with extra pages which you have to delete. It is easier to place the first part of the story manually, *Select all* with the text tool, change the size and then flow the rest of the story.

• Some import filters provide further options if you hold down the SHIFT key as you click OK in the *Place...* box.

Formatting paragraphs 18

Type

Font ▶
Size ▶
Leading ▶
Set width ▶
Track ▶
Type style ▶

Type specs... ⌘T
Paragraph... ⌘M
Indents/tabs... ⌘I
Hyphenation... ⌘H

Alignment ▶
Style ▶

Define styles... ⌘3

Paragraph specifications

Indents:

Left `0` mm
First `0` mm
Right `0` mm

Paragraph space:

Before `0` mm
After `0` mm

OK
Cancel

Rules...
Spacing...

Alignment: `Left`   Dictionary: `UK English`

Options:

☐ Keep lines together   ☐ Keep with next `0` lines
☐ Column break before   ☐ Widow control `0` lines
☐ Page break before   ☐ Orphan control `0` lines
☐ Include in table of contents

The paragraph specifications box (left) provides access to a wealth of formatting options. The Rules... and Spacing... buttons give you access to other specification boxes which are described later.

Select the paragraph to be formatted (with the text tool) and choose *Paragraph...* from the *Type* menu to reach the paragraph specifications box.

Click once with the text tool to position the insertion point anywhere in the paragraph to be formatted.

A single click with the text tool inside a paragraph (left) is sufficient to 'select' it.

Select a portion of each if several paragraphs are to be 'selected' for formatting (right).

tool to position the insertion point anywhere in the paragraph to be formatted.
If there are several, simply select a portion of each.

Setting the appearance of text has been described earlier—select the text and apply the required formatting to the selected words. Additional formatting can be applied at the paragraph level, of which alignment (left, centre, right or justify) is probably the most common.

The key to applying paragraph formats successfully is to use styles but before these are discussed it is worth becoming familiar with the method of formatting paragraphs manually—not only to set the groundwork for styles but also because local formatting has its uses too.

Selecting paragraphs. To specify formatting at the paragraph level you need to select the paragraph(s) to be formatted first. Since these specifications dictate how the whole paragraph will look, it is not necessary to select every character in the paragraph (as you would when changing the font, for example).

Instead, simply click once with the text tool to place the insertion point somewhere inside the paragraph. You can then format it. If you want to format several paragraphs at once, just ensure that a part of each paragraph is selected.

Specifications. Apart from the obvious *Alignment* (to specify the overall shape of a paragraph), the *Type* menu gives access to a wealth of formatting options through *Paragraph...*, which brings the dialog box for paragraph specifications on screen. This can look very intimidating to a newcomer but is worth investigating.

Indents. These are the distances by which the Left and Right margins of a paragraph can be made to move away from the edge of a column—for example, you might want a quotation to stand out by being offset within the column on both sides. First sets an indent on the first line only, typically used to make paragraph beginnings stand out in dense passages of text.

Space. You can add extra space at the beginning or end of a paragraph in the Before and After boxes. Additional space built into a paragraph will give you more flexibility than blank lines inserted manually since it is easier to change, especially as part of a style definition (described later).

Rules. The Rules... button provides a dialog box which allows you to attach a line (a rule) to the top or bottom of a paragraph. Not only does this save drawing it manually but the rule stays with the paragraph when it moves.

The exact placement of rules takes a bit of practice but it is not complicated. Click on the Rules... button and try some of the options offered. Rules are described in more detail later.

- Alignment options can be chosen from the Control palette, from a pop-up menu in Paragraph specifications (or from the *Type* menu) but it is often simpler to use the keyboard shortcuts for manual formatting.

- Use the force justify alignment option to justify a heading or the last line of a paragraph.

- Extensive use is made of paragraph specifications when defining styles so it is worth your while becoming familiar with the formatting options available in this box.

- Spacing... is critical to the overall typography of a paragraph and is discussed in detail later.

- Use styles to format paragraphs whenever possible.

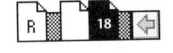

Leading

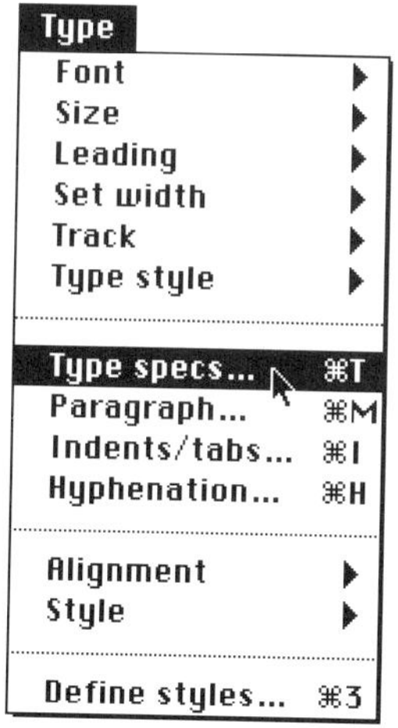

Type
Font ▶
Size ▶
Leading ▶
Set width ▶
Track ▶
Type style ▶

Type specs... ⌘T
Paragraph... ⌘M
Indents/tabs... ⌘I
Hyphenation... ⌘H

Alignment ▶
Style ▶

Define styles... ⌘3

Type specifications

Font: [Times]

Size: [9] ▷ points

Leading: [Auto] | ✓Auto
Set width: [Normal] | 8
Color: [Black] | 8.5
| 9
| 9.5
Type style: ⊠ Norm | 10 | alic
☐ Bold | 10.5 | derl
| **11**
| 13.5
| 18
| 27

Spacing attributes   [OK]

Word space: Letter space: [Cancel]
Minimum [75] %   Minimum [-5] %   [Reset]
Desired [100] %   Desired [0] %
Maximum [150] %   Maximum [25] %

Pair kerning: ⊠ Auto above [4] points

Leading method: Autoleading:
● Proportional   [120] % of point size
○ Top of caps
○ Baseline

To set leading, select the text using the text tool and choose either *Leading* or *Type specs...* from the Type menu.

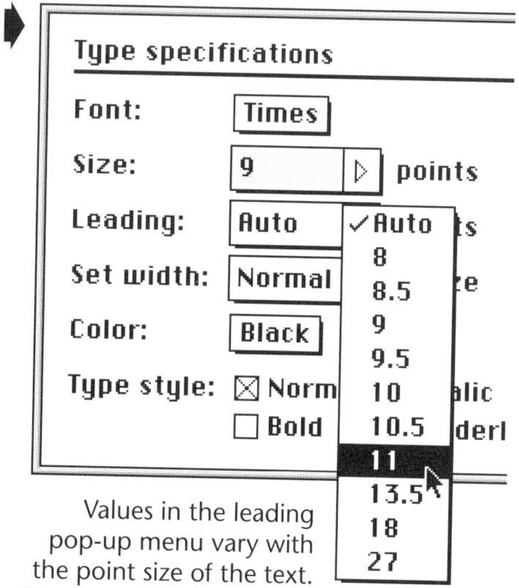

Values in the leading pop-up menu vary with the point size of the text. You can also type leading values into the box

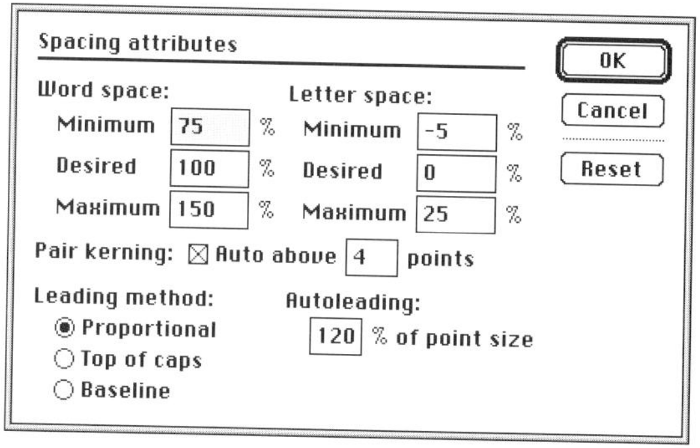

The Spacing... button in the *Paragraph...* box (described earlier) gives you access to the spacing attributes box where you can specify the leading method and the percentage for automatic leading. These are best set once at the program level (i.e. without a document open).

An example of each leading method (right). In each, a portion of text is selected to show the way vertical space is distributed.

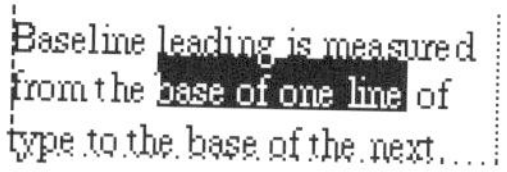

Baseline leading is measured from the base of one line of type to the base of the next.

Baseline leading

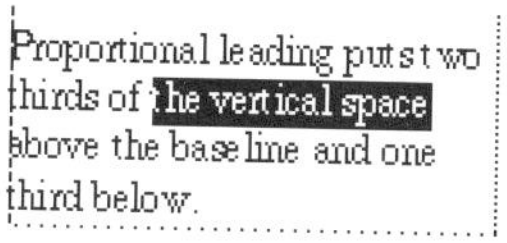

Proportional leading puts two thirds of the vertical space above the baseline and one third below.

Proportional

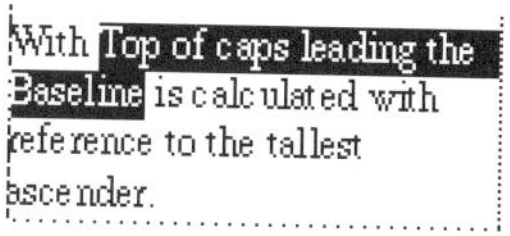

With Top of caps leading the Baseline is calculated with reference to the tallest ascender.

Top of caps

Control of the space around letters and words is the key to successful typography. When you are setting type on a page you should aim to make it as easy as possible to read, so space is an important consideration.

Although PageMaker does a lot of work for you, it is better to take some control—even if you are a complete novice.

Within blocks of text, space is distributed between lines, between words and between letters. Controlling the space between words and letters is complicated and is discussed later.

Leading. The space between lines is called *leading* and within PageMaker leading refers to the vertical space occupied by a line of type.

For example, you might expect a line with type set at a size of 10 points (10pt) to occupy 10 points vertically. However, PageMaker adds an additional 20% leading automatically so that the line actually occupies 12 points vertically (i.e. six lines to the inch). Within that space, the text will be smaller than you expect since the size (10pt) includes some space built into the structure of the character itself—this space varies and depends on the design of the individual typeface.

If typography is new to you, use automatic leading (Auto) until you begin to get a feel for what you are doing but you will eventually want to take more control.

Specifying. Leading is set by selecting text and choosing a value from the *Leading* submenu or in the *Type specs...* box (just below type size).

Leading methods. PageMaker provides three different leading methods—baseline, proportional and top of caps.

Baseline leading is measured from the base of one line of type to the baseline of the next and is the method used by professionals. Proportional leading distributes the space so that two-thirds is above the baseline with one-third below. Top of caps leading is calculated from the top of the highest ascender *in the font* and predicting the position of the baseline is difficult.

Use proportional leading to begin with (it makes type easier to select on screen) but you will eventually appreciate the extra control provided by baseline leading.

Choose the leading method which best suits your needs by choosing *Paragraph...* from the *Type* menu and click on the *Spacing...* button. Don't vary the method from paragraph to paragraph.

Check to see what method is preset and, if you want to change it, set it once at the program level (as explained earlier).

To see the vertical space occupied by a line of type, select some text with the text tool to see the line's 'slug' (another term from metal type).

- Type is measured in points. Although the term may be new to you, there is nothing complicated involved—it is simply a unit of measurement:

72 pts = 1 inch

It is worthwhile getting to know this system since designers and printers use it and it will allow you to develop a better understanding of what you are doing.

- Leading is pronounced 'ledding' and is a term originating from the days of metal type.

- Leading has a marked effect on the overall look (the colour) of text. You can make text dense (if you absolutely have to cram it all in!) or add extra leading to give text a light and open feel.

- The longer the line of type, the more generous the leading should be.

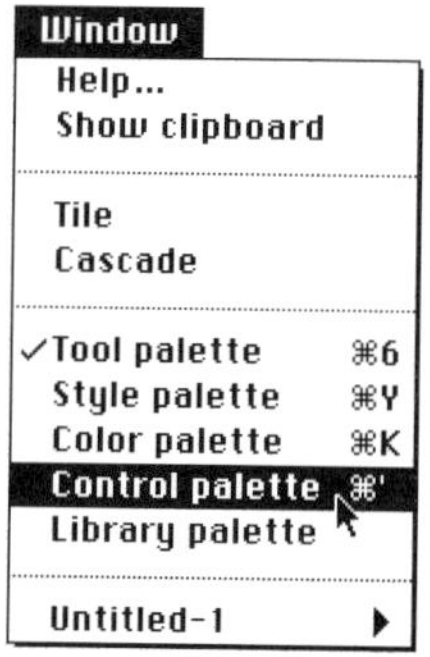

Text under control 20

Window
Help...
Show clipboard

Tile
Cascade

✓Tool palette   ⌘6
Style palette   ⌘Y
Color palette   ⌘K
Control palette ⌘'
Library palette

Untitled-1   ▶

Choose *Control palette*
from the *Window* menu
to make it visible.

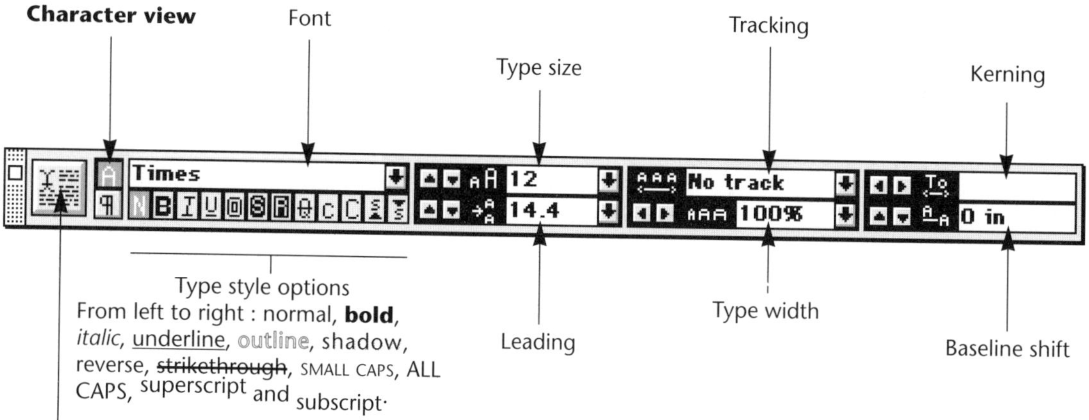

Character view   Font   Type size   Tracking   Kerning

Times   12   No track

14.4   100%   0 in

Type style options
From left to right : normal, **bold**,
italic, underline, outline, shadow,
reverse, ~~strikethrough~~, SMALL CAPS, ALL
CAPS, superscript and subscript·

Leading   Type width   Baseline shift

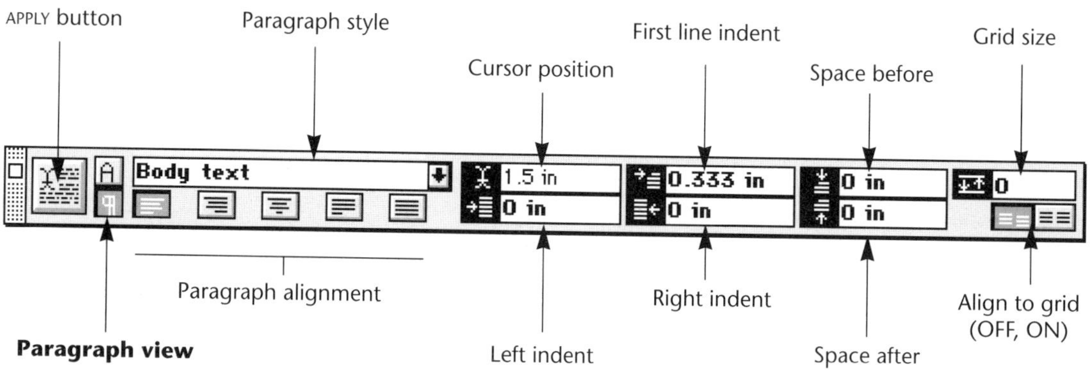

APPLY button   Paragraph style   Cursor position   First line indent   Space before   Grid size

Body text   1.5 in   0.333 in   0 in   0

0 in   0 in   0 in

Paragraph alignment   Right indent   Align to grid (OFF, ON)

Paragraph view   Left indent   Space after

Since you are probably already familiar with text and paragraph formatting in other programs you should have no difficulty formatting text using the *Type* menu. However, no matter how comfortable and familiar it feels to use menu options, make an effort to learn how to use the control palette too. The palette provides more immediate access to a wealth of formatting choices and will save you time.

You can use the palette to position, move and manipulate objects and also to format text.

The control palette displays different options depending on the tool you are using—each set of options is called a view.

Control palette. If it is not already visible, choose *Control palette* from the *Window* menu to make it available (and to hide it again).

Some options on the palette have drop-down lists and these are accessed by clicking on the downward-pointing arrows; other options have nudge arrows which you can click to modify the values in a field.

Formatting text. When the text tool is selected the control palette displays text formatting options and shows the attributes of any text selected. You use the palette by first selecting the text to be formatted (as described earlier) and then choosing the appropriate options in the palette.

If you select an option by clicking on it or by selecting one from a pop-up list, the effect is immediate. Otherwise, you will need to click the APPLY button (or press RETURN or TAB, or ENTER under Windows) for changes to take effect.

Character view. To the immediate right of the APPLY button in the palette are two buttons one above the other. Click on the top button (the letter A) when you want to format text at the character level—font, type style, leading, etc.

Paragraph view. Click on the lower of the two buttons next to the APPLY button to display paragraph-level formatting options—alignment, indents, space before and after, etc.

You can also apply paragraph styles (described later) using the pop-up menu in the palette.

Keyboard control. It takes some getting used to, but you can use the palette from the keyboard.

You can also use COMMAND-` (grave) to activate the palette (CTRL-` under Windows) and to move between palette and page. Use the TAB key to move between options (and arrow keys to move between multiple options). Use the SPACE bar to switch highlighted options on or off.

You can also apply a font or a style by tabbing to the appropriate field and then typing enough of the font or style name to uniquely identify it.

• Unless you have a small screen and need the space, choose *Control palette* from the *Window* menu before you open a document and it will be automatically displayed in all new documents.

• Don't forget that you need to select text or a paragraph before you can make formatting changes.

• Use COMMAND-SHIFT-` (grave) to alternate between character and paragraph views, and TAB to move between options.

• Hold down the COMMAND key as you click on nudge buttons for ten times their normal value.

• Position the cursor in a paragraph by eye and use the cursor position indicator to find its exact position if you want to type a value that you have worked out visually into an indent field.

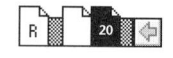

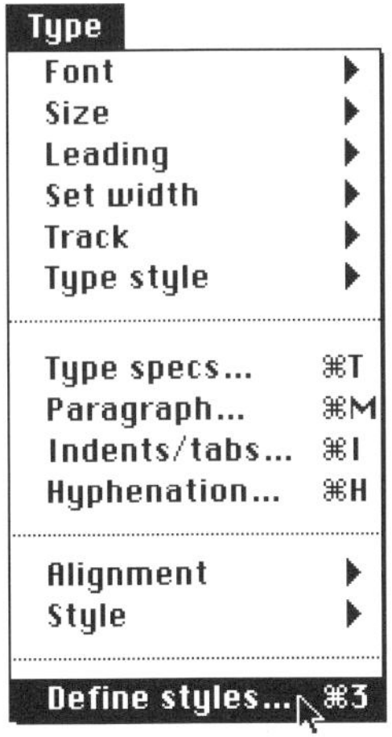

Defining styles

21

Type

Font	▶
Size	▶
Leading	▶
Set width	▶
Track	▶
Type style	▶
Type specs...	⌘T
Paragraph...	⌘M
Indents/tabs...	⌘I
Hyphenation...	⌘H
Alignment	▶
Style	▶
Define styles...	⌘3

Choose *Define styles...*
from the *Type* menu.

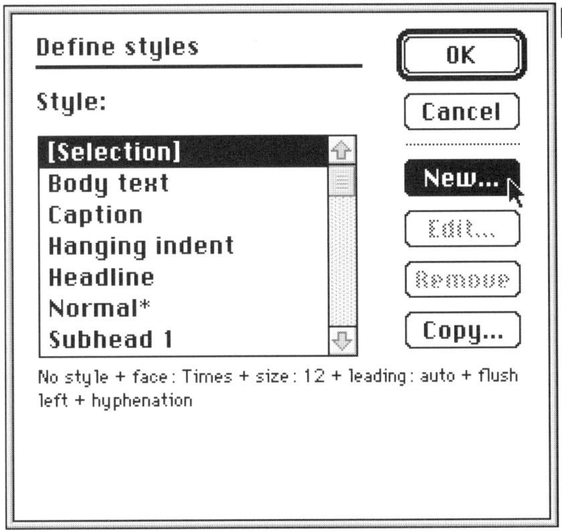

Define styles

Style:

[Selection]
Body text
Caption
Hanging indent
Headline
Normal*
Subhead 1

No style + face : Times + size : 12 + leading : auto + flush
left + hyphenation

[OK]
[Cancel]
[New...]
[Edit...]
[Remove]
[Copy...]

The Define styles box shows the styles already defined
(above). You can remove those you don't need by
selecting each in turn and clicking the Remove
button. Keep 'Hanging indent' for now. If you
position the cursor in a paragraph with a style
attached before you choose *Define styles...*, that style
name will be highlighted in the Style box and a
summary of its attributes will be shown.

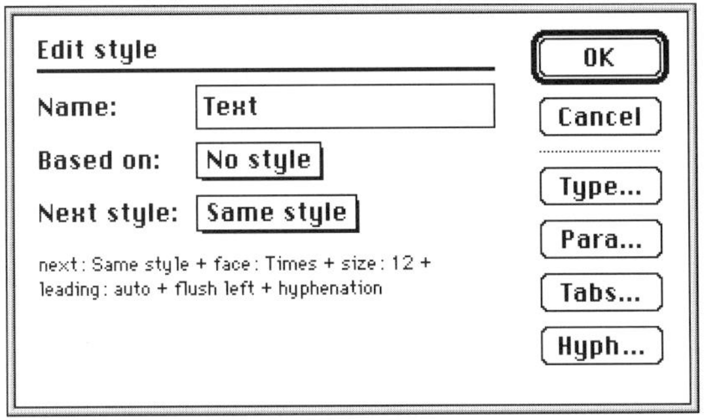

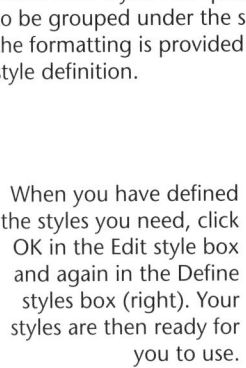

Edit style

Name:	Text
Based on:	No style
Next style:	Same style

next: Same style + face : Times + size : 12 +
leading : auto + flush left + hyphenation

[OK]
[Cancel]
[Type...]
[Para...]
[Tabs...]
[Hyph...]

To define a new style, click the New... button to
reach the Edit style box (above) and type a name for
the style. Then click the Type... and Para... buttons to
access the type and paragraph specification dialog
boxes where you can specify the formatting attributes
to be grouped under the style name. A summary of
the formatting is provided in the box as you build the
style definition.

When you have defined
the styles you need, click
OK in the Edit style box
and again in the Define
styles box (right). Your
styles are then ready for
you to use.

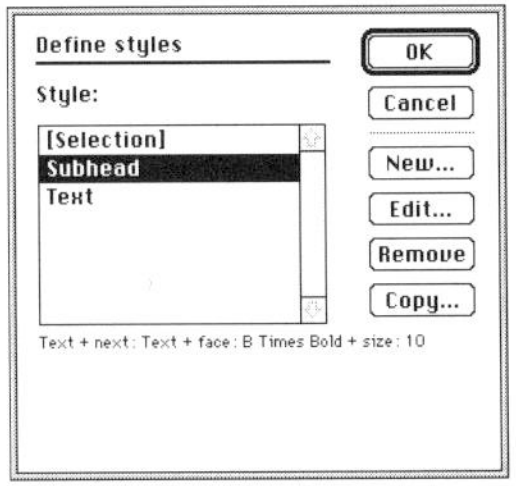

Define styles

Style:

[Selection]
Subhead
Text

Text + next : Text + face : B Times Bold + size : 10

[OK]
[Cancel]
[New...]
[Edit...]
[Remove]
[Copy...]

By far the most efficient way to manage the appearance of text in a publication is to use styles. Although you can format text (*Type specs…*) and paragraphs (*Paragraph…*) manually using the text tool, it is not efficient to work this way over a complete publication.

Styles allow you to group a range of type and paragraph attributes under a single name and thus to apply them all in one go.

For example, if the text of your publication (often called body text) is to be set justified in 9pt Times on 11pt leading, you could define a style called 'Text' to mean 'Times, 9pt type on 11pt leading, justified' and then format the appropriate paragraphs using that style name. Similarly, a style called 'Subhead' could mean 'Times Bold, 10pt on 11pt leading, left aligned' and could be used to format subheadings.

Design decisions. Before you define styles for use in a publication you must make some decisions (the design process). You will need, at least, to be aware of the hierarchy of headings and subheadings, and the various paragraph formats you intend to use. Is the text to be set in the same font as the subheads? Will some paragraph styles differ only slightly from others? You need to decide how you want the publication to look.

Styles are not difficult. They make layout so much easier that it is important to use them.

Defining styles. To define a style choose *Define styles…* from the *Type* menu. In the dialog box that follows you will save yourself a lot of confusion later if you first remove the existing styles supplied by PageMaker. Do this by clicking on each in turn to select it and then click on the Remove button.

To define your own styles, click on the New… button and give the first style a name. Then click on the Type… and Para… buttons in turn and specify the formatting attributes to be grouped under that name (the buttons give you access to dialog boxes which you should be reasonably familiar with by now). Click the OK buttons in the dialog boxes as you go. Tabs and Hyphenation will be described later.

Once you are satisfied with the style definition (double check it by looking at the summary list as it builds up), click OK. The style name appears in the list of styles. You can continue to define several styles by clicking on the New… button each time and repeating the sequence. Click OK in the Define styles box when you have prepared what you need.

Shortcut. You can also define a style by formatting a paragraph first and then typing a name into the style field on the control palette. You will then be given the option to add that style definition.

Try defining two or three styles and take them for a test drive (see Using styles).

• If you are using your own computer, remove the style names supplied by PageMaker at the program level (i.e. without a document open) to avoid confusion with your own style names.

• If you want to change some part of a style once it has been defined, for example the type size, select the style name from the list in the *Define styles…* box and click on the Edit button.

• Use meaningful style names—subFirst, subSecond, text, textIndented, etc.

• If a new style is similar to an existing one (suppose you have two kinds of text paragraph, one of which is indented), select the existing style name in the Based on: pop-up menu to save time.

• OPTION-click on OK or Cancel to close all boxes.

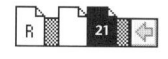

Using styles 22

Type

Font	▶
Size	▶
Leading	▶
Set width	▶
Track	▶
Type style	▶
Type specs...	⌘T
Paragraph...	⌘M
Indents/tabs...	⌘I
Hyphenation...	⌘H
Alignment	▶
Style	▶
Define styles...	⌘3

Style submenu:
- ✓[No style]
- Subhead
- Text
- Text indented

Styles
- [No style]
- Subhead
- Text
- **TextIndented**

Open the style palette (above) by selecting *Style palette* from the *Window* menu and click on a style name (above) to apply it.

Although you can apply styles using the *Style* submenu on the *Type* menu (above), it is quicker to use the style palette or the control palette.

To format a paragraph using a style definition, click the text tool inside the paragraph to position the text insertion cursor (top) and then click on the style name in the style palette. The attributes grouped under that style name will be applied to the 'selected' paragraph which will then be reformatted (right) as defined in the style.

To format a paragraph using a style, it is first necessary to 'select' the paragraph by clicking inside it with the text insertion cursor (text tool).

To format a paragraph using a style, it is first necessary to 'select' the paragraph by clicking inside it with the text insertion cursor (text tool).

Subheading

Dolor sit amet, adipiscing elit, sed diam nonummy nibh euismod tincidunt ut laoreet dolore magna aliquam erat volutpat.

Subheading

Ut wisi enim ad minim

Once you assign a style to a paragraph (as in subheadings, left), when you edit the definition of that style the paragraph is automatically reformatted according to the new definition (right). Changing subheadings throughout a document from 10pt Times Bold to 12pt Helvetica Bold with a 4pt rule above it, takes very little effort. (Illustrations enlarged.)

Subheading

Dolor sit amet, adipiscing elit, sed diam nonummy nibh euismod tincidunt ut laoreet dolore magna aliquam erat volutpat.

Subheading

Once you have defined the styles for your publication, you can use them to format text. The easiest way to apply styles is to use the style palette. If it is not already visible, choose *Style palette* from the *Window* menu. The palette shows a list of styles already defined and has a close box, a scroll bar and a resize box.

Applying styles. Suppose, for example, that you have initially defined two styles – Text (Times, 9/11, justified) and Subhead (Times, bold, 10/11, left aligned) – as described earlier.

To assign a style to a paragraph, click with the text tool to position the text insertion cursor inside the paragraph to be formatted. Once you have 'selected' the paragraph in this way, click on the appropriate style name (for example, the text style) in the style palette, or select it on the control palette, to apply all of the attributes grouped under that name to the paragraph. Watch, as PageMaker does the work for you, applying font, size and alignment attributes (and anything else you have included in the style definition) all at once. Then move the cursor to the next paragraph and again click on a style name in the style palette (this time possibly the subheading style), and so on.

Shortcut. If there is a predominant style, for example for paragraphs of text, use *Select all* from the *Edit* menu and apply the text style to the complete story. Then move through the story from the beginning and apply subheading styles where appropriate. You will find this quicker than applying a style to each individual paragraph.

Style benefits. Styles bring additional benefits beyond ease of formatting. Once a paragraph has a style name associated with it, any change in the style definition is automatically applied to that paragraph. For example, if having produced the first draft of your publication (and assuming that you have used styles) you decide that you want subheadings set in Helvetica not Times (a daunting manual task), edit the subhead style. Choose *Define styles…* again, select the style name and click on the Edit button. Change the font via the Type… button and click OK. Click OK in the Edit styles box when you have finished editing and watch as all of the subheadings are magically changed from Times to Helvetica—the style name is the same but you have changed its meaning.

Importing styles. Some word processors allow styles to be defined which PageMaker can understand. These can be applied as text is typed and carried with it when it is placed on the page. They can then be edited, as required, in the final publication. An asterisk (*) is added to these style names in the style palette to highlight the fact that they have been imported with the text.

• Styles can also be applied from the control palette in paragraph view.

• To edit a style quickly, hold down the COMMAND key (CTRL under Windows) and click on its name in the style or control palette. To define a new style, COMMAND-click [No style].

• Use the Copy… button in the *Define styles…* box to copy style definitions from another publication.

• Style names are shown on the left side of the story editor window. They can be applied in this window but you will not see the changes until you return to the layout view.

• Styles can be saved as part of a template.

• Styles encourage you to plan your publication before you begin to construct it—a good discipline, particularly if you do not have a design background.

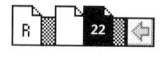

Style spin-offs

23

Utilities

Aldus Additions ▶

Find... ⌘8
Find next ⌘,
Change... ⌘9
Spelling... ⌘L

Index entry... ⌘;
Show index...
Create index...
Create TOC...

Choose *Create TOC...* from the *Utilities* menu to have PageMaker generate a table of contents for you—but paragraphs have to be marked for inclusion first.

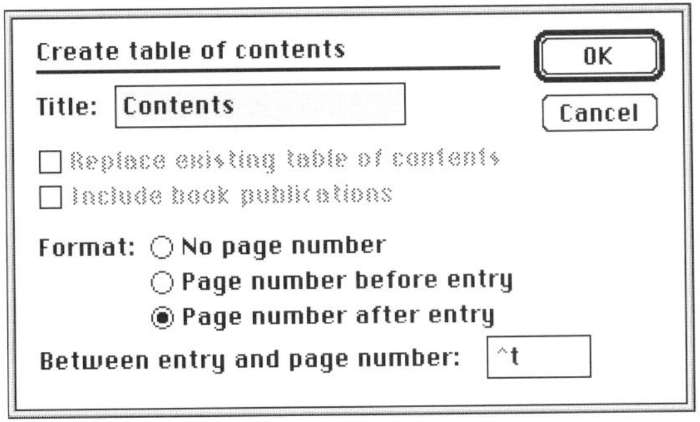

Create table of contents   [OK]   [Cancel]

Title: [Contents]

☐ Replace existing table of contents
☐ Include book publications

Format: ○ No page number
         ○ Page number before entry
         ◉ Page number after entry

Between entry and page number: [^t]

You can specify the structure of a table of contents in the *Create TOC...* box (above)—^t means tab.

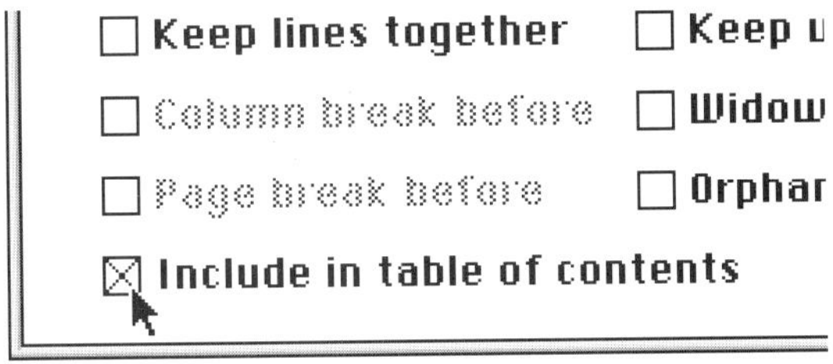

☐ **Keep lines together**   ☐ **Keep u**
☐ Column break before   ☐ **Widow**
☐ Page break before   ☐ **Orphar**
☒ **Include in table of contents**

The check box to mark paragraphs for inclusion in a table of contents is at the bottom of the paragraph box (above), reached via *Paragraph...* (on *Type* menu).

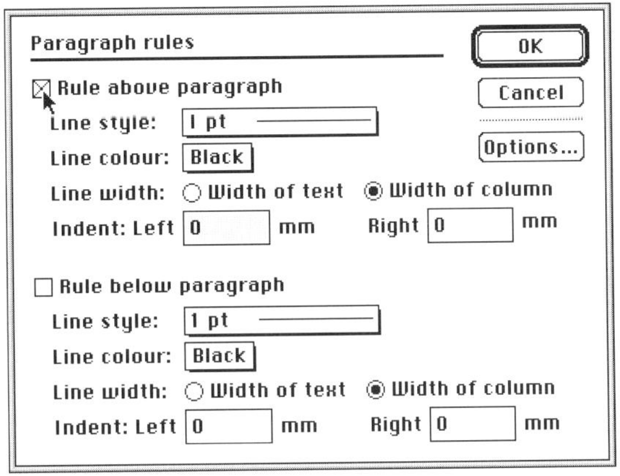

Paragraph rules   [OK]   [Cancel]   [Options...]

☒ **Rule above paragraph**
Line style: [1 pt ————]
Line colour: [Black]
Line width: ○ Width of text ◉ Width of column
Indent: Left [0] mm   Right [0] mm

☐ **Rule below paragraph**
Line style: [1 pt ————]
Line colour: [Black]
Line width: ○ Width of text ◉ Width of column
Indent: Left [0] mm   Right [0] mm

To include a rule (line) as part of a paragraph, click the Rules... button in the paragraph specifications box (from *Paragraph...* on the *Type* menu). Click the Options... button (left), to position it accurately (below).

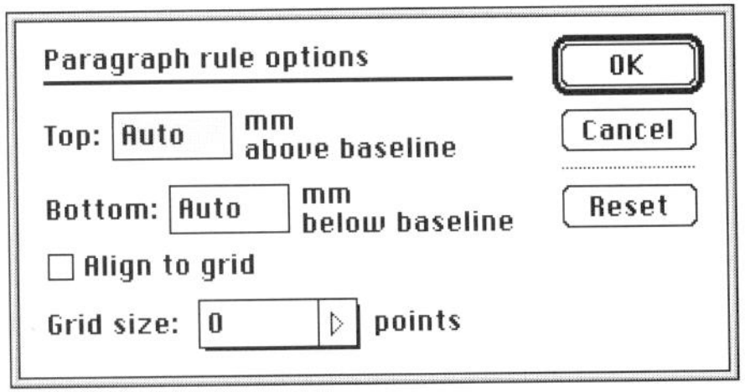

Paragraph rule options   [OK]   [Cancel]   [Reset]

Top: [Auto] mm above baseline

Bottom: [Auto] mm below baseline

☐ Align to grid

Grid size: [0] ▷ points

Keep in mind, when you are doing layout work, that you want PageMaker to do as much of the work as possible. Besides those already mentioned, styles bring many additional benefits.

Table of contents. You can produce a table of contents (TOC) by choosing *Create TOC...* from the *Options* menu. However, you must first indicate the paragraphs you want included—these will usually be headings and subheadings.

Tucked away at the bottom of the paragraph specification box (*Paragraph...* from the *Type* menu) is a powerful little checkbox labelled: Include in table of contents.

Although you can check this box to mark individual subheadings for inclusion in the table of contents, it is more sensible to include it in the style definition. That way you save additional effort and you are less likely to miss paragraphs which should be included.

Having marked the paragraphs for inclusion, when you choose *Create TOC...* you are presented with a box which allows you to specify the format of the contents list. When you click OK PageMaker builds the table of contents and loads it onto the cursor for you to place (just as though you had used *Place...* from the *File* menu).

Separate style definitions are automatically applied to the contents list and are shown in the style palette. You can edit these styles to format the table of contents—font, size, etc.

Paragraph rules. You might occasionally want a line (rule) drawn above or below a paragraph for emphasis. Again, this will usually be a heading or subheading. You can draw rules using the line drawing tools but they are independent of the text—if the text moves because you edit, delete or insert earlier text, the line does not move with it so you end up having to reposition it.

Paragraph rules are part of a paragraph and do stay with it if it moves. They are applied by clicking on the Rules... button in the paragraph specifications box. From the variety of options provided, you can customise the position and size of the rule.

To save effort, paragraph rules can (and should!) be used as part of a style definition.

Consistency. Styles can help to eliminate human error and to ensure consistency in a publication. If styles can be applied as text is typed in a word processor, particularly if it is being typed by the author who will be familiar with its structure and with the hierarchy of headings, then a lot of the formatting work on the final page will be easier—the style definitions can be edited in the final publication to match the design requirements.

• A table of contents can be generated across a series of publications which are part of a book (explained later).

• If at some stage you decide that a table of contents would be useful, and you have not planned for it, edit the heading styles and tick the box. PageMaker can then generate a TOC for you.

• You can take advantage of the fact that style definitions within PageMaker take precedence over styles with the same name coming from a word processor. When text is being drafted it is sensible that it be produced in a typeface and size suitable for editing—so the styles should be defined with that in mind. If the style name is already defined in PageMaker, text will be reformatted (according to the style definition in PageMaker) as it is placed on the page.

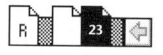

Text editing tools   24

Utilities

Aldus Additions ▷

Find...   ⌘8
Find next   ⌘,
Change...   ⌘9
Spelling...   ⌘L

Index entry...   ⌘;
Show index...
Create index...
Create TOC...

Inside the Story Editor, editing tools (*Spelling...,* *Find...* and *Change...*) become available on the *Utilities* menu.

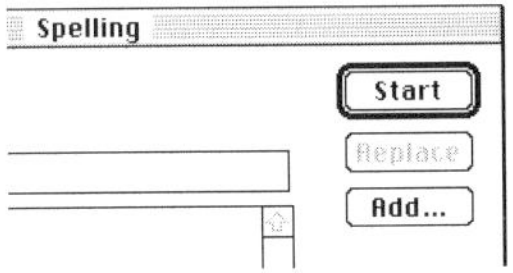

Spelling

[Start]

[Replace]
[Add...]

Choose *Spelling...* and click on the Start button to begin a spelling check (above).

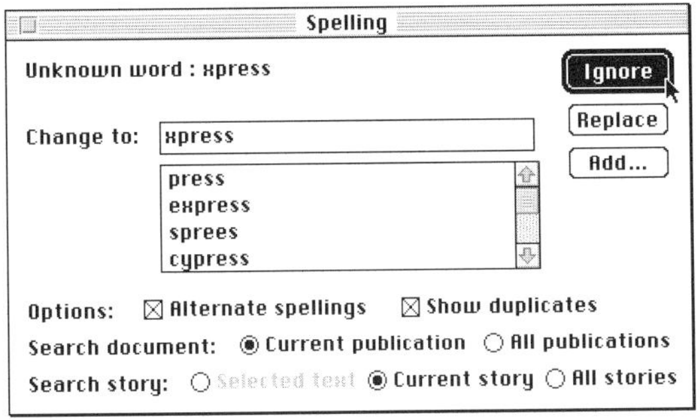

Spelling

Unknown word : xpress   [**Ignore**]

Change to: xpress   [Replace]

            press   [Add...]
            express
            sprees
            cypress

Options: ☒ Alternate spellings   ☒ Show duplicates

Search document: ⦿ Current publication ◯ All publications
Search story: ◯ Selected text ⦿ Current story ◯ All stories

Unrecognised words are shown in the Change to: box for you to edit (above). They are also highlighted in context in the text. By setting the various options you can extend the spelling check to all stories in the document or to all open publications.

Add word to user dictionary

Word: dic~~tion~ary
Dictionary: UK English
Add: ◯ As all lowercase
            ⦿ Exactly as typed

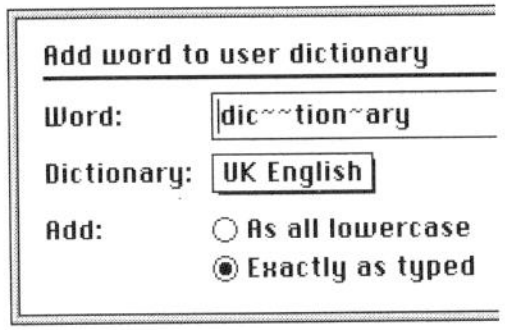

The Add... button (left) allows you to include an unrecognised word in the user dictionary (above). Type tildes (~) if you want to define hyphenation points.

Utilities

Aldus Additions ▷

Find...   ⌘8
Find next   ⌘,
Change...   ⌘9
Spelling...   ⌘L

Index entry...   ⌘;
Show index...
Create index...
Create TOC...

Choose *Change...* to find text and change it.

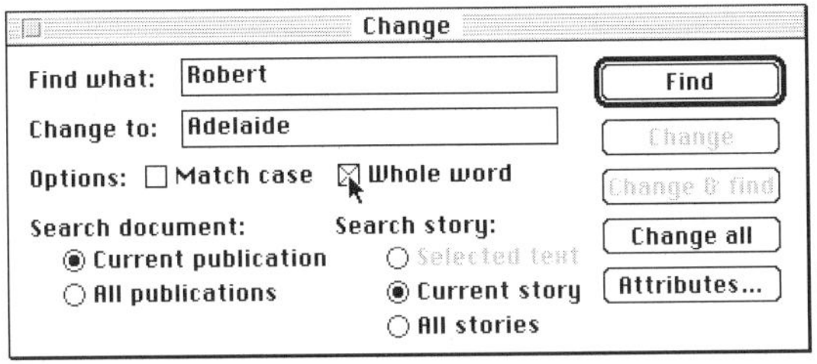

Change

Find what: Robert   [Find]

Change to: Adelaide   [Change]

Options: ☐ Match case   ☒ Whole word   [Change & find]

Search document: Search story: [Change all]
 ⦿ Current publication ◯ Selected text
 ◯ All publications   ⦿ Current story   [Attributes...]
                        ◯ All stories

You can extend the search to all stories in a document or to all open publications by setting the appropriate search option buttons.

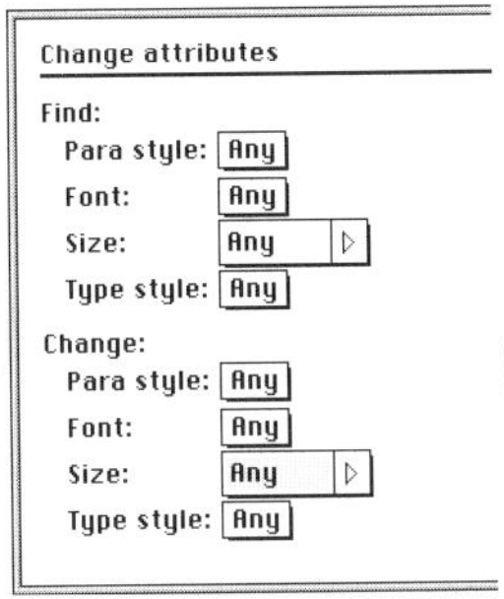

Change attributes

Find:
 Para style: Any
 Font: Any
 Size: Any   ▷
 Type style: Any
Change:
 Para style: Any
 Font: Any
 Size: Any   ▷
 Type style: Any

The Attributes... button allows you to limit a find or change to specific type formats via pop-up menus in the Change attributes box (left).

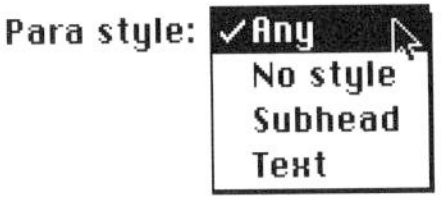

Para style: ✓Any
             No style
             Subhead
             Text

When you use the story editor, additional text editing tools are made available. You can use the spelling checker to find spelling mistakes in a particular story or in the document as a whole. You can also use it to spot typing mistakes, and some capitalisation and limited grammar errors. Also provided is a global search and replace facility which will allow you to find every occurrence of a word and replace it with another word, effortlessly—useful if a job title or a name has to be changed throughout a document at the last minute.

Both are features found in most word processors so you should have no trouble with the concepts.

Spelling. To check spelling, open the story in the story editor (*Edit story* from the *Edit* menu as described earlier) and choose *Spelling...* from the *Utilities* menu.

To begin, click the Start button in the dialog box (or press RETURN). Each word not recognised is shown in turn giving you the option to correct it. Correct the word in the Change to: box or double-click the correct one in the list of suggestions. To leave a word as it is click Ignore (or press RETURN). Add opens the box which allows you to add the unrecognised word to the user dictionary. PageMaker uses the same dictionary for hyphenation and spelling so you can add tildes (~) to the word when you add it to the dictionary to show where you want it to break—from one tilde for the best hyphenation position to three for the least favourable position.

Find and change. You can use *Change...* on the *Utilities* menu to find all occurrences of a particular word or text string and change it to something else (in a story, a publication or across several publications). Type the text you want to modify in the Find what: field, the text you want to change it to in the Change to: field and click on the Find or Change all button. The Options check boxes allow you to limit the search to whole words ('page' would not find 'PageMaker' if checked) and to specify an exact upper/lowercase match as typed. Use Change all with caution until you are familiar with it—you can use Change and find instead to show each occurrence of the located text in context so that you can make a decision.

The Attributes button allows you to limit a search based on the way the text is formatted – find words only when they occur within a specific style, for example – and to specify a typographic format for the replacement text. You can also leave the Find what: and Change to: fields empty if you need to search on typographic attributes only—for example, find unknown words highlighted in bold and change them to italic instead.

• The spelling checker is not a substitute for proof reading. It will not catch mistakes such as the use of the word 'there' instead of 'their'.

• The spelling checker window can be kept on screen and moved around just like any other window.

• If you want to check a particular block of text only, select it before initiating the spelling checker.

• You can use ^? as a wildcard in *Find...* (match any character). Use ^p to find end of paragraph marks or ^t for tabs.

• To remind you that you have set attributes for find and/or change, Find what: and Change to: are underlined in the Change box. OPTION-click on the Attributes button to reset all the fields back to Any.

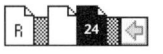

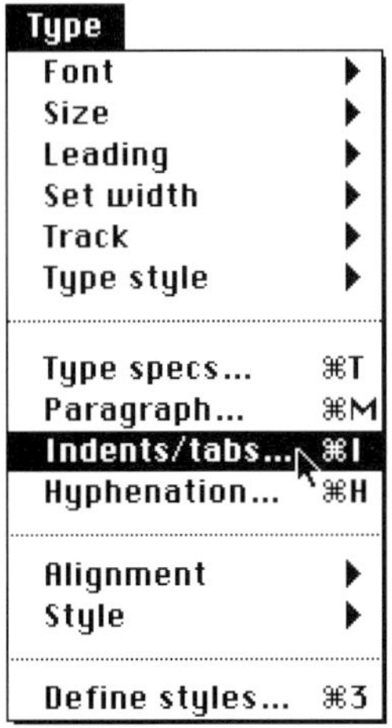

Indents and tabs   25

Type
- Font ▶
- Size ▶
- Leading ▶
- Set width ▶
- Track ▶
- Type style ▶

- Type specs...   ⌘T
- Paragraph...   ⌘M
- **Indents/tabs...   ⌘I**
- Hyphenation...   ⌘H

- Alignment ▶
- Style ▶

- Define styles...   ⌘3

To set indents or tabs, click to position the text cursor within the paragraph to be formatted and choose *Indents/tabs...* from the *Type* menu.

The Indents/Tabs window aligns the zero point of its ruler with the left-hand edge of the column. Tab positions are measured from there. The right margin of the column is also shown on the ruler.

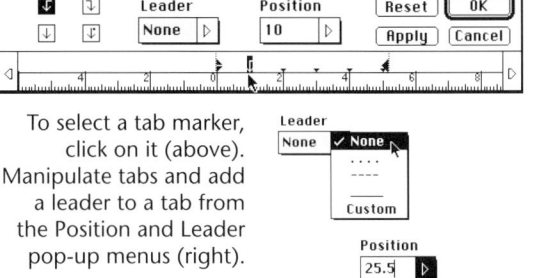

To select a tab marker, click on it (above). Manipulate tabs and add a leader to a tab from the Position and Leader pop-up menus (right).

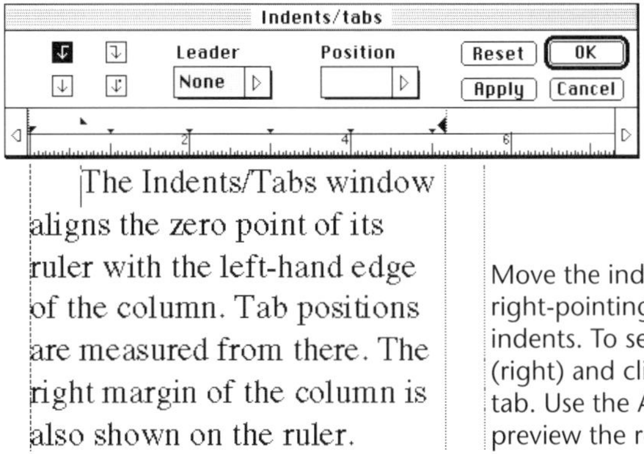

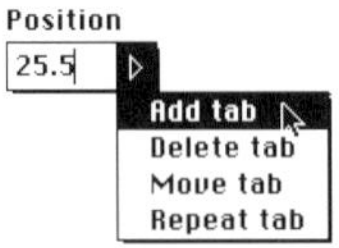

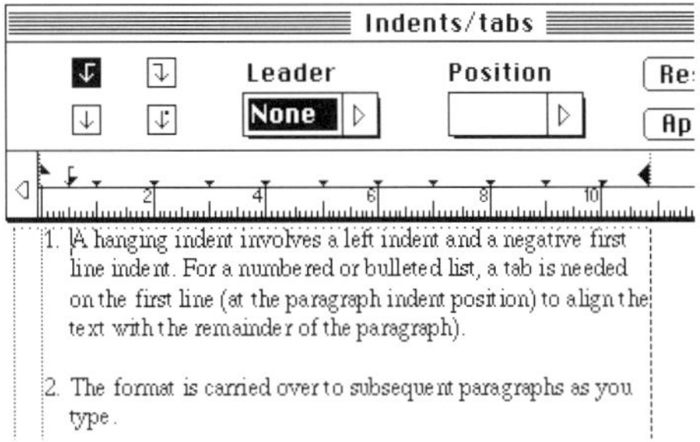

The upper part of the left indent marker (right) controls the first line and the lower part affects the paragraph as a whole. Preset tabs are shown as an inverted 'T'.

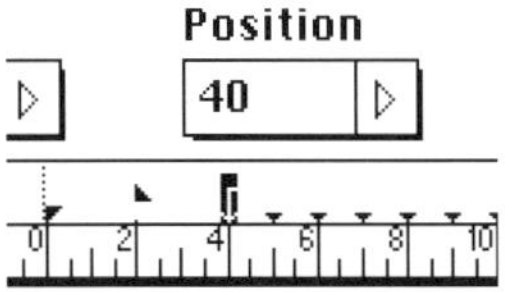

Move the indent markers (the left and right-pointing arrows) to set paragraph indents. To set a tab, select a tab icon (right) and click in the ruler to insert the tab. Use the Apply button if you want to preview the result.

Tab icons. Left, right; centre and decimal.

1. A hanging indent involves a left indent and a negative first line indent. For a numbered or bulleted list, a tab is needed on the first line (at the paragraph indent position) to align the text with the remainder of the paragraph).

2. The format is carried over to subsequent paragraphs as you type.

A hanging indent can be produced either by moving the indent markers as shown above; by using the *Paragraph...* box to set a paragraph indent and a negative first line indent, or by using the 'hanging indent' style provided in PageMaker.

When you produce tables in text, don't use spaces to align columns of text. Spaces worked on typewriters because the space occupied by each character was the same (Courier is a similar mono-spaced font available on computers). When setting type, characters occupy a space in proportion to their width so they don't all align in the same position—they are proportionally spaced. If you use spaces, characters won't align properly and the result will be unsatisfactory. The key is to use paragraph indents and tabs instead.

Indents and tabs are paragraph attributes you can set by choosing *Indents/Tabs*... from the *Type* menu. As with any paragraph formatting, you must first position the text insertion cursor within the paragraph you want to format.

Paragraph indents. Similar to those in other programs, the ruler within the Indents/Tabs... box has markers which show the left and right edges of the paragraph. The indent marker on the left is in two parts—the upper triangle marks the indent for the first line only while the lower triangle shows the left indent for the paragraph as a whole. You can move the upper marker independently, but to move the paragraph indent marker without moving the first line indent too, you must hold down the SHIFT key. When both are aligned with the left of the column, then the paragraph is not indented. To set or change either indent, drag the appropriate marker to the desired location.

Tabs. Ideal for lists and tables. To set a tab, click on a tab icon (left, right, centre or decimal) to select the alignment you want. Then click in the ruler at the point where you want the tab inserted (don't forget to put the text insertion cursor within the paragraph first). Tabs set by the program itself are shown in the ruler and the first tab you set clears all those to its left. You can change the position of a tab if you click on it to select it and then drag it to a new position or type its new location in the position field and select Move tab from the pop-up menu (nothing happens if you leave out this last step). You can also delete, add or set a series of tabs in this submenu.

Tab leaders. To lead the reader's eye across a wide column you can use a leader—a repeated pattern of dots or dashes. Choose the one you want from the leader pop-up menu before you set the tab.

Preview. Click the Apply button to see the result of changes before you close the ruler. If you are satisfied with the result, click OK; if not, try again, or click Reset (to start afresh) or Cancel.

• You can also set paragraph indents by typing values for the first line indent or for left and right indents in the *Paragraph specs*... box from the *Type* menu.

• If you need to indent the first line of a paragraph, use an indent rather than TAB, particularly when preparing text in a word processor. Tabs are retained as local formatting (just like an *italicised* word) and can only be manipulated and deleted manually. Indents are part of a paragraph's specification and can be altered in the *Paragraph*... dialog box, or as part of a style definition.

• Moving the first line indent marker on its own can be tricky at first.

• Type OPTION-8 if you need a bullet (•), for example in a hanging indent style.

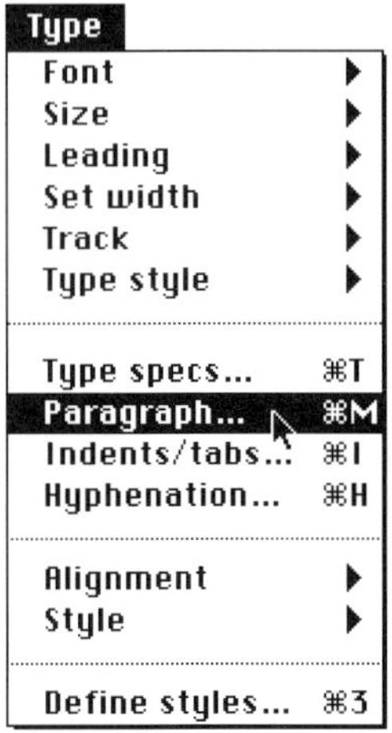

Word spacing 26

Type

Font	▶
Size	▶
Leading	▶
Set width	▶
Track	▶
Type style	▶

Type specs...	⌘T
Paragraph...	⌘M
Indents/tabs...	⌘I
Hyphenation...	⌘H

Alignment	▶
Style	▶

Define styles...	⌘3

To change the word spacing in a paragraph, position the text insertion cursor in the paragraph (or select a range of paragraphs) and choose *Paragraph...* from the *Type* menu as a first step.

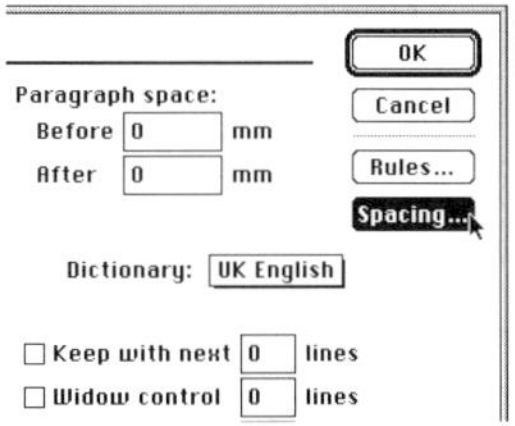

Paragraph space:
Before [0] mm
After [0] mm

[OK]
[Cancel]
[Rules...]
[Spacing...]

Dictionary: [UK English]

☐ Keep with next [0] lines
☐ Widow control [0] lines

Then, click on the Spacing... button in paragraph specifications box (above)...

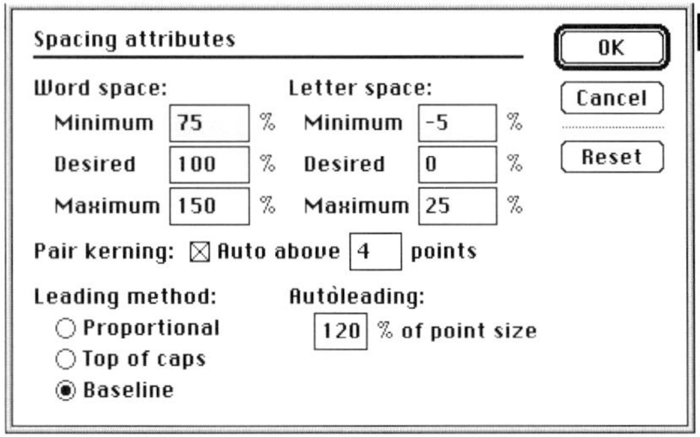

Spacing attributes

[OK]
[Cancel]
[Reset]

Word space:		Letter space:		
Minimum	75 %	Minimum	-5	%
Desired	100 %	Desired	0	%
Maximum	150 %	Maximum	25	%

Pair kerning: ☒ Auto above [4] points

Leading method: Autoleading:
○ Proportional   [120] % of point size
○ Top of caps
● Baseline

...and set the word space settings in the spacing box (above). Experiment with the Minimum, Desired and Maximum values to get the best result (right).

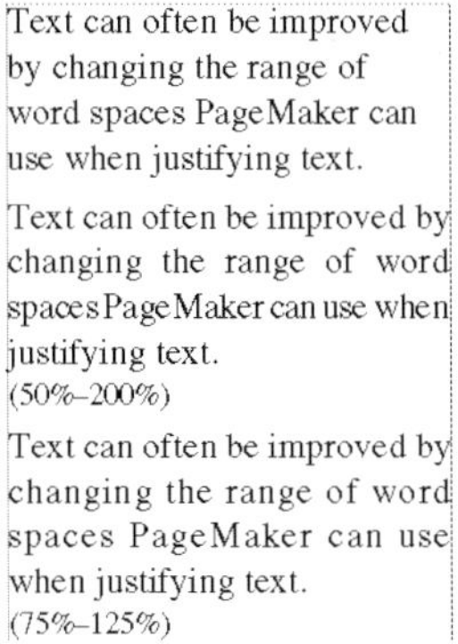

Hyphenation

[OK]
[Cancel]
[Add...]

Hyphenation: ● On   ○ Off
○ Manual only
● Manual plus dictionary
○ Manual plus algorithm

Limit consecutive hyphens to: [2]

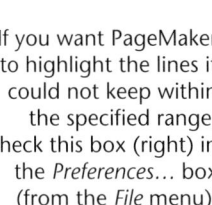

Hyphenation zone: [12] mm

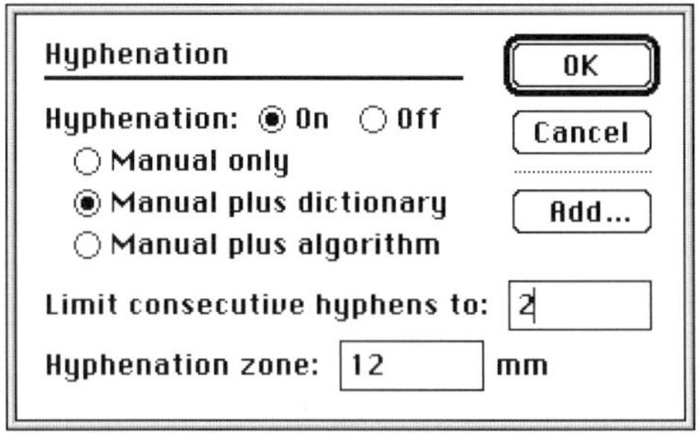

To access hyphenation controls (above), choose *Hyphenation...* from the *Type* menu.

Text can often be improved by changing the range of word spaces PageMaker can use when justifying text.

Text can often be improved by changing the range of word spaces PageMaker can use when justifying text.
(50%–200%)

Text can often be improved by changing the range of word spaces PageMaker can use when justifying text.
(75%–125%)

Unjustified text (top) for comparison. Notice how the 50–200% range (middle) produces a very tight third line. The 75–125% range (bottom) is better for this particular font and size.

If you want PageMaker to highlight the lines it could not keep within the specified range, check this box (right) in the *Preferences...* box (from the *File* menu).

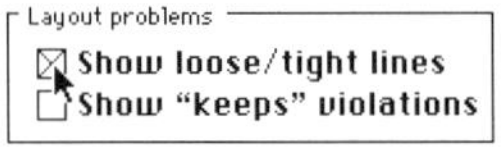

┌ Layout problems ────
☒ Show loose/tight lines
☐ Show "keeps" violations

You will need to take control of word spacing when you justify text. If you do not, preset values will be used which, although often appropriate, can have a detrimental effect on the appearance of a block of text.

Unfortunately, there is no magic formula. The appropriate spacing for justified text depends on the column width, on the typeface (font) being used and on the size of the type. Hyphenation further complicates the issue.

Before you embark on a layout, try different word space settings once you have chosen your typeface. If you can't find a satisfactory setting, try varying the type size a little. When you find a set of values that produces good-looking paragraphs, build them into a text style. If you use that setting regularly, consider changing the program's spacing defaults (i.e. without a document open).

Spacing. You can vary word spacing by clicking on the Spacing… button in the *Paragraph*… box.

Within the spacing attributes box you can define the amount of variation you will permit when PageMaker separates words (and letters, too). The word space values are expressed in this box as percentages of the space character (i.e. the space bar) in that particular font and size. Desired is where you specify your ideal, and Minimum and Maximum define the range of variation you will permit when text is justified.

If you want to alter the word spacing in text that is not justified, the easiest way is to set all three fields to the same value (e.g. 200%).

Justification. When text is aligned left or right, without hyphenation, PageMaker has a simple decision to make at the end of lines—if a word does not fit it must put it at the beginning of the next line. Justified text is more complicated because each line has to fill the column width. When it reaches the point on a line when a word won't fit, the program varies the word spacing within the range you have specified trying either to shrink them to fit the word on the line or to expand them so that the line fits the column (and the word can go on the next line). It will then try varying the letter spacing. Failing both it will vary the space between words, outside the range you have specified, if necessary.

Hyphenation. To give PageMaker a better chance of setting text satisfactorily you can let it break words at the end of a line.

Choose *Hyphenation*… from the *Type* menu and set the level you require (Manual relies on you doing it yourself). You can limit the number of consecutive lines which have hyphens and can set a zone, for unjustified text, within which lines can break without hyphens (e.g. on a space).

• Sometimes PageMaker will not be able to set text within the limits you have set and lines will end up with more space (loose) or less space (tight) than you specified. If you check the Loose/tight lines box under Layout problems in *Preferences*… from the *File* menu, PageMaker will highlight these lines for you so that you can adjust them manually—either by rewriting slightly or adding discretionary hyphens.

• Use COMMAND-HYPHEN to insert a discretionary hyphen into a word to break it manually at an acceptable point. These are not used if the word moves to a new location. Hyphenation must be on before you can insert a discretionary hyphen.

• Letter spacing is best left to the experts.

• You can also apply a 'desired' word space setting to unjustified text.

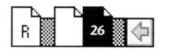

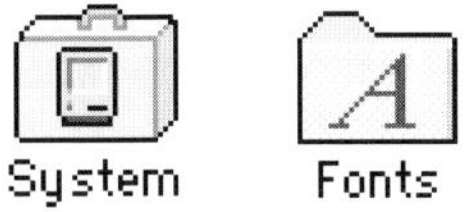

Fonts 27

System · **Fonts**

Depending on the version of system software you are using, fonts are installed in the System or in a Fonts folder (above), or both. (They can be stored elsewhere if you are using font management software.) TrueType fonts are stored as outlines—double-click an icon to see samples in different sizes (right)

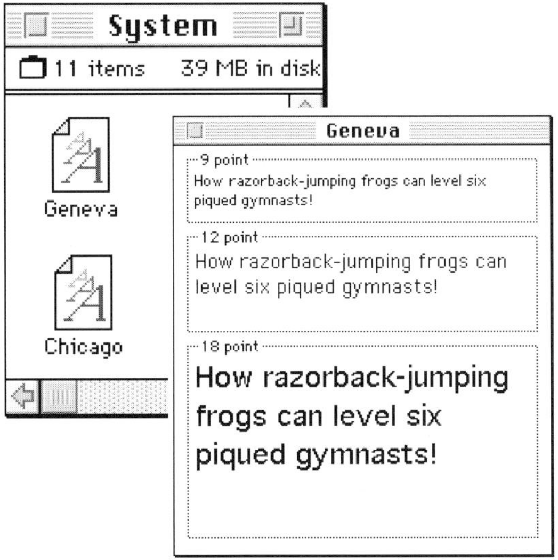

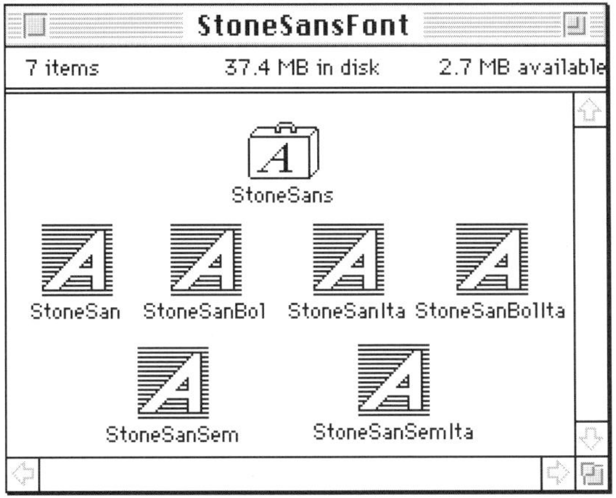

System
11 items   39 MB in disk

Geneva

Chicago

Geneva

9 point
How razorback-jumping frogs can level six piqued gymnasts!

12 point
How razorback-jumping frogs can level six piqued gymnasts!

18 point
How razorback-jumping frogs can level six piqued gymnasts!

StoneSansFont
7 items   37.4 MB in disk   2.7 MB available

StoneSans

StoneSan   StoneSanBol   StoneSanIta   StoneSanBolIta

StoneSanSem   StoneSanSemIta

PostScript fonts have separate screen (bit-mapped) and printer versions of each font (above).

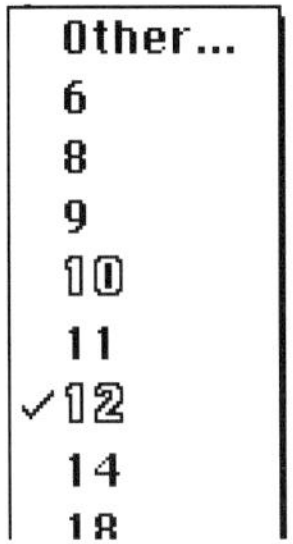

Other...
6
8
9
10
11
✓12
14
18

Look at the *Size* submenu (on the *Type* menu). If a font has limited sizes shown in outline (left) (meaning that a bit map is available for that size), it's a PostScript font. Fonts with most sizes shown in outline are TrueType fonts (right).

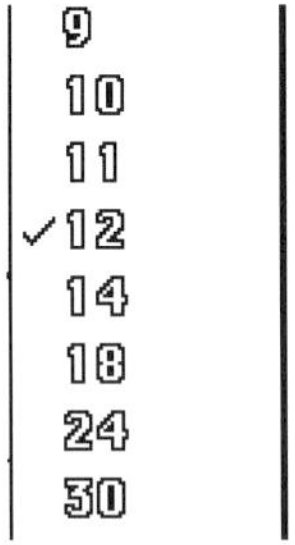

9
10
11
✓12
14
18
24
30

LaserWriter Fonts

PostScript screen fonts are stored separately (right) in individual sizes.

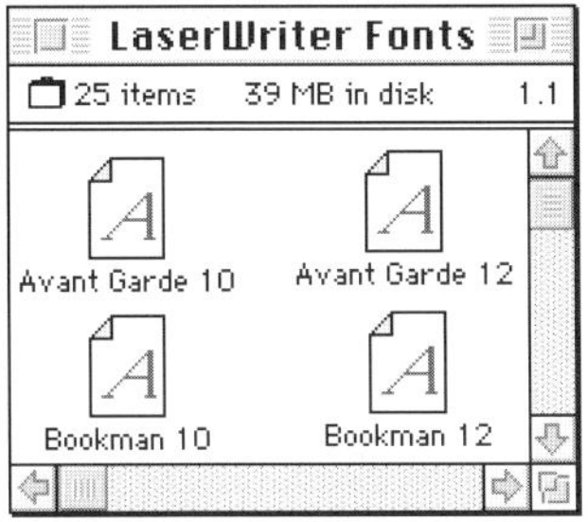

LaserWriter Fonts
25 items   39 MB in disk   1.1

Avant Garde 10   Avant Garde 12

Bookman 10   Bookman 12

When you use PageMaker you have access to the fonts that are installed on the particular computer you are using. You will see these listed under *Font* on the *Type* menu and in font pop-up menus.

Background. Fonts come in different shapes and sizes, and also in different flavours. There are many font vendors, each producing their own versions of fonts (sometimes even using the same name), and there are competing font formats.

Fonts needs to be displayed in two places—on the screen and at the printer. These devices are not equal in terms of the quality of type they can reproduce. Usually the printer is capable of producing crisper, sharper characters because it uses smaller dots (pixels)—it is, therefore, said to have a higher resolution.

Until recently, fonts used on the screen were a separate entity. They were a fixed size, often crude, representation (called a bit-map) for screen use only and were automatically replaced by the equivalent printer fonts when printed. A separate bit map was needed for each size.

Because printer fonts (also called outline fonts) are defined mathematically, they can be varied in size without loss of quality and can take advantage of the increased sharpness of a laser printer or imagesetter. Thus, as the resolution of the printer increases, the quality of the type keeps improving.

Formats. Nowadays, screen and printer fonts are much closer. The printer font can be used to render type on the screen as well as at the printer.

There are two competing formats each with their own strengths—TrueType (cheaper) and PostScript (well established). PostScript fonts retain the separate screen and printer fonts of old. (If you use ATM to render type on screen, the screen font is used to make the font name appear on the menu.) TrueType fonts make no distinction between screen and printer fonts—there is only one definition for both screen and printer.

Telling them apart. You can generally tell which format you are using by the way a font's sizes are displayed on the *Type* menu. If all the sizes are displayed in outline, it's TrueType; if only a few are outlined, such as 10pt, 12pt, it's a PostScript font. Each format has its own distinguishing icon.

Avoiding problems. When using a PostScript font, you must ensure that the appropriate printer font is available to the printer at print time—it must either be built into the ROM or available for downloading. If not, Courier is printed instead.

Take sample pages all the way through the production process, at an early stage, to make sure that no one is using mis-matched fonts, especially the printers or the imagesetting bureau.

• To avoid confusion it is best not to mix font formats. Above all, don't make different formats of a font with the same name available to a publication. It will not be obvious to you which you are using.

• You can also use a font management program, such as Suitcase, to handle fonts.

• Adobe Type Manager (ATM) needs access to printer font outlines to render type on screen.

• When printing, watch for a message indicating that a bit-mapped font is being down-loaded to the printer—it's not usually what you want.

• PageMaker's PANOSE font matching and substitution facility will allow you to overcome some difficulties when the fonts used in a document are not installed on your computer.

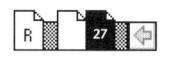

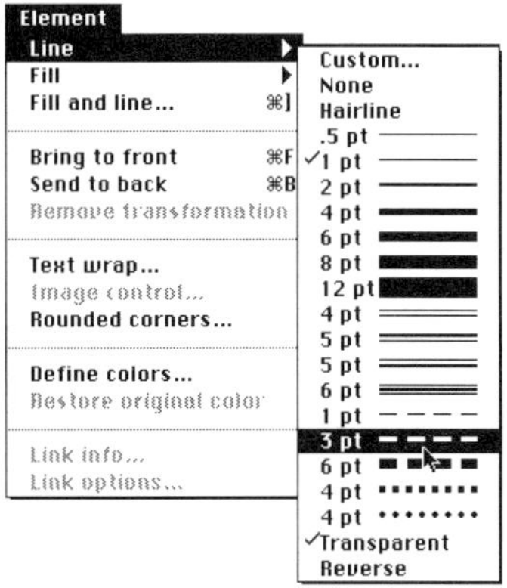

Lines and fills 28

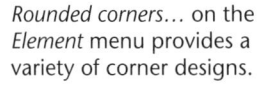

Element
Line ▶
Fill ▶
Fill and line... ⌘]

Bring to front ⌘F
Send to back ⌘B
Remove transformation

Text wrap...
Image control...
Rounded corners...

Define colors...
Restore original color

Link info...
Link options...

Custom...
None
Hairline
.5 pt ————
✓1 pt ————
2 pt ————
4 pt ————
6 pt ————
8 pt ————
12 pt ————
4 pt ————
5 pt ————
5 pt ————
6 pt ————
1 pt – – – –
3 pt ▭ ▭ ▭
6 pt ■ ■ ■
4 pt ▪ ▪ ▪
4 pt • • • •
✓Transparent
Reverse

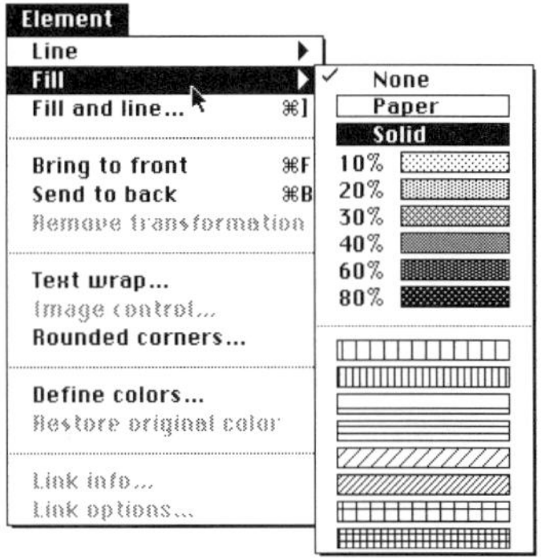

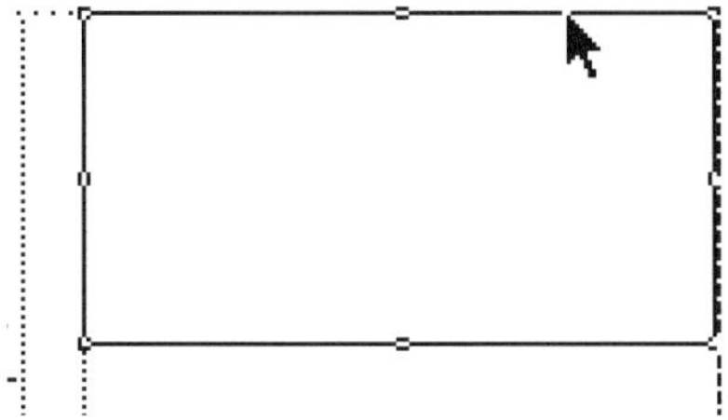

Apply line and/or fill styles immediately after drawing an element (while it is still selected), or select the element by clicking on it with the pointer tool (left)

Lines can flip edges as you draw. This is especially obvious on thicker lines. By moving your hand in the opposite direction as you draw (or having selected it) you can flip it back again.

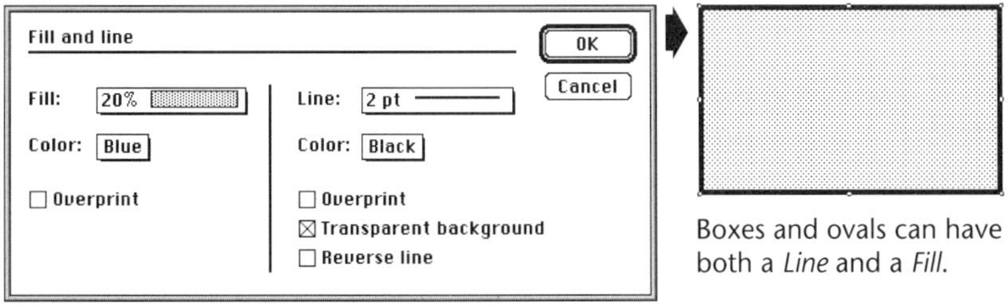

Select an item with the pointer tool and set its *Line* and/or *Fill* from the *Element* menu.

Element
Line ▶
Fill ▶
Fill and line... ⌘]

Bring to front ⌘F
Send to back ⌘B
Remove transformation

Text wrap...
Image control...
Rounded corners...

Define colors...
Restore original color

Link info...
Link options...

✓ None
Paper
Solid
10%
20%
30%
40%
60%
80%

Fill and line   OK   Cancel

Fill: [20% ▦]   Line: [2 pt ————]

Color: [Blue]   Color: [Black]

☐ Overprint   ☐ Overprint
                      ☒ Transparent background
                      ☐ Reverse line

Boxes and ovals can have both a *Line* and a *Fill*.

Fill and line... on the *Element* menu provides a box where you can apply both fill and line characteristics, and colour to both using pop-down menus.

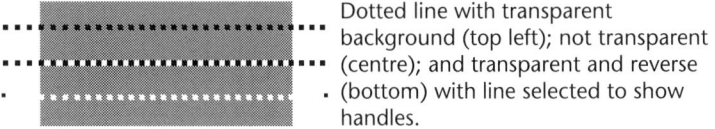

Rounded corners... on the *Element* menu provides a variety of corner designs.

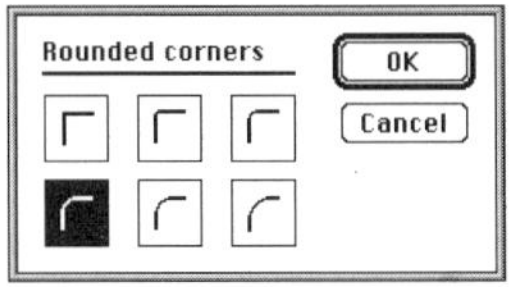

Dotted line with transparent background (top left); not transparent (centre); and transparent and reverse (bottom) with line selected to show handles.

Rounded corners   OK   Cancel

⌐ ⌐ ⌐
⌐ ⌐ ⌐

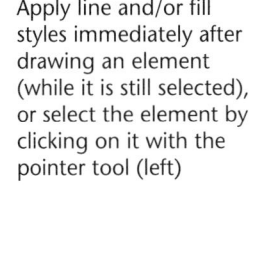

Even formal publications can benefit from lines (also called rules) and shaded areas on the page. They add variety and make a page more inviting to the reader. They are especially useful in newsletters and brochures.

Although it is not sensible to use PageMaker's drawing tools for anything but the most basic of illustrations (normally you use a drawing program and import graphics using *Place…*), nevertheless the tools can be used to separate elements on a page, for emphasis or to add impact.

Drawing tools. To draw a line, box or oval, select the appropriate tool from the toolbox and click to position the start point. Keeping the mouse button pressed, drag to the point on the page where you want the object to end. When you release the mouse button the item you have just drawn is selected and you can then modify it using *Line* or *Fill* from the *Element* menu.

For a line with a thickness of 4 points, for example, choose 4pt from the *Line* submenu while the line is still selected.

Variation. To modify an object already drawn on the page, select it first by clicking on it with the pointer tool and then choose the *Line* or *Fill* style required from the *Element* menu.

Choose *Fill and line…* if you want to apply both, or an attribute such as colour.

Check Transparent background on dotted lines if there are objects behind them which you want to show through the gaps in the lines.

If you don't want a line or fill to knockout (leave a hole in) objects underneath on colour separations, check Overprint.

Reverse line produces a line (or outline of an object) with the same colour as Paper.

Drawing lines. When you are drawing lines, you need to be aware that moving the mouse at right angles to the direction of the line being drawn – left or right on vertical lines, and up or down on horizontal lines – can flip the alignment of a line from one edge to another.

Squares and circles. When drawing boxes or ovals, hold down the SHIFT key if you want to draw a square or a circle.

Changing presets. You can change the preset line and fill within a document by choosing a style when nothing is selected. The style chosen will be used automatically from then on.

If you want to change *Line* and *Fill* presets at the program level, choose the styles you want when you do not have a document open. These styles will then be automatically preset in each new document thereafter.

• You can create custom lines to your own specifications, ranging from 0.1pt to 800pt wide.

• Use *Rounded corners…* on the *Element* menu to vary corner shapes.

• Fills don't apply to lines.

• The Transparent option on dotted lines styles affects the gaps between the dots.

• Be aware that lines thinner than 1pt can look wider on the screen than they do when printed, especially when printed on an imagesetter.

• If you want to draw a box around text, fit the box to the column guides and offset the text within the box (using left or right indents or a narrower text block). This looks much better than fitting the text to the column as normal and drawing the box outside the guides.

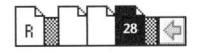

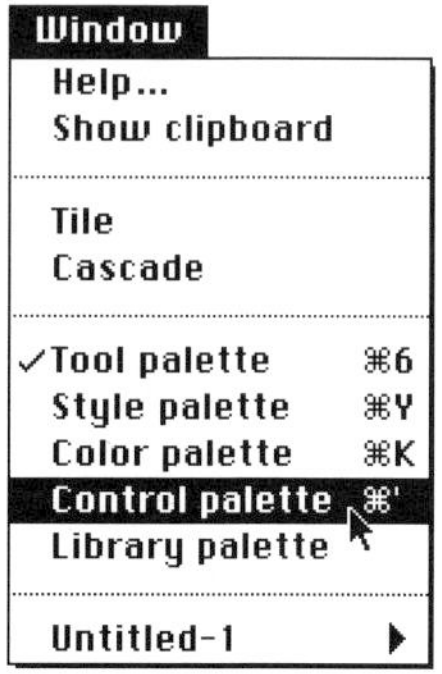

Graphics under control   29

Window
- Help...
- Show clipboard
- Tile
- Cascade
- ✓ Tool palette   ⌘6
- Style palette   ⌘Y
- Color palette   ⌘K
- **Control palette**   ⌘'
- Library palette
- Untitled-1   ▶

Apply button

Nudge buttons

Reference point co-ordinates (x,y)

Scale

Rotation (top) and Skewing (below)

X 190 mm

Y 255.75 mm

W 61 mm   100%

H 42.5 mm   100%

🔄 0°

↗ 0°

F+⊐

F+⊥

Active reference point (proxy)

Object size

Flip horizontal (top) and vertical (below)

Choose *Control palette* on the *Window* menu to make the palette visible.

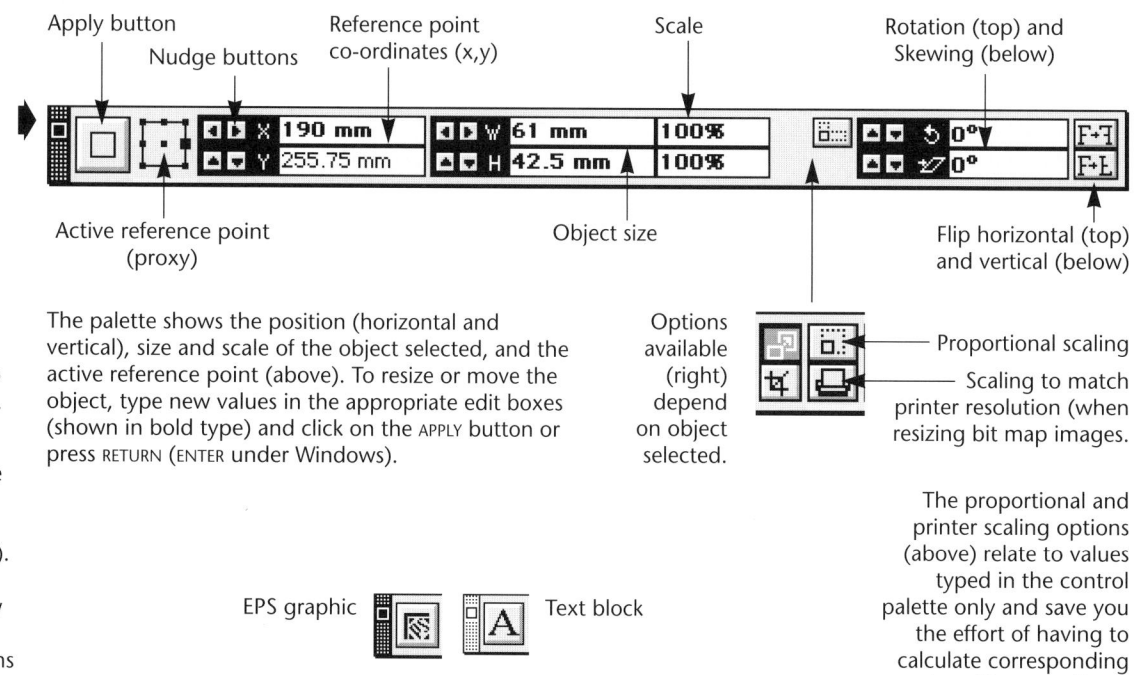

Select an object and use TAB to move from field (edit box) to field (or click in a particular field). The active field is highlighted. Type a new value, or press the SPACEBAR to switch options on or off. When the proxy is active, spacebar switches the reference point from handle (anchor) to double-headed arrow (drag).

The palette shows the position (horizontal and vertical), size and scale of the object selected, and the active reference point (above). To resize or move the object, type new values in the appropriate edit boxes (shown in bold type) and click on the APPLY button or press RETURN (ENTER under Windows).

EPS graphic   Text block

PICT (draw) graphic with proxy showing rotation.

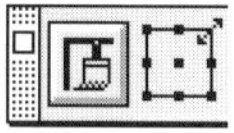

Paint-type graphic with reference point set to drag.

The APPLY button shows the type of object selected.

Options available (right) depend on object selected.

Proportional scaling

Scaling to match printer resolution (when resizing bit map images.

The proportional and printer scaling options (above) relate to values typed in the control palette only and save you the effort of having to calculate corresponding values. However, if you drag using the mouse to rescale, you will still need to hold down the SHIFT and/or COMMAND keys to achieve the same effect.

Occasionally you will want to position and resize elements accurately on a page using specific measurements. You can use the control palette for this purpose by typing new values into the appropriate boxes (fields) and clicking the APPLY button.

Control palette. If the palette is not already visible, choose *Control palette* from the *Window* menu.

You use it by selecting an object on the page and then changing its palette values to modify it. Palette contents vary with the object selected.

You can close the palette at any time (if it is taking up screen space) by clicking its close box.

Reference point. When you select an object, the values displayed in the control palette relate to one particular handle—the current reference point. You set the reference point by selecting an object and clicking one of its handles on the page or by clicking on a handle in the proxy icon. The palette shows the x and y co-ordinates of that particular handle on the selected object.

The reference point stays the same for objects subsequently selected, until you change it again.

Editing values. Only values shown in bold can be changed. If the reference point is a side handle, for example, it can be moved horizontally only, the 'Y' (vertical) and 'H' (height) fields are not accessible. You can use the TAB key to move from field to field (SHIFT-TAB to go backwards) or click the cursor within a field to enter new values.

Moving. When the palette is visible, type new co-ordinates into the 'X' and 'Y' field—remember these refer to the current reference point. Click on the nudge buttons for fine movement.

Even if the control palette is not visible, you can use the arrow keys on the keyboard to move the selected object in small increments (useful for fine positioning, particularly near guides) or larger increments if you press the COMMAND key too.

Manipulating. Typing new values into the Width (W) and Height (H) fields resizes the selected object. The 'Proportional scaling' option retains the aspect ratio of the graphic (it does not distort) and saves you having to work out new values.

If you click again on the active reference point in the proxy (or press SPACE when the proxy field is active) the handle changes to a double-headed arrow. It is then the handle, not the object itself, that will move when you type new values—i.e. you will resize the object instead of moving it.

Scale an object by typing a new percentage value in the scale fields (set the proportional option, if necessary).

- Choose *Control palette* without a document open if you want the palette visible in new documents.

- Since you type values into the palette, you can use it in any page view.

- The reference point is important and can give unpredictable results (particularly when rotating and skewing). If a result is not what you expected, double-check on the active reference point—it moves with rotated objects.

- x and y values are shown relative to the ruler origin.

- Use COMMAND-OPTION-M (or CTRL-F11 on Windows) to cycle measurement units in a field.

- The control palette can also be used to format text with the text tool.

- Nudge values can be set in *Preferences…* (*File* menu).

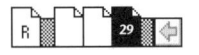

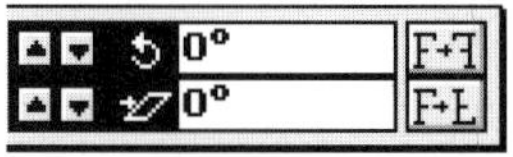

Rotating and skewing   30

To rotate an item precisely, enter an angle value (positive for anti-clockwise rotation) in the rotation field (above, right) of the Control palette. You can also click on the nudge buttons. The item will be rotated around the reference point selected in the proxy (left).

Notice that the reference point also rotates with the item (below, left).

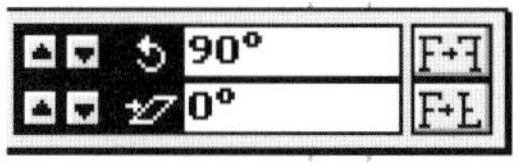

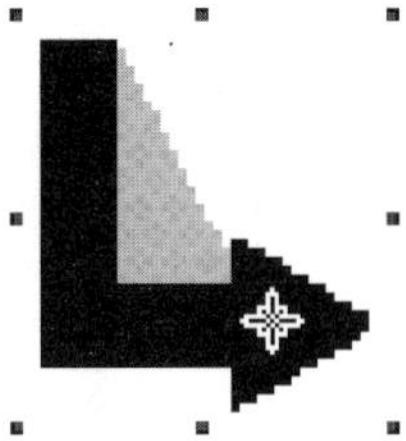

To rotate around a fixed point, click with the rotation tool to select the object (left), and then click and drag in the direction of the rotation you want (right). The object rotates as you drag around the fixed point at which you clicked.

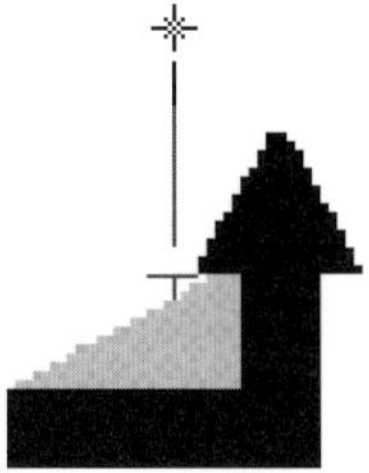

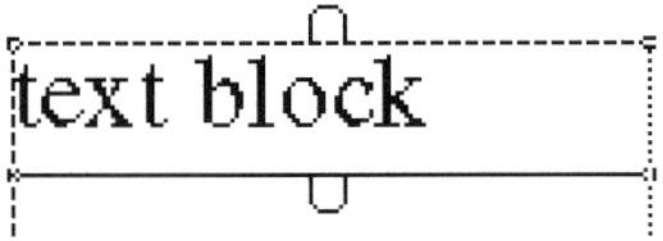

Depending on how you like to work, you will need to keep an eye on the reference point in the proxy when you skew an object. The result (below) might not be what you expect. If the reference point is solid, it stays fixed in its place.

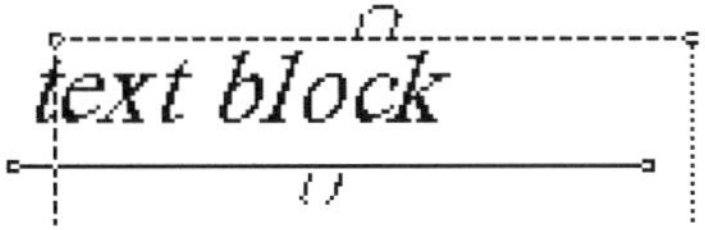

Either change the reference point before you start (below) or click it again to change it to a double-headed arrow which then defines it as the point that will move.

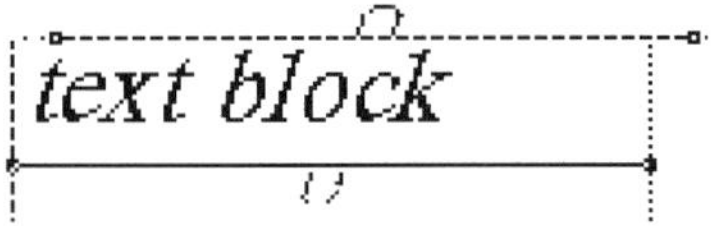

Choose *Remove transformation* on the *Element* menu (right) if you want to remove reflection and skewing.

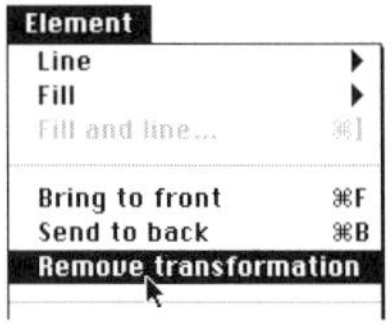

One way to jazz up a publication is to rotate text or graphic objects on the page. This not only adds variety but also increases impact. However, do try to exercise restraint—if you get carried away it is a sure signal to the reader that the layout was produced by a novice. In PageMaker you can rotate, reflect and skew (slant) objects, including text blocks, on the page.

Rotate. There are different ways of rotating objects. You can rotate manually using the rotation tool, or type a value into the rotation field on the Control palette if you want to be very precise; you can also use the nudge buttons next to the rotation field on the palette.

To rotate an object manually around a fixed point, you must first select the object to be rotated. Do this by clicking on the rotation tool in the toolbox (the pointer takes the shape of a starburst) and then clicking on the object (you could also use the pointer tool to select the object first and then choose the rotation tool).

Once the object is selected, click again to establish the point around which you want the object to rotate and drag in the direction you want it rotated (i.e. straight up for a 90° rotation). The further you drag, the longer the rotation lever becomes and the more fine control you have.

To rotate a selected object using the Control palette, simply type the value of the angle you require into the rotation field (positive values to rotate in an anti-clockwise direction and negative values for clockwise rotation). Alternatively you can click on the nudge buttons until the value you want to reach is shown.

When you use the Control palette, the object is rotated around the active reference point (handle) shown in the proxy. When the object is reflected, the reference point stays in the same place in relation to the original object, but changes in the proxy to show the rotation applied.

It pays to keep an eye on the reference point if you select rotated and non-rotated objects in turn—its movement takes a bit of getting used to.

Reflect. To flip (mirror image) a selected object, click on the horizontal or vertical buttons at the right-hand edge of the Control palette. Horizontal reflection is achieved by first reflecting vertically and then applying a rotation of 180°, this is why the rotation value changes to 180° in the palette.

Reflection is around the active handle in the proxy if solid. If an arrow, the point itself moves.

Skew. If you want to slant an object (for example a tinted copy to use as a shadow), type a value into the skewing field—positive values to slant the selected object to the right and negative values to slant to the left.

• You can remove rotation or skewing by choosing *Remove transformation* from the *Element* menu. The object will not always, however, move back to its original location.

• Hold down the SHIFT key to restrict manual rotation to 45° increments.

• Choose a reference point in the centre until you become familiar with the way rotation works—you will have fewer surprises.

• Skewed and rotated text can be edited on the page, but it can sometimes be difficult to select text. Triple-click with the pointer tool to view the text in the story editor if you have problems.

• Use negative values for clockwise rotation.

• If you click twice on the reference point in the proxy, it becomes an arrow (drag) indicating that it is no longer fixed.

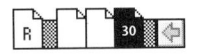

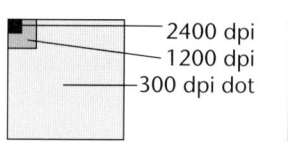

Using a scanner

2400 dpi	
1200 dpi	
300 dpi dot	

300x300	=	90,000
1200x1200	=	1,440,000
2400x2400	=	5,760,000

The resolution of a printer or scanner is expressed in dots per inch. Shown above are the relative sizes of a 300dpi dot, a 1200dpi dot and a 2400 dpi dot. The smaller the dot, the higher the resolution (detail).

Dots per inch is a linear measurement that applies both to width and to height. A square inch is composed of considerably more dots as the resolution of the printer or scanner increases.

To produce the illusion of grey when printing, smaller dots are clustering together to form a bigger dot. The number of dots printed in each cluster determines how grey the larger dot will be overall.

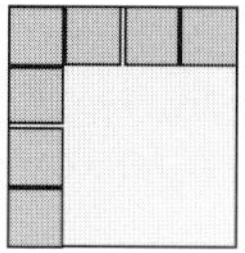

The number of greys that can be printed depends on the number of dots in the cluster. For example, if 16 dots are available, 16 different greys can be printed by printing any combination from 1 to 16 dots in the cluster—4 dots printed for 25% grey; 8 dots for 50%.

A 75 lines per inch screen on a 300 dpi means that a 4x4 cluster (300/75) is used for printing—16 greys.

A 75 lpi screen on a 1200 dpi printer uses a 16x16 cluster (1200/75)—256 greys possible.

1200 dpi/150 lpi = 8
8x8 = 64 greys
2400 dpi/150 lpi = 16
16x16 = 256 greys

The screen applied to an image and resolution of the printer affect the number of greys available in the printed image. The same line screen (150 lpi) applied to an image produces more grey levels as the resolution of the printer (dpi) increases (left).

You need to scan at one and a half to two times (1.5 – 2.0) the print screen you intend applying to an image to ensure that you capture sufficient detail. If you intend to increase the size of the image on the page, then you need even more detail (right).

(final height/original height) x screen x 1.5

for example, a photo 5 inches high which is to be printed 10 inches high (twice original size) with a screen of 150 lpi would need to be scanned at 450 dpi.

(10/5) x 150 x 1.5 = 450

When it comes to adding variety to a publication there are few accessories as useful as a scanner. With access to a scanner you can copy images from paper to disk and then *Place*… them into a publication.

The main benefit is that you retain control of the finished page. You can position the image accurately, resize and crop it until you are satisfied and then, if necessary, manipulate it for effect (such as apply a colour). Even if you only use it to put rough images on the page to indicate to your printers where you want them to position high-quality images at the plate-making stage, you will save time and effort.

Although a scanner is very similar in use to a photocopier, there are some considerations (and jargon) to take into account before you begin. To make the best use of a scanner you need to know something about its characteristics, but you also need to know how an image is to be treated on the printing press, and what the final size of the printed image is to be.

Printing press. Apart from line drawings consisting of a single colour (line art), a printing press needs images such as photographs, with different levels of grey, to be broken down into dots of varying sizes before it can print them—clusters of larger dots to produce dark shades and smaller dots for lighter shades of black (grey is only an illusion).

Manually an image is broken into these dots by photographing it through a screen with a mesh suitable for the paper being used—for example, a coarse screen (88 dots per inch) for absorbent paper, and fine (150 dpi) for a better quality paper.

The same principles apply if you are supplying the images from your computer—you have to screen the images. You need to know what value is appropriate for your images on the paper being used, so ask your printers to tell you.

Imagesetter. You must also take the resolution (dot size) of the imagesetter into account. Does it have dots that are small enough that, when they are clustered to produce the image screen, the level of detail (number of grey shades) you want can be produced?

Scanner. Having done the sums, you can then decide how to scan the image, taking into account the screen ruling, the size of the scanned file on disk and whether or not the image is to be resized on the page.

To capture enough detail, scan at one and a half or two times the final image screen.

If necessary you can compromise to suit your needs—if the file becomes to big to fit on your disk, for example, you can scan or screen at a lower resolution.

- Responsibility, too, comes with control, so you will not be able to blame anyone else if things go wrong. Run some tests first or use the scanner on a smaller project until you become familiar with it.

- Scan line art at the highest resolution possible.

- If a photograph has a textured image (such as a landscape or a tiger's face) you can usually scan at a lower resolution.

- PageMaker applies a pre-set screen ruling to images unless you apply another using *Image control…* or change the pre-set value when you choose *Print…* (under the Colour option).

- Increase contrast if scanning colour photos as black and white images.

- Refer to the Commercial Printing Guide that comes with PageMaker for more information.

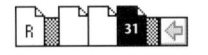

Improving images   32

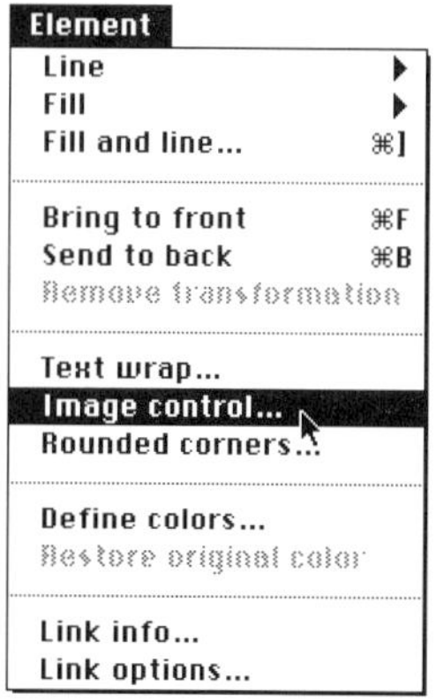

Element

Line	▶
Fill	▶
Fill and line...	⌘]
Bring to front	⌘F
Send to back	⌘B
Remove transformation	
Text wrap...	
Image control...	
Rounded corners...	
Define colors...	
Restore original color	
Link info...	
Link options...	

Image control

○ Black and white
○ Screened   ● Grey

Screen

Angle: DFLT

Lines/in: DFLT

Lightness   Contrast

OK
Cancel
Reset
Apply

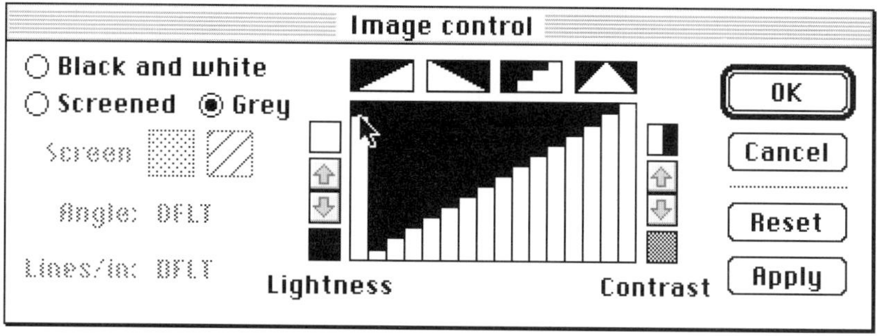

Select one of the image effects (by clicking on it) at the top of the box. Left to right they are normal, negative, posterise and solarise. You can also move individual control bars in greyscale images—black being changed to white is shown (left). Move the sliders to vary brightness and contrast.

You can modify a black and white bitmapped image (or one scanned to retain levels of grey) by selecting it with the pointer tool and choosing *Image control...* from the *Element* menu.

Images with no grey can be modified (below) if you click Screened for a line or dot screen.

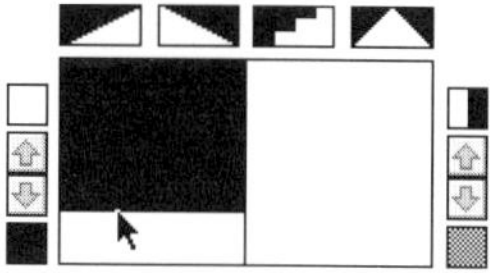

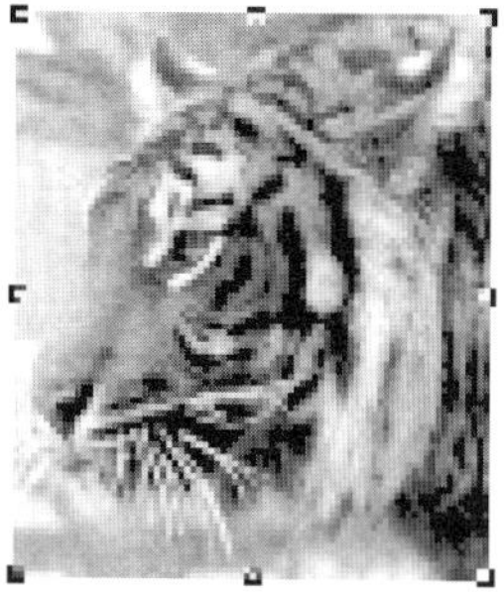

Scanned photos can be improved and previewed effectively if you are using a monitor that can display greys. Screened images coarsen on screen (above right) so you should make changes to the image prior to screening so that you can preview the result.

Clicking the negative option (below) reverses the image, i.e black in, white out.

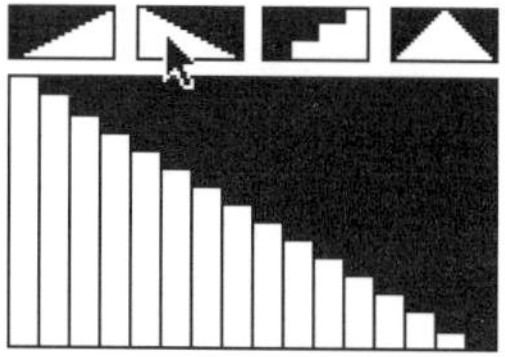

Scanned photographs and graphics from paint programs can often be improved using the image controls provided in PageMaker. You can lighten or darken an image, improve contrast or apply a screen (break it into lines or dots of a particular size) for special effect. Only images composed of dots (pixels), such as TIFF and paint (bit-mapped) files can be modified.

Taking control. Select the image to be modified and choose *Image control...* from the *Element* menu. Make the changes using the controls provided and click OK, or use Reset to return the image to its original state. You can preview the changes you make by clicking the Apply button.

Photographs. If you are using a monitor capable of displaying greys you will be surprised at the quality of the screen image and at the ease with which you can manipulate photographs that have been scanned as greyscale images. Such images look terrific on screen and can be manipulated and previewed very successfully before printing—your skill will improve with experience.

Use the presets provided along the top of the dialog box if they are suitable, or adjust individual levels of grey by moving the control bars (click where you want them to go). To lighten or darken a complete image or improve the contrast, use the slider bars to the left and right of the control bars. Sixteen control bars are shown for greyscale images, each of which represents a band of 16 greys if an image is saved with 256 grey levels.

Apply a screen by clicking on the Screened button and typing the values you require into the Angle and Lines/in fields. The on-screen preview can be very coarse with some settings and you will need to print the image to view the effect.

With experience you will learn how best to manipulate images but to begin with set the image slightly lighter than what looks best on the screen. Images tend to darken when printed.

Black and white. Images produced in basic paint programs or scanned as line art contain two levels of grey—black and white. When such images are selected for manipulation two control bars only are provided. It may not look as if you can do much with them but you can move these control bars up or down to modify the image.

By applying a screen to such images you can lighten them so that they become grey overall (or a lighter tint of whatever spot colour you apply). This is a particularly useful technique when you want text to be printed over a graphic and need to lighten the graphic so that the text is still readable.

- The control bars and image effects are not available under Windows.

- If, having selected the graphic, *Image control...* is shown in grey on the *Element* menu it means that the format of the graphic is not suitable (because it is in PICT or EPSF format, for example) and you can't modify it. Only Paint and TIFF formats can be modified.

- You can't use *Image control...* to modify colour images.

- For best on-screen preview, change the number of grey levels to the maximum available on your screen.

- Ask your printer's advice on the screen frequency (or ruling) to use for photographs. PageMaker applies a preset screen (DFLT, for default) so you should take control.

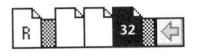

Graphics in text   33

File

New... ⌘N
Open... ⌘O
Close

Save ⌘S
Save as...
Revert
Export...

Place... ⌘D

Links... ⌘=
Book...
Preferences...

Page setup...
Print... ⌘P

Quit ⌘Q

To place an inline graphic, click first to position the cursor at the point in the text where you want to insert the graphic and choose *Place...* from the *File* menu (above).

Place:
○ As independent graphic
● As inline graphic
○ Inserting text

In the *Place...* dialog box the inline button will be set (above), indicating that the graphic will be placed as part of the story (in-line).

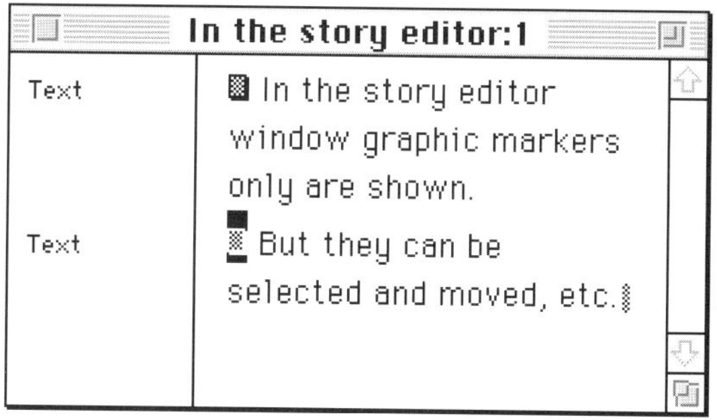

In the story editor:1

Text   ▨ In the story editor window graphic markers only are shown.

Text   ▧ But they can be selected and moved, etc.▨

The position of a graphic is shown by a marker within the story editor (above). Markers can be selected and then cut, copied or deleted as though they are text.

▲▼ ⌂ 12.7 mm   ◄ ▷ W 35.3 m   ▲▼ H 38.1 m

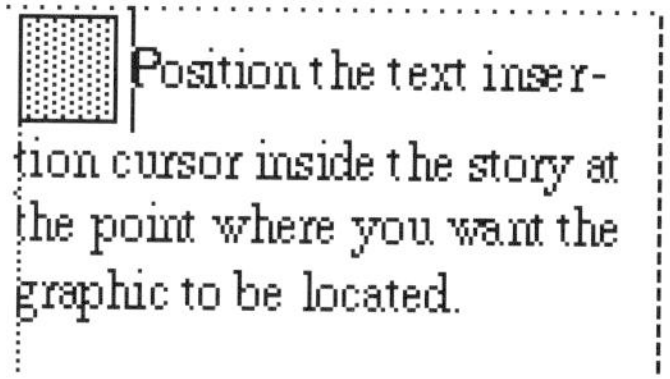

Position the text insertion cursor inside the story at the point where you want the graphic to be located.

Position the text insertion cursor inside the story at .. resize as normal.

Position the text insertion cursor inside the story at ... move the graphic up or down.

To position an inline graphic (in this case a box drawn with the rectangle tool), click in the story and use *Place...* or *Paste* (top left).

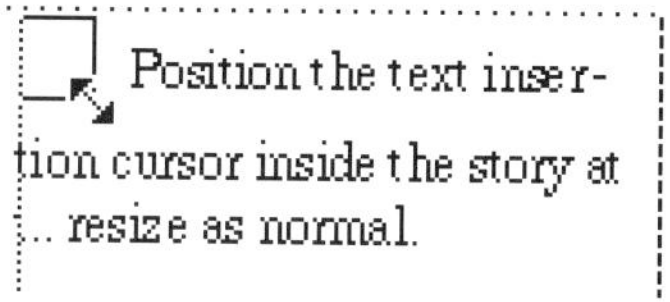

Resize as normal by dragging a handle (centre) using the pointer tool.

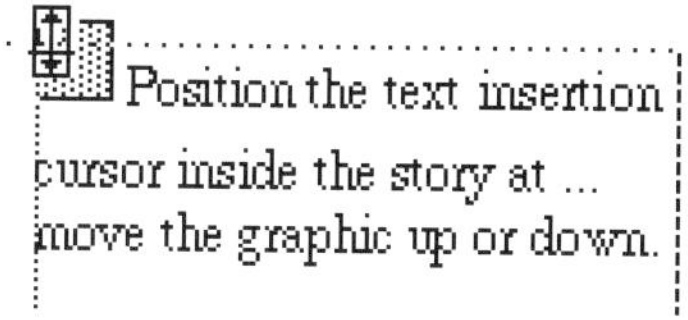

Drag the graphic up or down to vary its position relative to the baseline (below).

You can also adjust the vertical position of an inline graphic using the control palette (left). When you select an inline graphic using the pointer tool, a baseline offset field is displayed in the palette instead of X and Y.

If, before you *Place...* or *Paste* a graphic, you click with the text tool to position the text insertion cursor, the graphic is placed at that point in the paragraph and remains associated with it. This is useful when you want to ensure that a graphic stays with text—graphics embedded in text (called inline graphics) move with the surrounding text.

Think of an inline graphic as simply another text character and you won't go far wrong.

Inline graphics. To anchor a graphic to a particular piece of text, click first with the text tool to position the insertion cursor and choose *Place...* from the *File* menu in the usual way (or *Paste* one from the Clipboard). The As inline graphic button will be automatically set in the *Place...* box.

The graphic is placed within the text and you will usually need to resize it or to change its vertical position. Inline graphics can be altered like independent graphics if you select them with the pointer or cropping tool, and can sometimes be treated as type (leading, for example, can be applied) if you select with the text tool.

If you select using the text tool and choose *Type specs...* you will see an inline specifications box where you can apply leading and tracking.

Inline boxes. To position a box within text you can draw one using PageMaker's drawing tools and, while it is still selected, *Cut* it to the Clipboard. Then position the text cursor at the point in the text where you want the box to appear and *Paste* it back.

Baseline offset. Often, particularly when using graphics to highlight items in a list or to use as checkboxes, you will want to change the vertical position of the graphic relative to the text around it. Do this visually by selecting the graphic with the pointer tool and dragging the graphic up or down—you are moving the graphic relative to the baseline of type.

For accurate control use the Control palette. The X and Y fields are replaced by a Baseline offset field which you can modify by changing its value in the palette (or by using the nudge icons). By varying the baseline offset you change the vertical position of the graphic relative to the type.

Story editor. You can also import a graphic within the story editor using *Place...* from the *File* menu. It is automatically placed as an inline graphic and is shown as a graphic marker only. Markers can be cut, copied, pasted and deleted but you will not see the graphic itself until you return to the page.

Transformation. An inline graphic is rotated, etc, if its text block is rotated. Select the graphic itself using the pointer to transform it independently.

- If you place a graphic as inline by mistake, press DELETE to remove it. Or turn it into an independent graphic by selecting it with the pointer tool and using *Cut* and then *Paste*.

- Graphics already within text in a word processor are imported with the text (when you use *Place...*).

- A graphic can be embedded in a paragraph of its own and aligned using the paragraph alignment options (centred, etc).

- When you modify the baseline offset of an in-line graphic, it stays with the graphic even when it is copied and pasted. If, for example, you want to use a graphic as a bullet to highlight several paragraphs, modify the baseline alignment of one and then paste it into the other paragraphs.

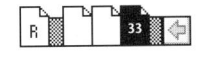

Text around graphics 34

Element
Line	▶
Fill	▶
Fill and line...	⌘l
Bring to front	⌘F
Send to back	⌘B
Remove transformation	
Text wrap...	
Image control...	
Rounded corners...	
Define colors...	
Restore original color	
Link info...	
Link options...	

Select an independent graphic with the pointer tool and choose *Text wrap...* from the *Element* menu.

Text wrap

Wrap option:

Text flow:

Standoff in mm:

Left	4	Right	4
Top	4	Bottom	4

OK

Cancel

Select the characteristics you want from the options provided in the text wrap box (left).

Centre option applies a wrap; left removes. (Right indicates manual customisation.)

Stop and jump to next column (left); jump over graphic (centre) and wrap around (right).

The distance by which you want text to be pushed away from the graphic.

You can also split a text block manually by moving the bottom handle upwards, clicking on it to load the cursor with the next part of the story and then clicking the loaded text cursor lower in the same column leaving sufficient room for the graphic. Text wrap is more efficient.

Graphic on top of text.

Instead of manually making space for a graphic, you can make text flow around it by applying a text wrap to the graphic. Then, no matter where you move the graphic, text will continue to flow around it. You can modify the text wrap perimeter in all sorts of ways and, if to change the size of the graphic, the text wrap boundary will be resized too. This particular feature can save you a lot of layout effort.

Text wrap applied.

Instead of manually making space for a graphic, you can make text flow around it by applying a text wrap to the graphic. Then, no matter where you move the graphic, text will continue to flow around it. You can modify the text wrap perimeter in all sorts of ways and, if to change the size of the graphic, the text wrap boundary

Moving a handle.

Instead of manually making space for a graphic, you can make text flow around it by applying a text wrap to the graphic. Then, no matter where you move the graphic, text will continue to it. You can modify the text wrap perimeter in all sorts of ways and, if to change the size of the graphic, the text wrap boundary

Customised wrap.

Instead of manually making space for a graphic, you can make text flow around it by applying a text wrap to the graphic. Then, no matter where you move the graphic, text will continue to flow around it. You can modify the text wrap perimeter in all sorts of ways and, if to change the size of the graphic, the text wrap boundary will be resized too. This particular feature

Design gets more complicated when you add graphics to a page. Although they add visual interest, graphic images require additional decisions if they are to be effective. Location and size are obviously important, as is the relationship with other elements on the page, particularly text.

Although graphics are sometimes used as a background behind text (in such cases, you must ensure that the text is still legible), it is more usual for a graphic to be separated from text.

Space can be set aside manually by resizing and splitting text blocks but if the graphic is moved the space will have to be closed up and created again at the new location.

Text wrap. Creating space manually can be time consuming, but is sometimes unavoidable. Fortunately a text wrap feature is available which defines a boundary around an element – usually a graphic – into which text may not intrude.

To repel text from a graphic (or, seen from the text's point of view, to wrap text around a graphic), select the graphic with the pointer tool and choose *Text wrap*… from the *Element* menu.

The box has three levels. In Wrap option you click the type of wrap you want—this is usually the centre (wraparound) option. The left and right options, respectively, remove the text wrap from a graphic or show that the text wrap has been customised (see below). The Text flow options define how you want text to flow around a graphic—to stop when a graphic is encountered (left), to jump over it (centre) or to wrap itself completely around the graphic (right). The Standoff level allows you to specify the distance to be put between each side of the graphic and the text—use the TAB key to move from field to field.

When you apply a text wrap, a graphic shows dotted lines around its perimeter indicating the area which will repel text. The text wrap has its own diamond-shaped handles at the corners.

Text wraps are rectangular by default but can be customised to any shape you require.

Custom wrap. You can move a diamond by clicking on it and dragging it to a new location. If you do, the text is reflowed around the new boundary. If you click on the dotted line of a text wrap, you create an additional diamond. These, too, can be moved. By adding and moving additional diamond handles you can create a text wrap to suit your graphic which can, if you wish, even be made to follow the contour of the graphic. An irregular wrap stays with a graphic when it moves and is resized if the graphic is resized.

To remove a customised wrap, click the regular text wrap option or click the overlapping option to remove it altogether.

• Text wraps define a boundary around an independent graphic that stays with the graphic even if you move it.

• Hold down the SPACE bar while customising a text wrap to stop the screen redrawing after every action—when you release it, all of the modifications are applied in one go.

• To delete a text wrap diamond, move it over another one nearby.

• A text block wholly within the perimeter of a text wrap is not affected by it.

• To remove a text wrap, select the graphic with the pointer tool and click on the left wrap icon which shows text overlapping the graphic, i.e. no wrap.

• Don't just use a graphic for the sake of it. To be effective, a graphic should be relevant and should enhance the text.

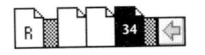

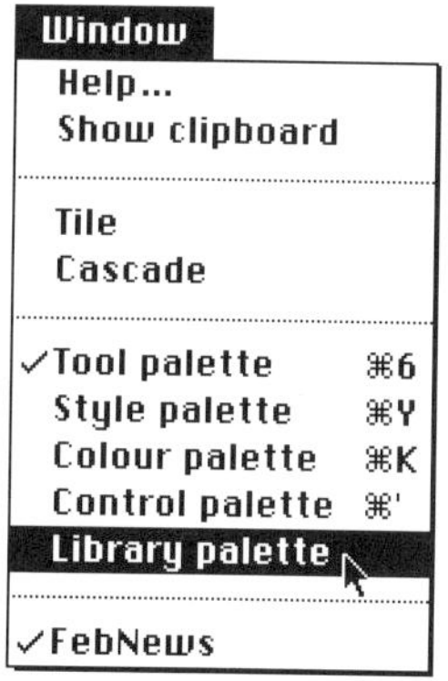

Building a library   35

Window
Help...
Show clipboard

Tile
Cascade

✓Tool palette   ⌘6
Style palette   ⌘Y
Colour palette   ⌘K
Control palette   ⌘'
Library palette

✓FebNews

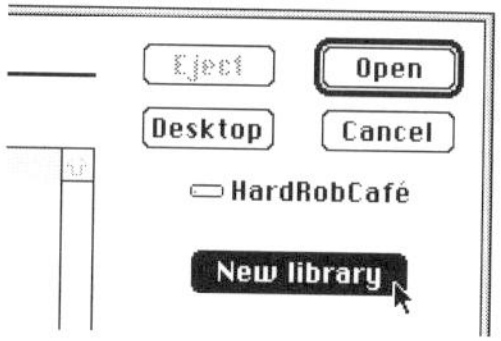

To create a new library
(or open an existing one)
choose *Library palette*
from the *Window* menu.

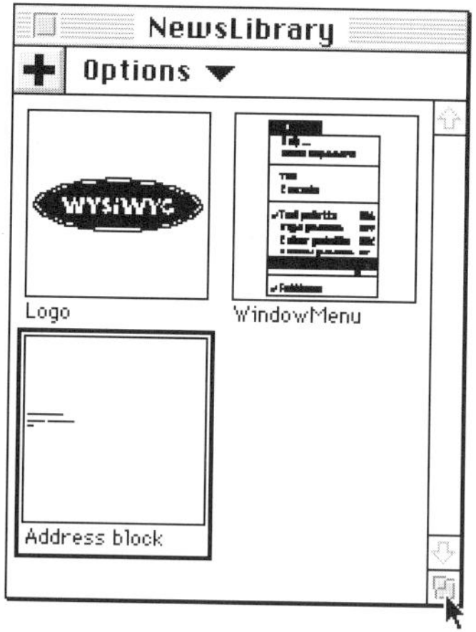

Eject   Open
Desktop   Cancel

⊂ HardRobCafé

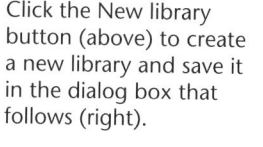

New library

Click the New library
button (above) to create
a new library and save it
in the dialog box that
follows (right).

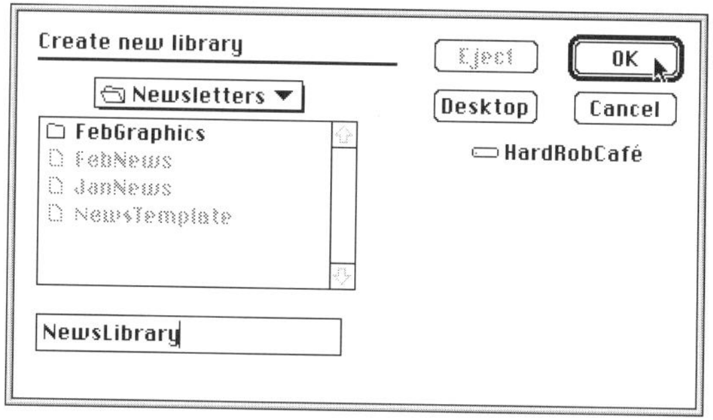

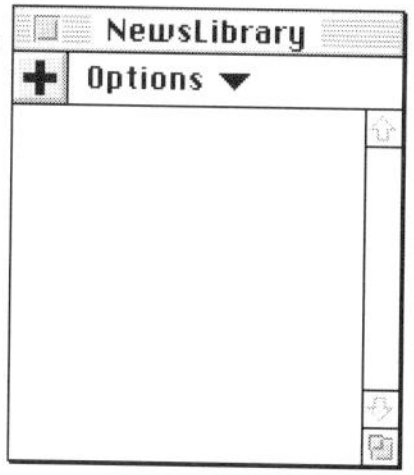

Create new library

⊏ Newsletters ▼

☐ FebGraphics
☐ FebNews
☐ JanNews
☐ NewsTemplate

NewsLibrary

Eject   OK
Desktop   Cancel

⊂ HardRobCafé

NewsLibrary
➕ Options ▼

The new library palette
opens on screen (above)
and is initially empty.

NewsLibrary
➕ Options ▼

WYSiWYG

Logo

WindowMenu

Address block

Select the item you want
to add to the library, and
click the add (+) button
in the palette (right).

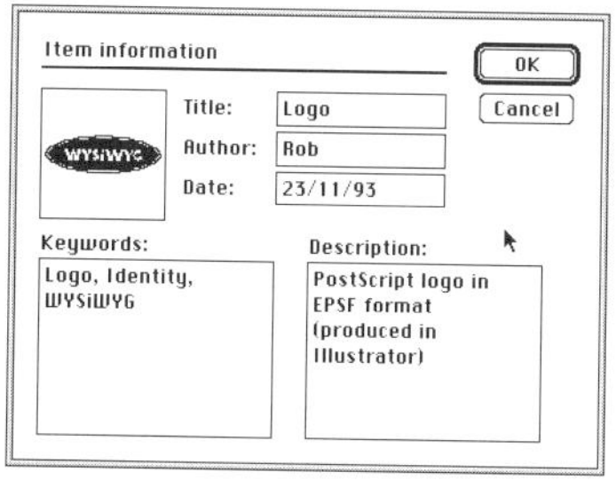

Item information   OK   Cancel

WYSiWYG

Title: Logo
Author: Rob
Date: 23/11/93

Keywords:
Logo, Identity,
WYSiWYG

Description:
PostScript logo in
EPSF format
(produced in
Illustrator)

You will be able to attach details to the item
(above) if you set Edit items after adding in
the palette's menu preferences (right). Use
the menu to open libraries and use *Search
library...* to locate items based on the details
(title, keyword, author, etc.) stored with them.

Copy an item from the
library by dragging it on
to a page and using the
loaded icon (left) to
position it (as in *Place...*).

Options ▼
New library...
Open library...
Search library...
Remove item...

Show all items
Import Fetch items
Preferences...

Display images
Display names
✓Display both

When you find yourself using the same text blocks and graphics regularly in publications – issues of a newsletter, for example – you should construct a template to save yourself the repeated effort of locating and *Placing*… the items each time. If templates are not appropriate (because the documents do not have a consistent structure), you can save effort by creating a library catalogue in which to store the items. You can view the contents of a catalogue in a separate library palette, which makes them easier to locate, and place items onto a page by copying them from the palette.

Creating a library. To create a new, empty library, (or to open the one previously opened), choose *Library palette* from the *Window* menu. Click the New library button in the dialog box that follows (or select an existing library if PageMaker can't find the previous one). If you are creating a new library, you will see another box which allows you to give the library its own name and to specify where on the disk you want to locate it. Once you have given the new library a name, it opens in a separate library palette and is initially empty.

Adding images. To add a graphic or text block to a library, select the item on the page (using the pointer tool) and then click on the add button (+) in the palette. If you have set *Edit items after adding* in the library's own *Options* menu (or its *Preferences*… on the Macintosh), you will be given an opportunity to store details of the item with it in the library. A thumbnail of the item is then added to the library palette.

Using a library. To copy an item from a library to a page, first locate the item within the palette and click to select it. Then drag it onto the page, using the loaded-cursor icon to position it accurately.

To delete an item from a library, select it in the palette and choose *Remove item*… from the library's *Options* menu.

Over time you can build extensive libraries and you will then find *Search library*… useful in finding the item you need. Items are retrieved on the basis of the information you store with an item when it is added to the library—you can find items by title, author, date or keyword (or by multiple keyword using And, Or or But not if you want to limit the search further). Only items which match the search criteria are then displayed in the palette so that it is easier for you to make a selection. Choose *Show all items* from the library's *Options* menu to display the complete library again after a search.

You can move items from one library to another by copying them to a page and then opening the destination library to add them again.

- Try to keep your libraries in a single folder, or close to the projects they serve. If you scatter them around a disk you will waste effort trying to find the one you want to open.

- You can create many libraries but can have only one library palette open.

- When you open a library palette, the library last used is re-opened. You can open a different one using *Open library*… from the palette's *Options* menu.

- You can move and resize the library palette.

- Items that you move to and from the palette are copied to the Clipboard in the process.

- Double-click a palette item if you want to edit the details stored with it.

- You don't need spaces or commas to separate keywords, but you will find it helpful to use them.

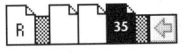

Managing graphics 36

File

New...	⌘N
Open...	⌘O
Close	
Save	⌘S
Save as...	
Revert	
Export...	
Place...	⌘D
Links...	**⌘=**
Book...	
Preferences...	
Page setup...	
Print...	⌘P
Quit	⌘Q

To manage the links to external graphics, choose *Links...* from the *File* menu.

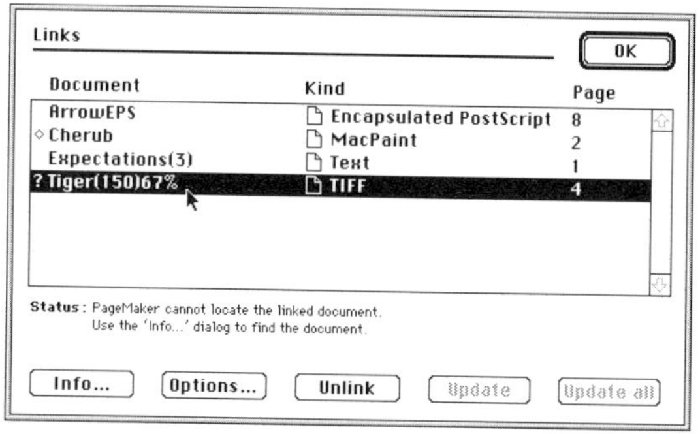

Links

OK

Document	Kind	Page
ArrowEPS	📄 Encapsulated PostScript	8
◊ Cherub	📄 MacPaint	2
Expectations(3)	📄 Text	1
? Tiger(150)67%	📄 TIFF	4

Status : PageMaker cannot locate the linked document. Use the 'Info...' dialog to find the document.

[Info...] [Options...] [Unlink] [Update] [Update all]

The *Links...* box (above) shows the documents you have placed in the publication. Select a document by clicking on it and click the Info... button for more information, or to update or relink it. Icons to the left of a document name indicate that the document has moved or has been modified since it was placed.

If you *Place...* a graphic larger than the size set in *Preferences...*, PageMaker asks if you really want to.

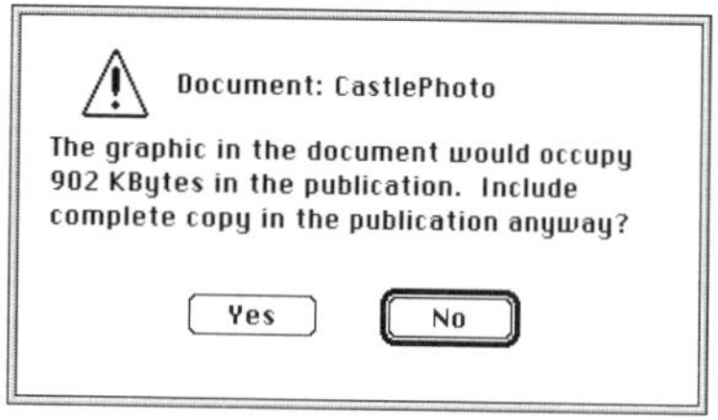

⚠ **Document: CastlePhoto**

The graphic in the document would occupy 902 KBytes in the publication. Include complete copy in the publication anyway?

[Yes] [No]

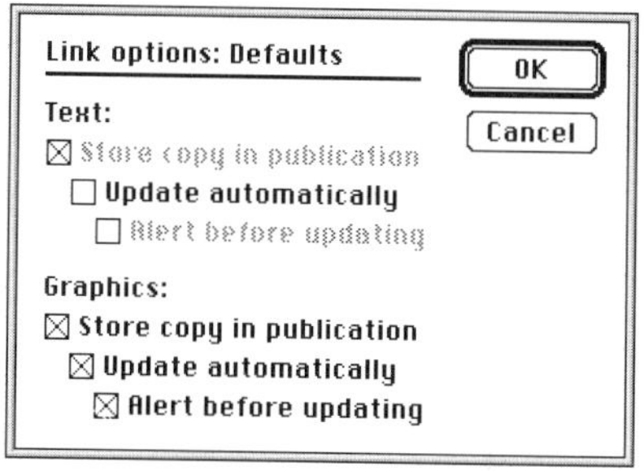

Link options: Defaults

OK

Cancel

Text:
☒ Store copy in publication
☐ Update automatically
☐ Alert before updating

Graphics:
☒ Store copy in publication
☒ Update automatically
☒ Alert before updating

Choose *Link options...* from the *Element* menu to set link options (above). Settings apply to selected documents or to those subsequently placed (if none is selected). The options shown above are a good set to begin with.

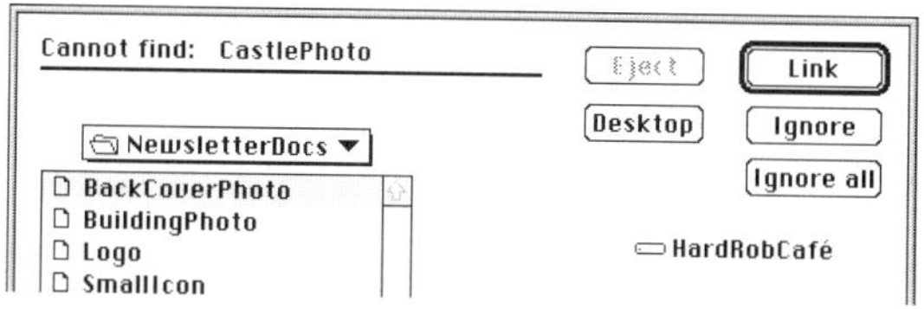

Cannot find: CastlePhoto

[Eject] [Link]

📁 NewsletterDocs ▼

[Desktop] [Ignore]

[Ignore all]

📄 BackCoverPhoto
📄 BuildingPhoto
📄 Logo
📄 SmallIcon

⊂ HardRobCafé

If PageMaker can't find a graphic (above), because you have moved or deleted it, it invites you to find it and re-establish a link to it (if you have set update automatically). Re-establish links before printing, otherwise graphics might not print properly.

When you *Place*... a graphic or scanned image in a publication you might be doing so 'for position only' to show your printers the precise position and size of a graphic which you want them to include (strip in), at the plate-making stage. (This can also help to avoid misunderstandings, and save you the effort of calculating the dimensions of resized images.)

You might, however, want to include high-quality images on the page yourself. The drawback with high-resolution images and complex graphics is that they can make your publications grow to an unmanageable size.

Big files. Once placed, PageMaker keeps its own internal copy of the text you use in a publication so it does not need access to the original word processing file in order to produce the publication. Graphics, however, are handled differently. Smaller graphic files are retained within a publication but it is more usual to keep larger graphics on the outside with a link to them which allows them to be substituted to obtain maximum quality when you use *Print*... (from the *File* menu).

Link preferences. If you *Place*... high-resolution scans and complex graphics in a publication you can choose to include only a screen representation (internal bitmap) to keep the publication size down, or you can import the complete file if you need to view the graphic at its highest resolution on screen.

Choose *Link options*... from the *Element* menu to set the options you require for future graphics, or select a graphic to set link options on individual graphics. Even if you choose to include graphics in a publication, you will be warned when you try to *Place*... files that are larger than the limit set in Other Preferences (*File* menu) and will be given the option to keep them separate at that stage.

Link management. When you *Open*... or *Print*... a document with Update automatically set, if PageMaker is unable to find the external graphic (because you have moved it or deleted it), it gives you a warning to say so and invites you to find the graphic and re-establish the link.

Links... on the *File* menu provides a dialog box showing all of the links, their kind, where they are located within the publication and their status. An Info... button is provided which provides more information on individual files and allows you to change the links to associated files; you can also set link options using the Options... button.

Updates. Use *Edit original* on the *Edit* menu (System 7 only) to edit a linked graphic by launching the application used to generate it. You can also OPTION-double click on the graphic to edit the original file.

• *Display pub info*... under *Aldus Additions* on the *Utilities* menu also provides information on links, and on fonts and styles in use.

• Links are retained to graphics positioned using *Place*... only. Graphics imported using *Paste* are not linked. However, linked graphics which are cut or copied and pasted back into a publication, or between publications, carry the link information with them.

• The *Publish* and *Subscribe* feature of System 7 can also be used to manage graphics in PageMaker. It is controlled via *Editions* on the *Edit* menu.

• PageMaker provides powerful facilities for ensuring that graphics and text used in publications produced on a network are always up to date, but to use them requires discipline and well-established work management procedures.

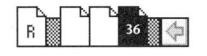

Spot colour

Element
Line ▶
Fill ▶
Fill and line... ⌘]

Bring to front ⌘F
Send to back ⌘B
Remove transformation

Text wrap...
Image control...
Rounded corners...

Define colours...
Restore original colour

Link info...
Link options...

To define or edit colours, choose *Define colours...* from the *Element* menu.

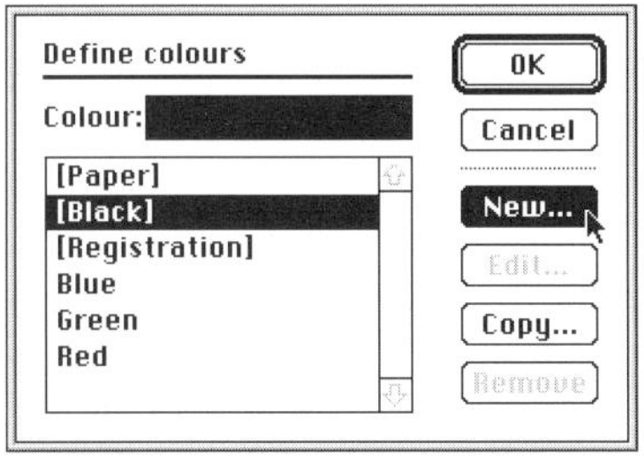

Define colours

Colour: ▮

[Paper]
[Black]
[Registration]
Blue
Green
Red

[OK]
[Cancel]
[New...]
[Edit...]
[Copy...]
[Remove]

To use a Pantone colour, for example, click on New... in the define colours box (above).

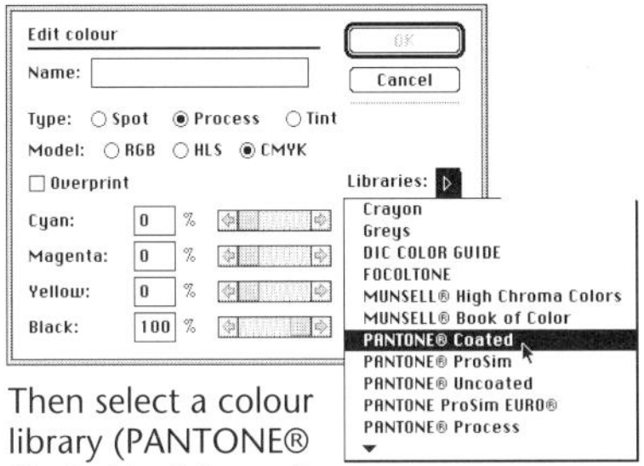

Edit colour
Name: ▮
[OK]
[Cancel]
Type: ○ Spot ● Process ○ Tint
Model: ○ RGB ○ HLS ● CMYK
☐ Overprint   Libraries: ◰
Cyan: [0] %
Magenta: [0] %
Yellow: [0] %
Black: [100] %

Crayon
Greys
DIC COLOR GUIDE
FOCOLTONE
MUNSELL® High Chroma Colors
MUNSELL® Book of Color
PANTONE® Coated
PANTONE® ProSim
PANTONE® Uncoated
PANTONE® ProSim EURO®
PANTONE® Process

Then select a colour library (PANTONE® Coated in this case) from the Libraries submenu. The colours available in that library are then displayed.

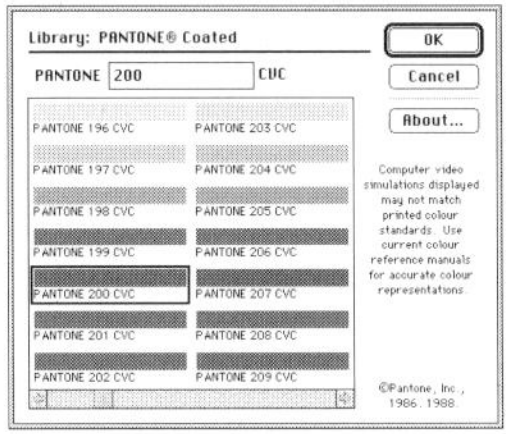

Library: PANTONE® Coated
PANTONE [200] CVC
[OK]
[Cancel]
[About...]

PANTONE 196 CVC   PANTONE 203 CVC
PANTONE 197 CVC   PANTONE 205 CVC
PANTONE 198 CVC   PANTONE 206 CVC
PANTONE 199 CVC   PANTONE 207 CVC
PANTONE 200 CVC   PANTONE 207 CVC
PANTONE 201 CVC   PANTONE 208 CVC
PANTONE 202 CVC   PANTONE 209 CVC

Computer video simulations displayed may not match printed colour standards. Use current colour reference manuals for accurate colour representations.

©Pantone, Inc., 1986, 1988

Select a colour, or type its number if you know it (above). When you click the OKs, the colour is made available in the colour palette.

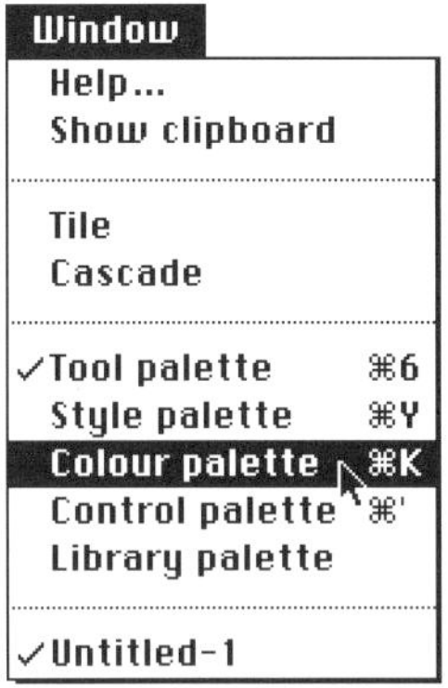

Window
Help...
Show clipboard

Tile
Cascade

✓Tool palette ⌘6
Style palette ⌘Y
Colour palette ⌘K
Control palette ⌘'
Library palette

✓Untitled-1

Choose *Colour palette* on the *Window* menu to make the palette visible.

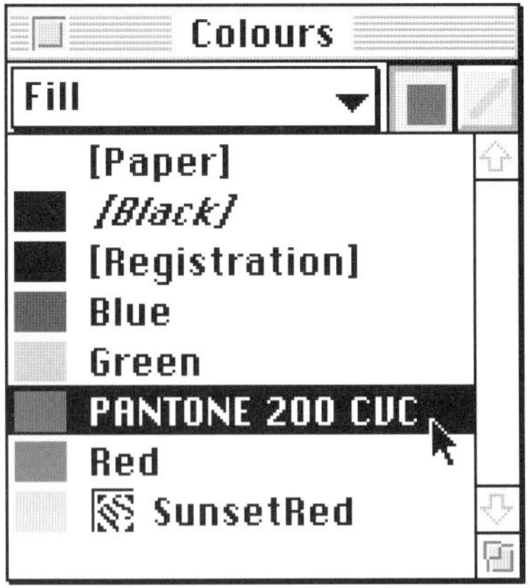

Colours

Fill ▼

[Paper]
[Black]
[Registration]
Blue
Green
PANTONE 200 CVC
Red
▨ SunsetRed

To apply colour, select the element on the page (use the text tool for text) and click on the required colour in the palette (left). Note, for example, that the Pantone colour defined above is available.

Colour names with the EPS icon are spot colours defined in imported graphics.

You can apply colour to the fill or line (or both) of objects drawn in PageMaker. Select the object, click the fill or line button on the colour palette (or choose *Line*, *Fill* or *Both* from the palette menu) and then click the colour you want to apply. You can also apply colour to both by holding down SHIFT as you click the unselected button.

Colour adds impact but it also increases printing costs. It is vital that you speak to your printers at an early stage if you are considering colour in your publication. They will advise you on costs and, if appropriate, on ways of minimising cost (for example, by adding colour to pages on the same printing plate only).

Process printing involves the use of four printing masters, one for each of the colours Cyan, Magenta, Yellow and Black (or Key, hence CMYK), and is both complex and costly. Spot colour, on the other hand, where a single colour is used to emphasise particular elements on a page, involves one extra printing master and is usually within most budgets. In addition, spot colour is easy to use and can be very effective.

Applying colours. Colours are applied from the colours palette. To make this palette visible, choose *Colour palette* from the *Window* menu. This is very similar in use to the style palette described earlier—you select the object to be coloured and click on the colour you want in the colours palette.

To select text to be coloured you must use the text tool; for everything else use the pointer tool. You can apply colour to lines and boxes and to imported graphics. Even if you are using a black and white screen you can still apply colours, but you will not see them on screen. Some imported graphic formats (for example, PICT and EPSF) will not show the colour you apply even on colour screens but they will print on the appropriate master.

Defining colours. Ask your printers what inks they use and, if possible, use a library (Pantone® for example) to save the effort of defining colours yourself. Libraries are sets of numbered colours (inks) which are well known and widely used within the printing industry. Don't, however, use the computer screen to select colours—they are not accurately represented. Use a book of printed samples (your printers will have one) and use what you see on screen as a guide only.

To add a Pantone colour to the palette, choose *Define colours…* from the *Element* menu and click on the New… button. Next, click on the Libraries submenu to select the library, and then choose the colour from the display that follows (if you know the number of the colour, you can type it). Click back through the OKs and the colour will be added to the palette for you to use.

Printing colours. Click on the Colour button in the *Print…* dialog box to reach the colour printing options. Print all inks produces a separate master (overlay) for each colour used in the publication, but you should discuss requirements with your printers before you proceed.

• Colour can also be applied to text in the *Type specs…* box and can be part of a style definition.

• You can create a colour library containing the colours you regularly use with the *Create colour library…* addition..

• Objects to which the registration 'colour' is applied appear on each master plate (overlay).

• Colours leave a gap (called a knockout) for other colours to prevent unsightly blending. Check Overprint in the *New…* box when defining colours if you want colours to print on top of one another. Seek the advice of your printers.

• Registration marks (if selected) are printed outside the page area (if the paper is big enough).

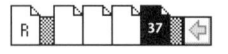

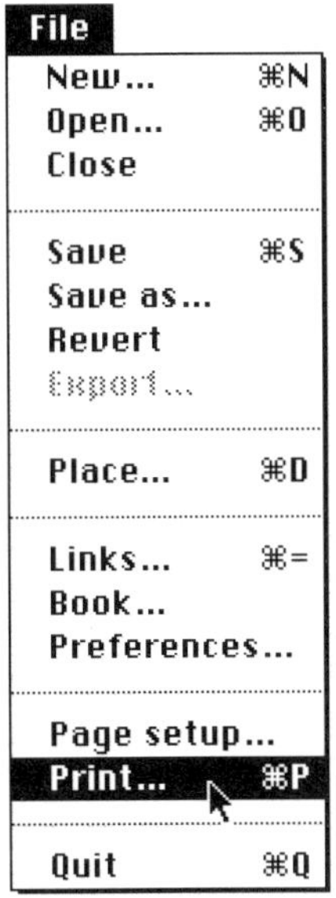

Colour separation 38

File

New...	⌘N
Open...	⌘O
Close	
Save	⌘S
Save as...	
Revert	
Export...	
Place...	⌘D
Links...	⌘=
Book...	
Preferences...	
Page setup...	
Print...	⌘P
Quit	⌘Q

To separate pages into their component colours, choose *Print...* from the *File* menu.

| Print |
| Cancel |
| Document |
| Paper |
| Options |
| **Colour** |
| Reset |

Then click the Colour button in the *Print...* dialog box.

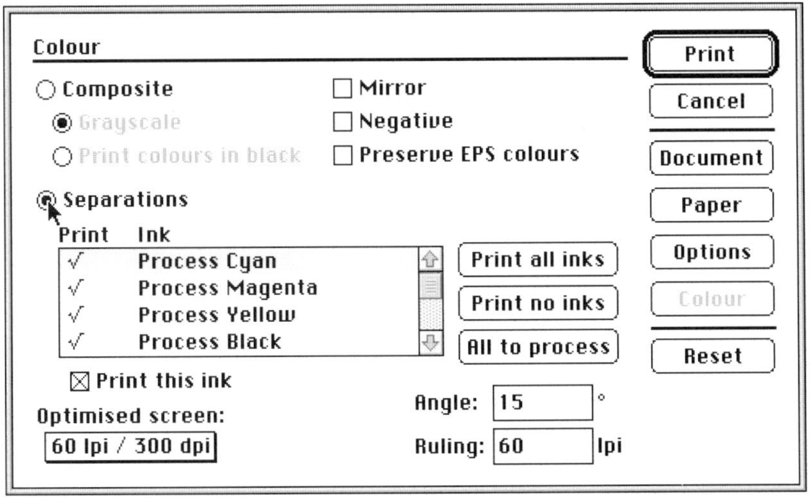

Colour

○ Composite
  ◉ Grayscale
  ○ Print colours in black

☐ Mirror
☐ Negative
☐ Preserve EPS colours

◉ Separations

Print	Ink
√	Process Cyan
√	Process Magenta
√	Process Yellow
√	Process Black

☒ Print this ink

Optimised screen:
| 60 lpi / 300 dpi |

[Print all inks]
[Print no inks]
[All to process]

Angle: | 15 | °
Ruling: | 60 | lpi

| Print |
| Cancel |
| Document |
| Paper |
| Options |
| Colour |
| Reset |

In the Colour box, click the Separations button and set the colour printing options that then appear according to your needs (above).

Notice, in particular, the Print all inks button—set this if you want to print a separate plate for each colour used. Print no inks is a quick way of deselecting all inks so that you can click on individual colours in the scrolling window when you want to print particular plates only.

The screen dot size (lines per inch) and angle are those stored in the PPD file for the printer being used, so it is important to select the correct destination printer in the *Print...* box. You should not vary these values without good reason.

Colour printing is expensive so mistakes can be costly. The advice given at several points throughout this book to consult with your printers is particularly relevant to colour work—you should not even think about embarking on a full-colour publication without first talking to the printers.

Some printers will be willing to accept a disk from you, while others will want to do the colour work themselves. Even if they are prepared to work with you, they will need to be convinced that you know what is involved and that you can deliver publications conforming to their specifications. So, be prepared for questions about line screens, screen angles, knockouts and trapping. You must also be prepared to accept full responsibility if something is not as it should be.

Proofing. Knowing what colours will look like when printed is one of the major problems associated with colour work. And the first rule is—never trust your computer screen.

Colours on a computer are produced by projecting red, green and blue (RGB) light onto a screen. Colour printing, on the other hand, uses cyan, magenta and yellow (CMY) inks which absorb and reflect light in varying degrees to produce different colours. Since they are based on different colour models, you can't rely on an RGB image to display CMY colours faithfully.

Four-colour printing. For printing purposes, a colour image must first be separated into its component CMY colours. One separated, a different printing plate is made for each colour and these are then printed, using each ink in turn, to reproduce the original image on paper.

A fourth ink, black, is also used in the process to improve density and also to sharpen up the image. Black is known as the Key colour, hence CMYK.

Separation is conventionally achieved by photographing an image, or page, through filters. PageMaker can now also do that work for you.

Separation. In the *Print…* dialog box, click on the Colour button and then click the Separations button.

Click the colours you want printed on separate masters (CMYK usually) and the Print all inks button if you are also using special spot colours for which you want a separate printing plate. The All to process button separates all colours, including spot colours in imported graphics, but that might not be what you want.

Depending on the plate-making and printing process used by your printers, you might need to provide Negative masters or Mirror images. If so, check the appropriate boxes.

• The Help information within PageMaker has a lot of useful information on colour printing.

• Click the Composite button if you are printing a proof on a colour printer.

• If you are unsure of the whole process, experiment by printing separations on a laser printer to get a feel for what is involved.

• You will need some kind of reference print (proof) to compare with the final printed copy.

• PageMaker will not separate TIFF images saved in RGB format.

• Red, green and blue (RGB), when combined, produce white. Cyan, magenta and yellow combine to produce black.

• Cyan is a bright blue colour; magenta a reddish purple.

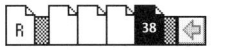

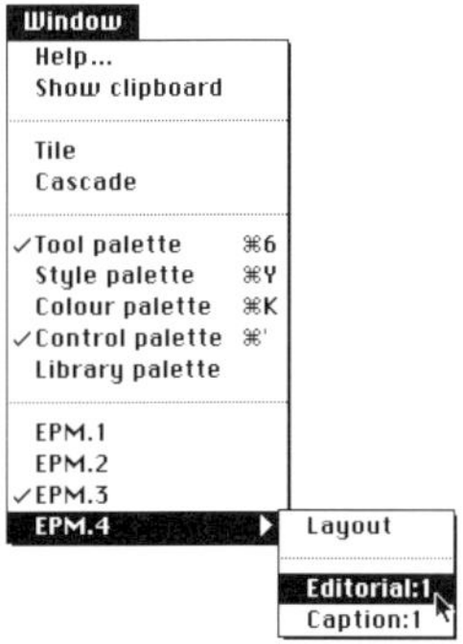

Multiple publications   39

When you have several publications open, you can select the window you want to work on from the list on the *Window* menu. The publication you are currently working on has a tick against it in the list. Note that you can reach open story editor windows, too, if necessary, via a submenu (above).

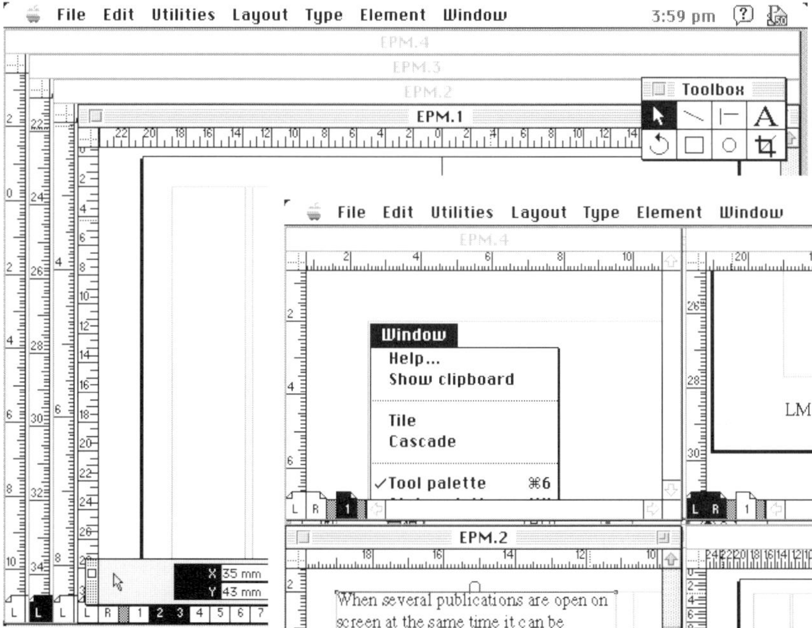

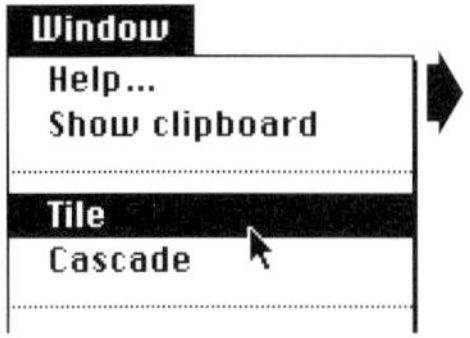

To manage several open publication windows, you can *Cascade* (above) or *Tile* them (right) by selecting the arrangement you want from the *Window* menu (left).

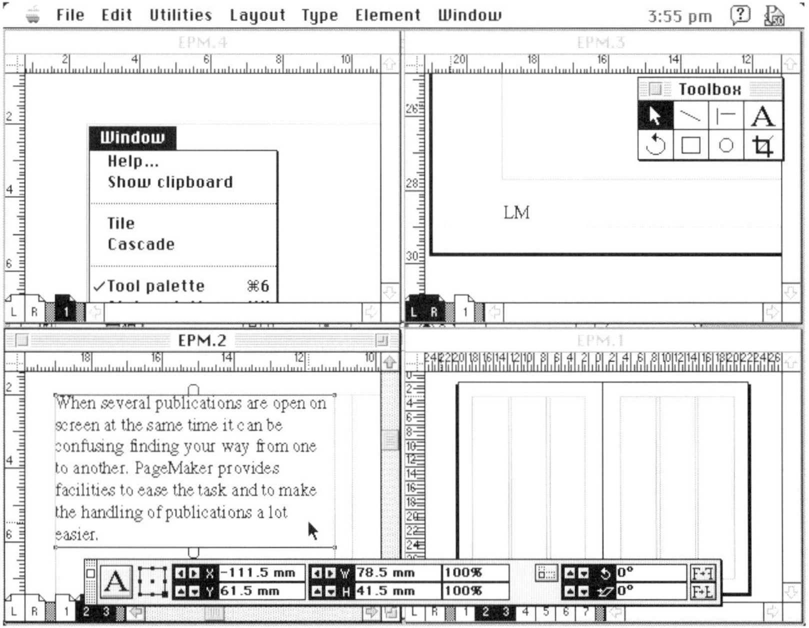

Depending on the amount of memory (RAM) available on the computer, you can have more than one publication open on screen. To begin with, you will probably concentrate on a single publication at a time. But gradually, as you complete one publication after another, you will want to open earlier publications to copy items to a new publication or to compare earlier solutions to particular layout problems. There will also be occasions when you need to change some detail throughout a publication (an address, a name or a telephone number, for example), at which time it would be sensible to make the change (before you forget) in existing publications, too, as part of the updating process.

It takes time to get used to working with several publications at once and the larger the size of your monitor the better—to give you space to navigate and manipulate layout and story editor windows, and to prevent the screen becoming too cluttered with windows and palettes.

PageMaker also has features designed to overcome some of the problems involved and to allow you to work comfortably with several publications open at once.

Multiple windows. When you have more than one publication open, one only can be active at any given time, but you can move between them by selecting the one you want to work on from the list of open publications provided on the *Window* menu (the active publication will have a tick against it in the list). If a publication has story editor windows open, these can be reached individually by using the submenu associated with that particular publication on the *Window* menu.

You can also move from window to window by clicking on the one you want, but only if you can see part of it on screen.

To put some order on publication windows you will find *Tile* and *Cascade* on the *Window* menu useful. *Cascade* places windows one on top of another but leaves the title bar of each visible; *Tile*, on the other hand, puts open windows side by side on screen.

Unless you are within the story editor, *Tile* and *Cascade* affect all open windows. Within the story editor, only the open story editor windows of the active publication are affected.

Copying items. *Tile* is very useful when you want to move items from one publication to another. Even on a small screen, you can click on an item in one window and drag it across to another to drop a copy of it into another publication—the view magnification does not have to be the same in both windows.

• When you have more than one publication open, if you hold down the OPTION key on the Macintosh (SHIFT under Windows) *Close* and *Save* become *Close all* and *Save all* on the *File* menu.

• With the OPTION key held down (SHIFT under Windows), *Tile* on the *Window* menu will tile all open story editor windows in all open publications.

• Don't worry when a window starts scrolling as you reach its boundary during drag and drop copying—PageMaker will put it back where it was once the copy is made.

• Drag and drop requires System 7 on Macintosh.

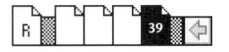

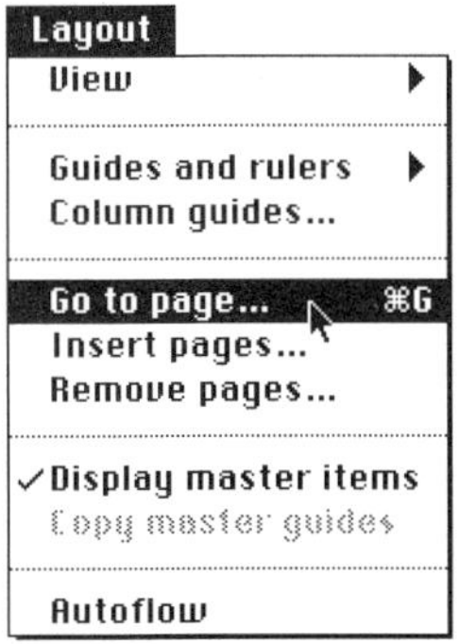

Managing pages — 40

Layout
View ▶
Guides and rulers ▶
Column guides...
Go to page... ⌘G
Insert pages...
Remove pages...
✓ Display master items
Copy master guides
Autoflow

Move to any page by choosing *Go to page...* on the *Page* menu.

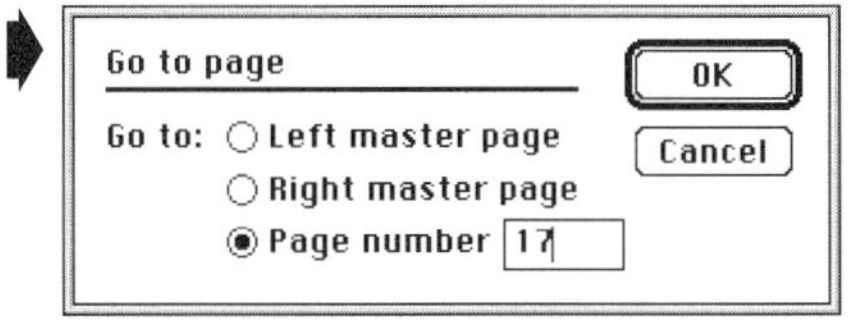

Go to page

Go to: ○ Left master page
○ Right master page
● Page number │1 7│

OK Cancel

Move from page to page using the page icons at the bottom of the window (below). You might have to scroll the page icons, using the arrows, to see the icon for the page you want to reach. As an alternative, use the *Go to page...* box (above) from the *Page* menu .

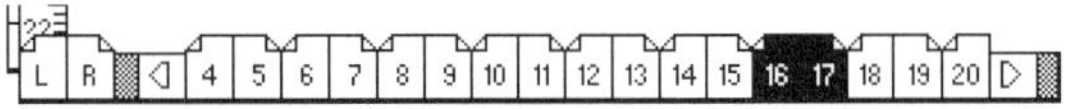

L R ◁ 4 5 6 7 8 9 10 11 12 13 14 15 16 17 18 19 20 ▷

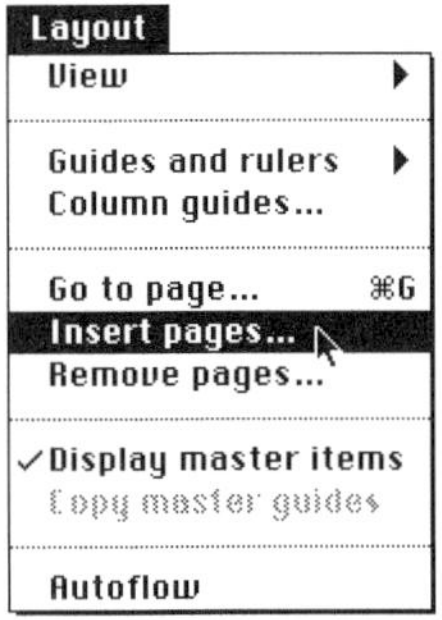

Layout
View ▶
Guides and rulers ▶
Column guides...
Go to page... ⌘G
Insert pages...
Remove pages...
✓ Display master items
Copy master guides
Autoflow

Insert and Remove pages via the *Page* menu.

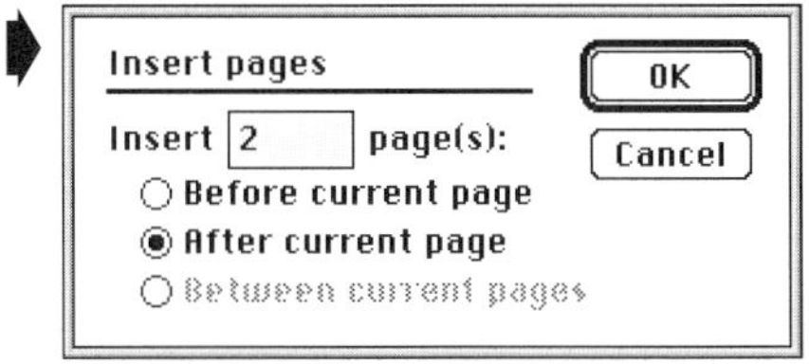

Insert pages

Insert │2│ page(s):
○ Before current page
● After current page
○ *Between current pages*

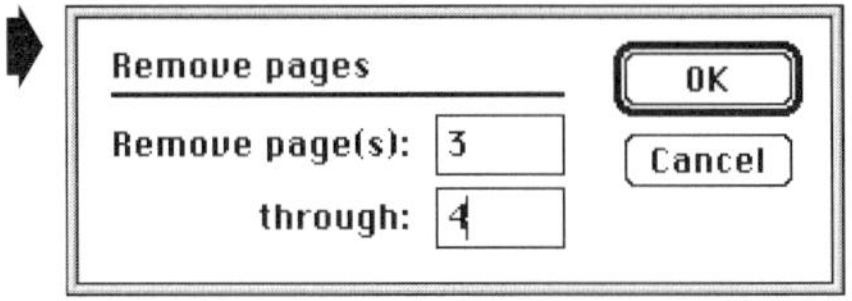

OK Cancel

Remove pages

Remove page(s): │3│
through: │4│

OK Cancel

Sort pages... at the base of the *Additions* list lets you move pages around within the page sorter window (below). Click and drag the pages you want to move. Use the SHIFT key as you click, to select multiple pages, or the COMMAND key (CTRL on Windows) to select a single facing page.

Utilities
Aldus Additions ▶

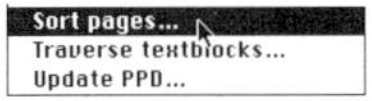

Sort pages...
Traverse textblocks...
Update PPD...

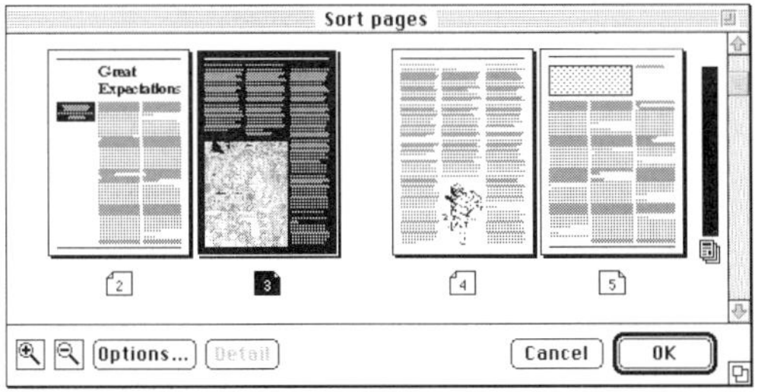

Sorting (above) with vertical bar showing where selected page is to go. Original page numbers are shown beside new ones (below) after the move.

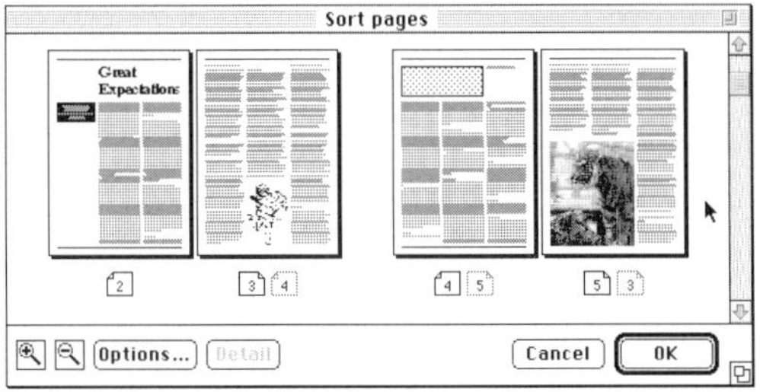

Up to this point, pages have been discussed in isolation. However, as you construct a publication you will want to move from page to page, to add, move and delete pages, and to view your publication as a complete entity. You need an impression of your publication as a whole to ensure consistency of design. As part of the production process you will need to move around within your publication and to manage individual pages as part of the overall document.

Navigating. The easiest way to move from page to page within a publication is to click on a page icon at the bottom of the window. However, in larger publications you might find that scrolling the page icons to find the one you want is time consuming.

An alternative is to use *Go to page…* on the *Page* menu. This produces a box in which you can type the number of the page you want to reach. Or use COMMAND-G (CTRL-G under Windows), type the page number and press RETURN. With practice you can learn to do this as one step, without stopping for the screen to redraw.

You can use COMMAND-TAB as a shortcut to move to the next page (CTRL-TAB under Windows), or COMMAND-SHIFT-TAB to move to the previous page.

Hold down SHIFT and choose *Go to page…* from the *Layout* menu to see each page briefly as a slide show. Click when you want it to stop.

Inserting and deleting. You can add or delete pages using *Insert pages…* or *Remove pages…* from the *Layout* menu. When you insert pages a box is provided for you to specify the number of pages you want to insert and where you want them to go (before or after the current page, or between facing pages). When you remove pages you are warned that items on the pages will be lost.

Sorting. To move pages around in a publication you can select everything on a page (*Select all*) and *Cut* it to the clipboard, or move it off the page on to the pasteboard, before going to the destination page to move or *Paste* it back again. *Sort pages…* on the *Aldus Additions* submenu of the *Utilities* menu makes the job easier by showing the publication in a special page sorter window.

Pages are shown as thumbnail miniatures and you can change their position within the publication by dragging them to a new location—a bar indicates the new location and the pages are dropped into place when you release the mouse button. Click OK to save the re-ordered pages.

You can move and resize the window and bring pages into view using the scroll bars. Use the magnifying glass icons to zoom in and out.

Click the Options… button to vary the level of detail shown on pages in the window (or *Detail* to vary detail on selected pages only).

• Pages can also be added by changing the Number of pages value in the *Page setup…* box.

• You can go to master pages in the *Go to page…* box. However, clicking on the master page icons (which don't move) at the bottom of the window is usually the quickest way to display the master pages.

• The page sorter addition is a useful way of looking at your publication as a whole, even if you do not intend to move pages. If the pages are grey, click the Options… button to change the level of detail.

• Choose a page view from the *Layout* menu with OPTION pressed to change all pages to that view—useful before a final run through (or slide show).

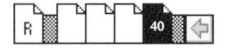

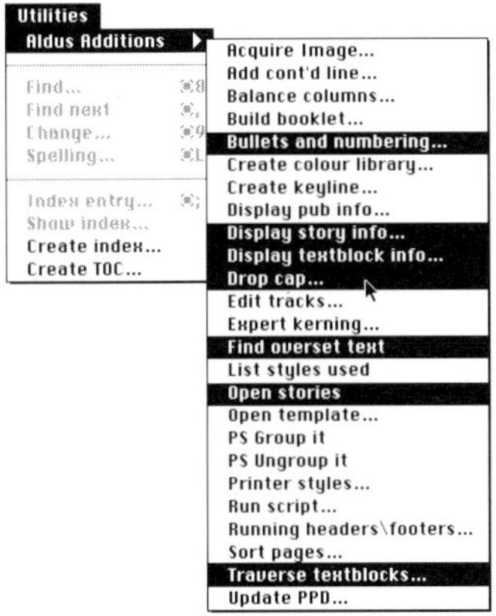

Text additions   41

Utilities
Aldus Additions ▶

Find...	⌘8
Find next	⌘,
Change...	⌘9
Spelling...	⌘L

Index entry... ⌘;
Show index...
Create index...
Create TOC...

Acquire Image...
Add cont'd line...
Balance columns...
Build booklet...
Bullets and numbering...
Create colour library...
Create keyline...
Display pub info...
Display story info...
Display textblock info...
Drop cap...
Edit tracks...
Expert kerning...
Find overset text
List styles used
Open stories
Open template...
PS Group it
PS Ungroup it
Printer styles...
Run script...
Running headers\footers...
Sort pages...
Traverse textblocks...
Update PPD...

Click to position the text cursor within a paragraph and choose *Drop cap...* from the *Aldus Additions* submenu (above). The other text additions are also highlighted in the menu.

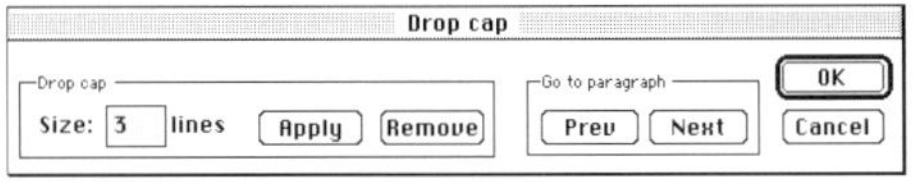

Drop cap

Drop cap — Size: 3 lines [Apply] [Remove]

Go to paragraph — [Prev] [Next]

[OK] [Cancel]

Specify the depth of the letter in lines (above) and watch PageMaker do the work of constructing the enlarged capital (right).

Bullets and numbering... inserts a number or bullet character (and a TAB) at the beginning of paragraphs. Click with text tool first.

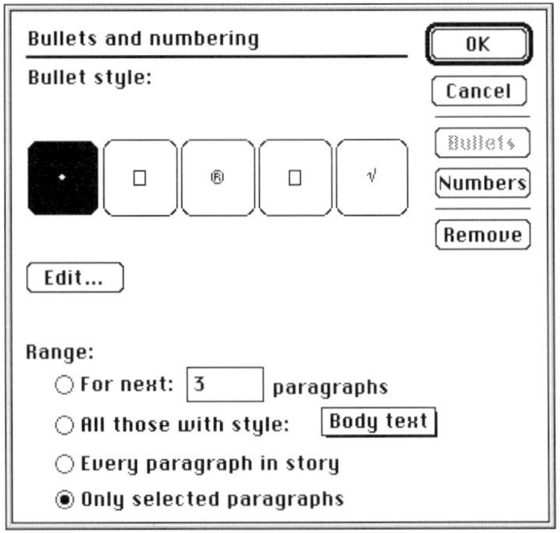

Bullets and numbering

Bullet style:

[•] [□] [®] [□] [√]

[Edit...]

Range:
○ For next: 3 paragraphs
○ All those with style: [Body text]
○ Every paragraph in story
● Only selected paragraphs

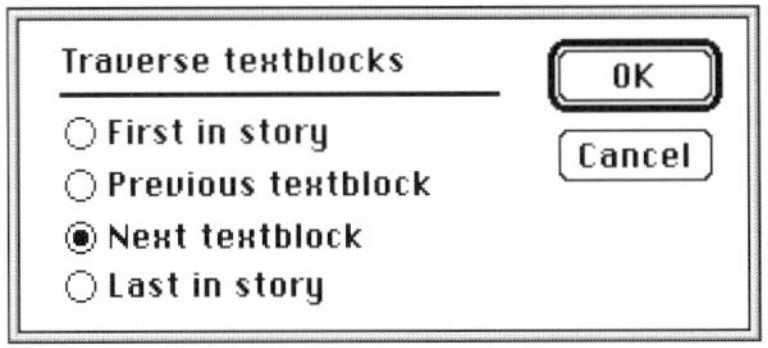

[OK]
[Cancel]
[Bullets]
[Numbers]
[Remove]

Drop capitals occupy the number of lines you specify in the dialog box (3 in this case). Don't forget to position the insertion cursor first.

Traverse textblocks

○ First in story
○ Previous textblock
● Next textblock
○ Last in story

[OK]
[Cancel]

Select a textblock with the pointer tool and use *Traverse textblocks* to move from one textblock to another within the same story.

Use *Find overset text* to find text not yet placed. Overset text is easy to overlook when a story is edited and extended on the page (it can easily be pushed off the lower right corner of a page).

to offer a degree of typographic control which, with care and attention, can be used to improve the quality of the output.

Additions add features to the program to simplify everyday tasks. To use an addition, choose it from the *Aldus Additions* submenu on the *Utilities* menu, but you need to select an object on the page first, if appropriate.

Drop cap... Click with the text tool to position the text insertion point within the paragraph to be formatted and choose *Drop cap...* to have the first letter of that paragraph enlarged (as at the top of this column). Then, in the dialog box, specify the Size (in number of lines) of letter you want. The drop capital is automatically generated using some complex formatting (by subscripting the initial character, shifting its baseline, and inserting tabs and line ends). It is best to use this addition once you are sure that no other edits are necessary in the affected lines of the paragraph. Use the Apply button if you want to see what the result looks like before you finally decide. To remove a drop cap, use the addition again and click Remove.

Bullets and numbering... Click first with the text tool to select a paragraph and use this addition to number paragraphs, or to call attention to paragraphs with bullets or some other character. You can specify the range of paragraphs you want numbered or apply numbers only to specific styles. Click the Numbers button to set the kind of numbers you want (arabic, roman, etc.) or Edit to choose the character to be used or to change its font or size.

Conveniently, this addition does not number empty lines separating paragraphs (unless they contain a space character).

It does not, however, renumber paragraphs already numbered—it adds an extra number instead. Use the Remove button first and then add the numbers again if you have to add or delete paragraphs after adding numbers. It is best to complete editing text before using this addition.

Display story/textblock info... These additions either display information about a textblock or about the story it belongs to (such as area occupied, character count and pages). You must first select a textblock with the pointer tool.

Traverse textblocks. Select a single textblock with the pointer tool and use this to move to the first, last, next or previous textblock in the story.

Find overset text. Useful for finding text not yet placed (accidentally or otherwise), or text pushed out of the last textblock by earlier editing.

Open stories. Opens all stories in the active publication in cascaded story windows.

• If any of the additions mentioned here do not appear on the *Aldus Additions* submenu, you can install them from disk. Additions are stored in a separate folder within the Aldus folder.

• Additions lack the polish associated with PageMaker itself and are not dimmed on the submenu when they are not relevant.

• Additions cannot be used in the Story editor.

• If you want the first line of a drop cap to have the same indent as the others in the paragraph (as used in this book), put a TAB between the drop cap and the next letter.

• The *Expert kerning...* addition improves the spacing between selected characters.

• *Edit tracks...* is best left to experts.

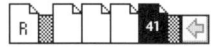

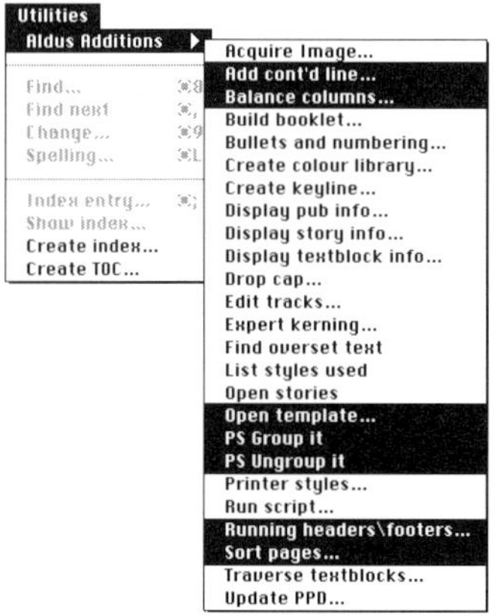

Layout additions 42

Utilities
Aldus Additions ▶

Find...   ⌘8
Find next   ⌘;
Change...   ⌘9
Spelling...   ⌘L

Index entry...   ⌘;
Show index...
Create index...
Create TOC...

Aldus Additions submenu
Acquire Image...
Add cont'd line...
Balance columns...
Build booklet...
Bullets and numbering...
Create colour library...
Create keyline...
Display pub info...
Display story info...
Display textblock info...
Drop cap...
Edit tracks...
Expert kerning...
Find overset text
List styles used
Open stories
Open template...
PS Group it
PS Ungroup it
Printer styles...
Run script...
Running headers\footers...
Sort pages...
Traverse textblocks...
Update PPD...

Balance columns   OK

Alignment: Cancel

Add leftover lines:

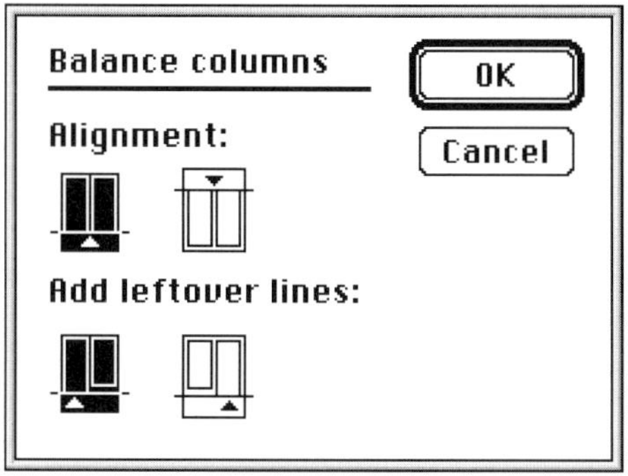

In the *Balance columns...* box (left) click the icons to specify how you want columns to align and where you want remainder lines to go.

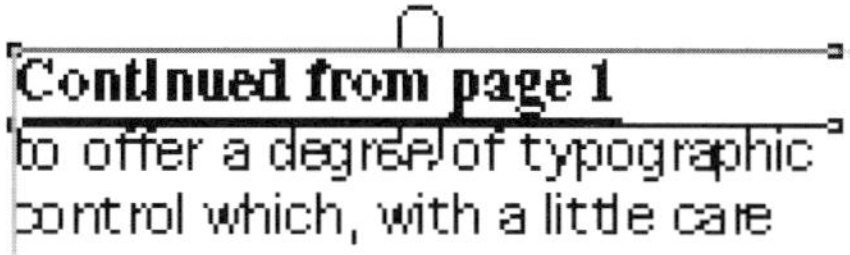

Contlnued from page 1
to offer a degree of typographic control which, with a little care

Use *Add cont'd line...* to add a continued on/from line to a text block (above).

A

Group selected items with *PS Group it.* When ungrouping with *PS Ungroup it* you are reminded that groups are external (below).

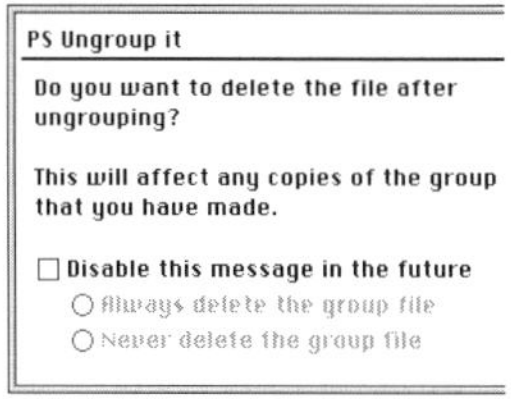

Using the pointer tool, select the textblocks (use SHIFT for multiple selection) and choose *Balance columns...* from the *Aldus Additions* submenu (above). The other additions for layout are also highlighted in the above menu.

Specify the text and position of headers/footers in the *Running headers\footers* box (below).

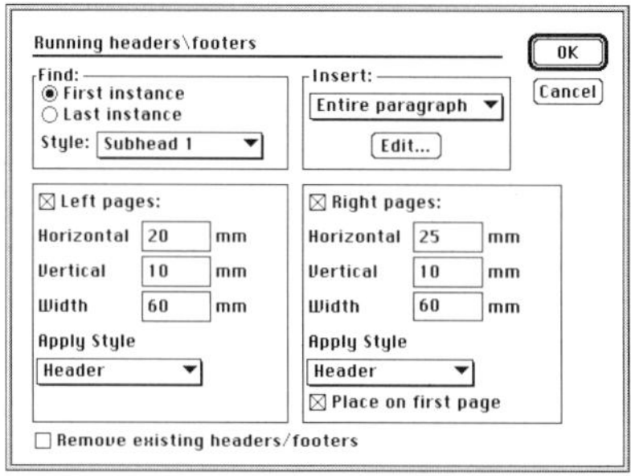

Running headers\footers   OK
─Find:───────── ─Insert:─────   Cancel
● First instance   Entire paragraph ▼
○ Last instance
Style: Subhead 1 ▼   Edit...

☒ Left pages: ☒ Right pages:
Horizontal 20 mm   Horizontal 25 mm
Vertical   10 mm   Vertical   10 mm
Width   60 mm   Width   60 mm
Apply Style   Apply Style
Header   ▼   Header   ▼
                       ☒ Place on first page

☐ Remove existing headers/footers

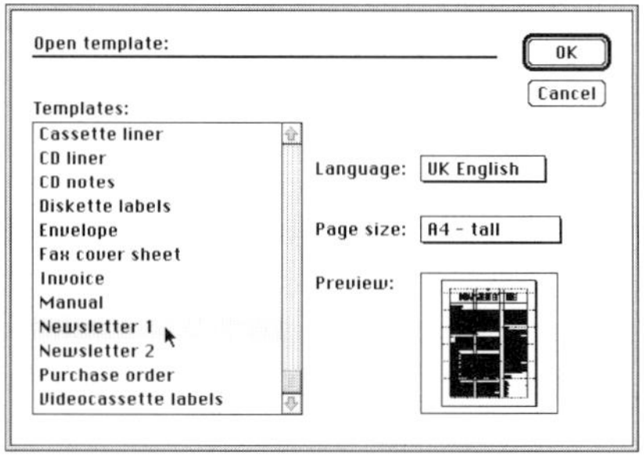

Open template: OK
                                      Cancel
Templates:
Cassette liner
CD liner   Language: UK English
CD notes
Diskette labels
Envelope   Page size: A4 – tall
Fax cover sheet
Invoice
Manual   Preview:
Newsletter 1
Newsletter 2
Purchase order
Videocassette labels

Use the *Open template...* box to select the pre-constructed document you want to use (above).

PS Ungroup it

Do you want to delete the file after ungrouping?

This will affect any copies of the group that you have made.

☐ Disable this message in the future
  ○ Always delete the group file
  ○ Never delete the group file

Layout additions help take the effort out of common layout tasks. To use an addition, choose it from the *Aldus Additions* submenu on the *Utilities* menu but, if appropriate, select an object on the page first.

Balance columns... Using the pointer tool, select two or more text blocks and use this addition to resize and align the blocks (at the top with the highest or at the bottom with the lowest) and to distribute the text evenly amongst them. You can also specify how you want any remainder lines to be treated.

Running headers\footers... A useful addition, particularly when one master page is not enough.

Based on a search that you define in the dialog box, text in the story is located and added to a separate text block at the location you specify on the pages containing that story. You could, for example, use it to add the section name to pages in each section of a publication.

Don't forget to select a textblock first. Headers/footers are added in a forward direction only and will not overlap existing text blocks.

Construct a text block manually first to help you decide what you want and then, if you need help, take location details (measured from the left edge of each page) from the Control palette.

Separate .HDR and .INI files are associated with headers/footers and these should be moved too if the document goes to another computer. They should not be deleted.

Add cont'd line... Stories sometimes jump from one page to another in a way that might not be obvious to the reader. Adding continuation lines to the story using this addition helps. Continuation lines can indicate the page number containing the next textblock in the story (...on) or the previous one (...from). Separate continued on/from styles are also constructed for you.

The selected text block is shrunk by one line and the continuation line is inserted in the space. If you delete a continuation line you will have to readjust textblocks manually.

PS Group/Ungroup it. Use this addition to group objects on a page if you want to move and manipulate them as a single entity. You must first select the objects you want to group together.

It works by creating a separate external EPS (PostScript) graphic of the objects and establishing a link to it (as though you had placed it).

The PageMaker document must have a name before you can use the addition (i.e. it cannot be untitled). The name of the document is used to construct the external filename for the new graphic—docname.PMGn.

• *Sort pages...* is described earlier.

• The *Library palette* is also an addition but appears on the *Window* menu.

• Complex text patterns can be specified (via the Edit... button) to construct headers/footers.

• *Run script...* PageMaker has its own scripting language which you can use to perform a sequence of commands and actions. Open one of the supplied scripts (or templates) in a word processor to get a feel for what is involved. You can also write your own scripts but you will need the Script Language Guide.

• PageMaker's templates are supplied as scripts to save disk space. Use the *Open template...* addition to construct and open the templates.

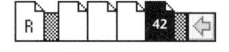

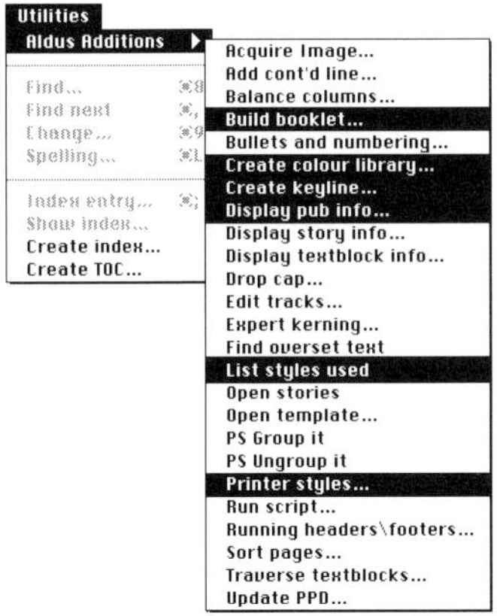

Printing additions   43

Utilities
Aldus Additions ▶

Find... ⌘8
Find next ⌘?
Change... ⌘?
Spelling... ⌘?

Index entry... ⌘;
Show index...
Create index...
Create TOC...

Acquire Image...
Add cont'd line...
Balance columns...
Build booklet...
Bullets and numbering...
Create colour library...
Create keyline...
Display pub info...
Display story info...
Display textblock info...
Drop cap...
Edit tracks...
Expert kerning...
Find overset text
List styles used
Open stories
Open template...
PS Group it
PS Ungroup it
Printer styles...
Run script...
Running headers\footers...
Sort pages...
Traverse textblocks...
Update PPD...

Choose the printing or
colour addition you need
from the *Aldus Additions*
submenu. They are
highlighted above.

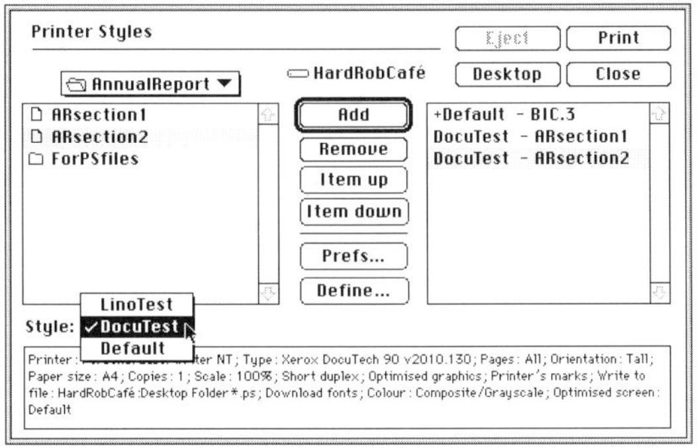

Printer Styles   Eject   Print

🗀 AnnualReport ▼   ☐ HardRobCafé   Desktop   Close

☐ ARsection1   Add   +Default – BIC.3
☐ ARsection2   Remove   DocuTest – ARsection1
🗀 ForPSfiles   Item up DocuTest – ARsection2
                  Item down
                  Prefs...
                  Define...

Style: ☐ LinoTest
       ✓ DocuTest
       ☐ Default

Printer : ___ NT ; Type : Xerox DocuTech 90 v2010.130 ; Pages : All ; Orientation : Tall ;
Paper size : A4 ; Copies : 1 ; Scale : 100% ; Short duplex ; Optimised graphics ; Printer's marks ; Write to
file : HardRobCafé :Desktop Folder * .ps ; Download fonts ; Colour : Composite /Grayscale ; Optimised screen :
Default

In the *Printer styles...* box (above), select
the publications you want added to the
queue and click the Add button (or double-
click). Assign a printer style as you go (or
by selecting the publication already in the
queue) from the Style drop-down menu.
Click Define... to create or edit a style.

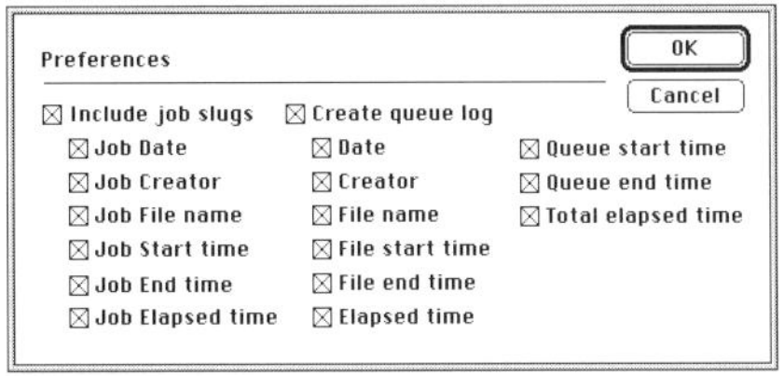

Preferences   OK
                    Cancel

☒ Include job slugs   ☒ Create queue log
☒ Job Date   ☒ Date   ☒ Queue start time
☒ Job Creator   ☒ Creator   ☒ Queue end time
☒ Job File name   ☒ File name   ☒ Total elapsed time
☒ Job Start time   ☒ File start time
☒ Job End time   ☒ File end time
☒ Job Elapsed time   ☒ Elapsed time

The Prefs... button gives access to a box
where you can print an accounting page
(called a job slug) or keep a log of printing
in a file (stored as PQLOGn.TXT in PStyles
in the Additions folder).

Use *Create colour library...* to save colours used in a
publication for future use (below). You can then select
the new library when defining colours in other
publications—to ensure consistency.

Create colour library   Save

Library name: Newsletter   Cancel
File name: Custom.bcf
                               Save as...
Preferences
   Colours per column: 5
   Colours per row: 3
Notes: Colours used in monthly newsletters (for
         example) and any other comments you want
         to appear in the About... box.

Create keyline... (right) is
useful if you want to put
a box around a graphic
or text. It also has
advanced uses in colour
printing (it can be used
to 'trap' colours).

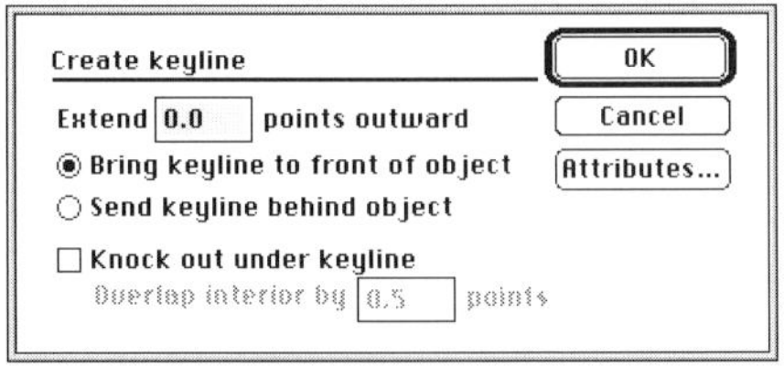

Create keyline   OK

Extend 0.0 points outward   Cancel
● Bring keyline to front of object   Attributes...
○ Send keyline behind object

☐ Knock out under keyline
   Overlap interior by 0.5 points

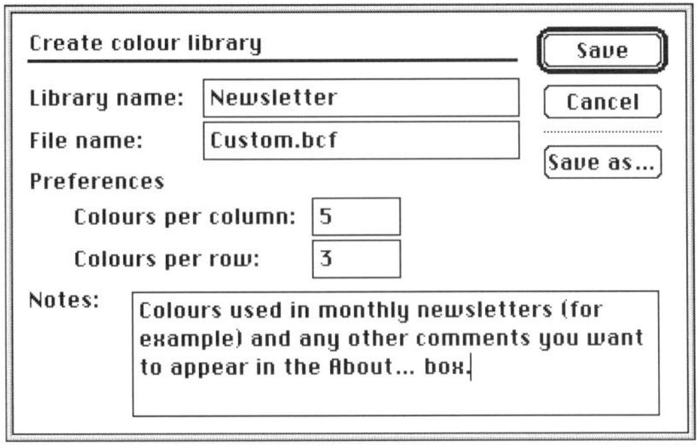

Additions are also provided to ease certain printing and colour-related tasks. To use an addition, choose it from the *Aldus Additions* submenu on the *Utilities* menu but, if appropriate, select an object on the page first.

Create colour library… If you go to the trouble of creating your own colours, or of selecting a specific set of colours from a colour library, save the colours in that palette in a library of your own so that they can be used in other publications. This not only saves effort but also helps to ensure a consistent use of colours across a range of publications.

The new library name will be added to the Libraries pop-up menu in the New box when you choose *Define colours…* from the *Element* menu.

Printer styles… When it comes to saving effort, this addition is hard to beat. It comes into its own when you use more than one printer, particularly when you have to save publications as PostScript files—you can automate printing to disk.

When you proof your publications on one printer and then need to change some of the *Print…* button options to produce final masters on another printer, it is easy to make costly mistakes by setting the wrong options.

You can save the printing options you use in different situations by creating a printer style for specific destination printers. The *Printer styles…* addition presents you with a box where you can Define… printer styles (a set of printing options). To use a style, select publications to add to the print queue and then assign a style to them as you go (these do not change the print settings within individual publications).

Within the box you can manipulate the queue by moving publications up or down and, via the Prefs… button, you can elect to have information about the queue's progress printed (job slug) or stored in a file (queue log).

Create keyline… Select a textblock or graphic with the pointer tool and use this addition to create a rectangular frame around it. You can also apply a fill and/or line to the frame (keyline).

Display pub info… This opens a window giving information on the fonts and style names in a publication, and on the status of linked (placed) elements. Use Save as… in the box to save a copy if you want to print the information later.

List styles used. Select a textblock with the pointer tool and this addition will construct and place a small textblock showing the names of paragraph styles used in the story and the number of times each is used.

• Double-click the name of a document in the *Printer styles…* queue to override settings temporarily. A plus sign (+) is then added to its name.

• The *Printer styles…* addition can also be used to construct a queue of publications for printing.

• *Create keyline…* has important uses in trapping colours when colour printing. Trapping helps to prevent unexpected colours (when colours overlap) and unsightly gaps between different colours. You should talk to your printers before you trap colours.

• Printer styles are stored in the Additions folder.

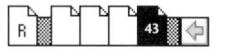

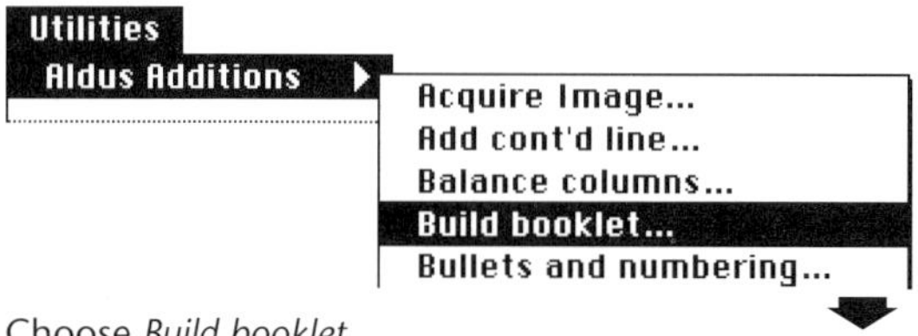

Producing booklets   44

Utilities
Aldus Additions ▶
- Acquire Image...
- Add cont'd line...
- Balance columns...
- **Build booklet...**
- Bullets and numbering...

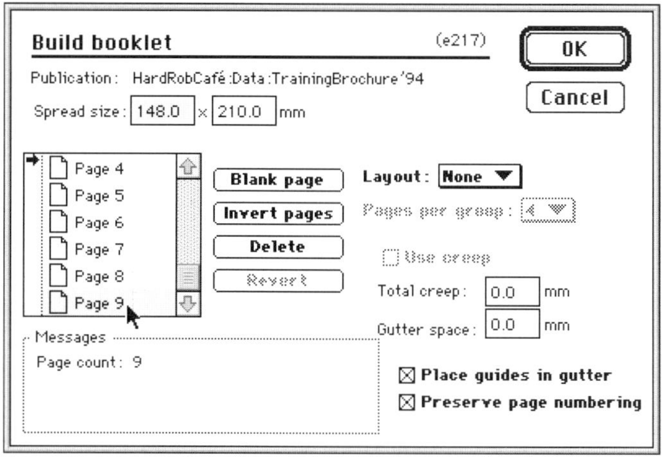

Choose the kind of booklet you want from the Layout pop-up menu (below). 2-up puts two of your pages onto one page in the correct sequence for printing, for example two A5 pages side by side on a single A4 sheet.

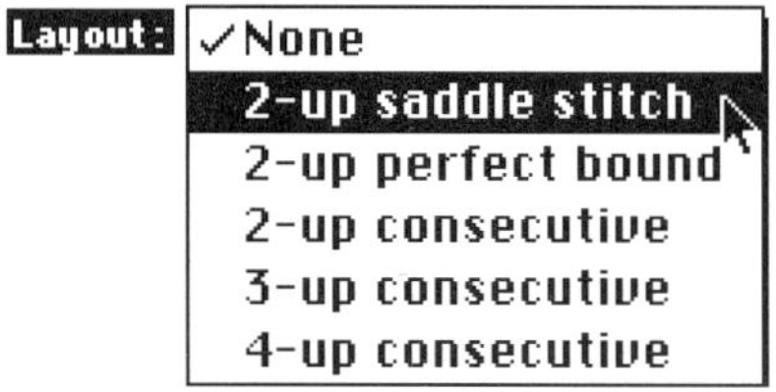

Choose *Build booklet...* from the *Additions* submenu (above) if you want to produce a booklet. In the booklet box (right) you can add blank pages and move or delete pages to match the necessary page count. Click the Revert button if you want to get back to where you started.

Layout: ✓None
2-up saddle stitch
2-up perfect bound
2-up consecutive
3-up consecutive
4-up consecutive

A saddle stitch is a simple staple binding so the first and last pages are on the same sheet, and the second and second-last on another, and so on. Perfect binding requires that pages are organised into smaller groups (below).

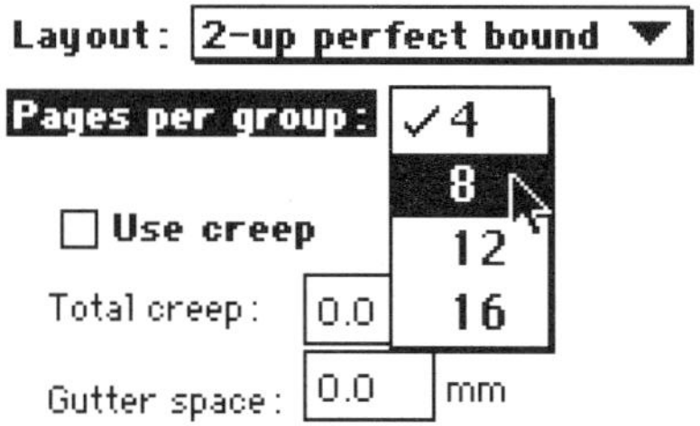

Build booklet   (e217)   [OK]

Publication: HardRobCafé:Data:TrainingBrochure'94

Spread size: [148.0] × [210.0] mm   [Cancel]

- ▶ □ Page 4
  □ Page 5
  □ Page 6
  □ Page 7
  □ Page 8
  □ Page 9

[Blank page]   Layout: [None ▼]
[Invert pages]   Pages per group: ◄ ▼
[Delete]   ☐ Use creep
[Revert]

Total creep: [0.0] mm
Gutter space: [0.0] mm

Messages
Page count: 9

☒ **Place guides in gutter**
☒ **Preserve page numbering**

Layout: [2-up perfect bound ▼]

Pages per group: ✓4
                      8
                      12
                      16

☐ **Use creep**

Total creep: [0.0]
Gutter space: [0.0] mm

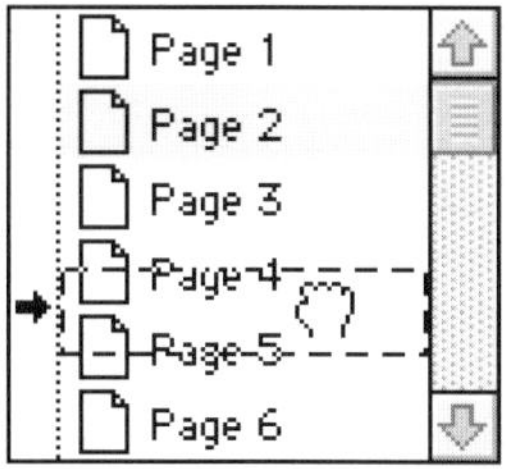

□ Page 1
□ Page 2
□ Page 3
▶ □ Page 4
  □ Page 5
  □ Page 6

When moving pages and adding blank pages, the arrow shows where pages will go (left).

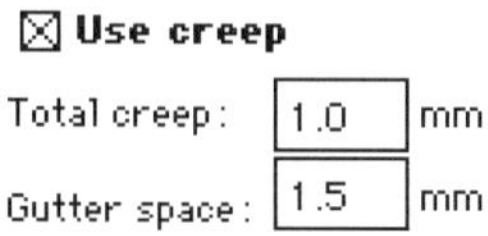

☒ **Use creep**

Total creep: [1.0] mm
Gutter space: [1.5] mm

When pages are folded for saddle stitching the edges of pages in the centre do not align with those at the outside—this 'creep' increases as the number of pages increases. Adjust the creep value (left) to compensate as instructed by your printers.

One of the most useful Aldus Additions is *Build booklet…* on the *Utilities* menu. It is especially useful when you are publishing an A5 publication and you are using a laser printer (with A4 paper usually) to produce final masters for printing.

If you are using a photocopier for volume printing, or you are taking the masters to a high-street print shop, you will need to produce A4 masters with two A5 publication pages on each sheet of paper (called 2-up). When you get tired of using scissors and glue, and of working out which pages go with which and where, take a look at the *Build booklet…* addition.

Build booklet… takes the effort and frustration out of producing brochure and pamphlets of all sorts by doing the print planning (working out the correct page sequence) for you.

Your publication should be finished and saved to disk before you use this addition—PageMaker makes another copy of the publication on the larger paper size you specify.

Build booklet… Choose the addition in the normal way from the *Additions* submenu on the *Utilities* menu. You will be presented with a box where you can specify the kind of booklet you want to produce and you can select layout options.

When you click OK, you are asked to save your publication and then another copy is constructed automatically for you according to the options you chose. It is fascinating to watch as PageMaker copies the items from the master pages and the publication pages into the correct place in the new publication.

Number of pages. You need to consider the number of pages in your original publication. For example, if you are producing an A4 publication from A5 pages you need an even number (two A5 pages on each sheet of paper). You can add blank pages to make up the numbers—move the little arrow by dragging it first to indicate where you want the Blank page inserted and click the button. If you do nothing, PageMaker will add the blank pages, as required, at the end.

You can also remove pages by clicking the Delete button.

Moving pages. You can move pages around within the little window by holding down the OPTION key (ALT on Windows) and dragging to a new location. To move more than one, SHIFT-click to select them first. If you also hold down the COMMAND key (Mac) or CTRL key (Windows) you can select non-consecutive pages.

Binding. You need to know what binding method will be used before you use this addition.

- You need free disk space equivalent to about two and a half times the size of the original publication.

- Only the active publication can be made into a booklet—booklets can not be constructed from book lists.

- Generate your table of contents and index before producing the booklet so that the original page numbers are referenced.

- Use the Revert button if you make a mistake setting the booklet options.

- You must have master page number markers in the original publication for pagination to transfer.

- You might find it easier to insert/delete blank pages to make up the numbers needed before using *Build booklet…*

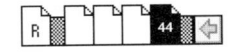

Longer publications   45

File

New...   ⌘N
Open...   ⌘O
Close

Save   ⌘S
Save as...
Revert
Export...

Place...   ⌘D

Links...   ⌘=
Book...
Preferences...

Page setup...
Print...   ⌘P

Quit   ⌘Q

To combine publications which you want to treat as a single unit, choose *Book...* from the *File* menu.

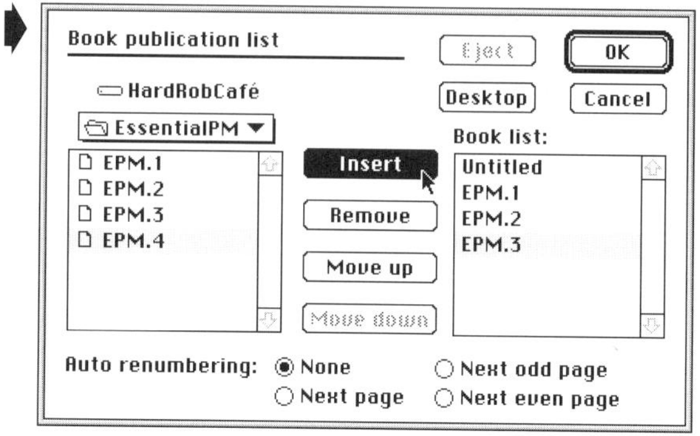

Book publication list

⊏ HardRobCafé
⊟ EssentialPM ▼

▫ EPM.1
▫ EPM.2
▫ EPM.3
▫ EPM.4

[Eject]   [OK]
[Desktop] [Cancel]

Book list:
Untitled
EPM.1
EPM.2
EPM.3

[**Insert**]
[Remove]
[Move up]
[Move down]

Auto renumbering: ● None   ○ Next odd page
                   ○ Next page   ○ Next even page

In the box on the left (above), select each document in turn and click the Insert button (or double-click) to build a book list (in the right-hand box). In the above example, the list is being constructed in an untitled document, which is automatically included in the book list. Note the buttons for moving documents within the list and the page renumbering options.

Utilities

Aldus Additions   ▶

Find...   ⌘8
Find next   ⌘,
Change...   ⌘9
Spelling...   ⌘L

Index entry...   ⌘;
Show index...
Create index...
Create TOC...

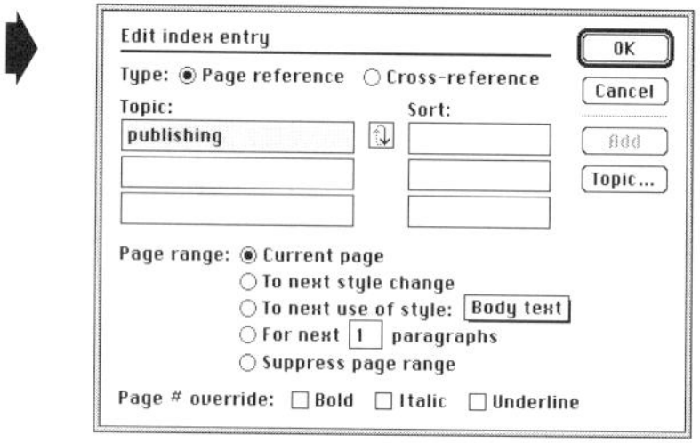

Edit index entry

[OK]
[Cancel]
Type: ● Page reference ○ Cross-reference
Topic: Sort:
publishing   [↓]

[Add]
[Topic...]

Page range: ● Current page
            ○ To next style change
            ○ To next use of style: [Body text]
            ○ For next [1] paragraphs
            ○ Suppress page range
Page # override: □ Bold □ Italic □ Underline

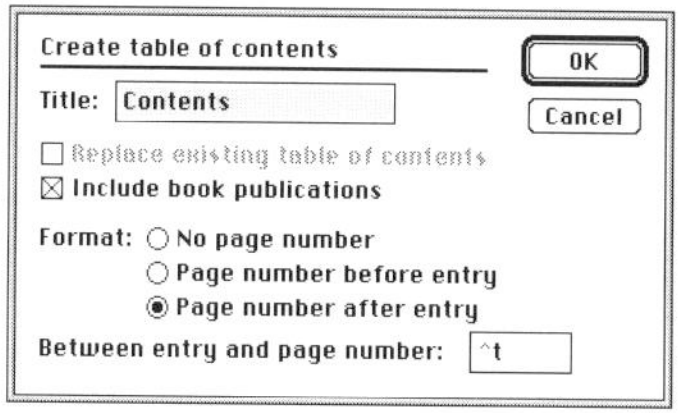

To create an index entry, select the text to be indexed and choose *Index entry...* from the *Utilities* menu.

To print the publications in a book list together, click the button in the *Print...* box (right).

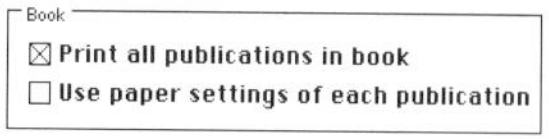

┌─ Book ──────────────────────┐
│ ⊠ Print all publications in book   │
│ □ Use paper settings of each publication │
└─────────────────────────────┘

If you want to restart page numbering in individual documents when printing, check that box in *Page setup...* of the individual documents (below).

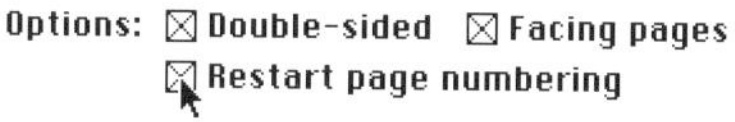

Options: ⊠ **Double-sided**   ⊠ **Facing pages**
         ⊠ **Restart page numbering**

To produce a table of contents for all publications in a book list, choose *Create TOC...* from the *Utilities* menu and check that option (right).

Create table of contents

[OK]
Title: [Contents]   [Cancel]

□ Replace existing table of contents
⊠ Include book publications

Format: ○ No page number
        ○ Page number before entry
        ● Page number after entry

Between entry and page number: [^t]

This box gives you access to comprehensive indexing facilities, but for simple indexes click OK. Click Topic... if you want to see or edit index entries. Use *Create index...* (*Utilities* menu) to produce and place the final index.

You can see index markers in Story Editor.

been a superb ▯publishing tool
r visual ▯standards than

If you produce long or complex documents, or there are several people working on different sections of the same publication, or documents are simply becoming too large to handle, you will find book lists useful. A book list is a means of connecting several documents for the purposes of pagination, printing, indexing or table of contents production. You can also continue to work on individual documents included in a book list.

Books. To construct a book list, choose *Book…* from the *File* menu. You will be presented with a box in which you can nominate the individual publications that you want to treat as a single entity—the book. Select the document you want to add to the list on the left side and click the Insert button (or double-click) to include it in the book list on the right side of the box.

As the list builds up you can select publications in the list and use the Move up and Move down buttons to change their order or the Remove button to delete them from the list. The order of publications in the list is significant and represents their position in the book.

Create the list with one of the publications in the list open (a new document which is to contain the table of contents, for example). You can then print the complete publication, or generate a table of contents or index (spanning all of the documents in the list) from that document.

Printing. When you want to print the complete publication, *Open…* the document containing the book list and choose *Print…* from the *File* menu. The Print all publications in book option becomes available in the print box (under Book).

You can renumber the publications in the list automatically (Auto renumbering in the book list box) so that they are numbered consecutively. If you need to Restart page numbering in some documents, click that button (in the *Page setup…* box) of the individual publications.

TOC. To generate a table of contents that spans the publications in a list, choose *Create TOC…* from the *Utilities* menu (when you have the document containing the book list open) and check the Include book publications option. Place the TOC using the loaded icon. You need to nominate the paragraphs (usually headings and sub-headings) beforehand as described under style spin-offs.

Indexing. To create a simple index entry, select the text (or click the cursor to enter a word manually) and choose *Index entry…* (or COMMAND-;). This displays a box where you can type an entry not in the text, or develop multi-level entries and define sorting order. The Topics… button helps prevent slightly differing entries being produced. Use *Create index…* to produce the index—you will be invited to *Place…* it using a loaded-text icon.

- You can copy a book list to each publication in the list if you hold down the COMMAND key (CONTROL under Windows) and choose *Book…* from the *File* menu when the document containing the list is active. You can then *Print…*, etc., from any publication in the list.

- You must use page number markers on master pages for page numbering to work.

- For consistency in design across a range of documents in a book list, use master pages and styles, and start each publication from the same template.

- Use COMMAND-SHIFT-; to create an index entry quickly if you don't need to see the index entry box.

- Select a marker and use COMMAND (or CONTROL) – ; in the Story Editor to see the index entry associated with a particular marker.

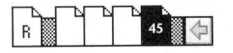

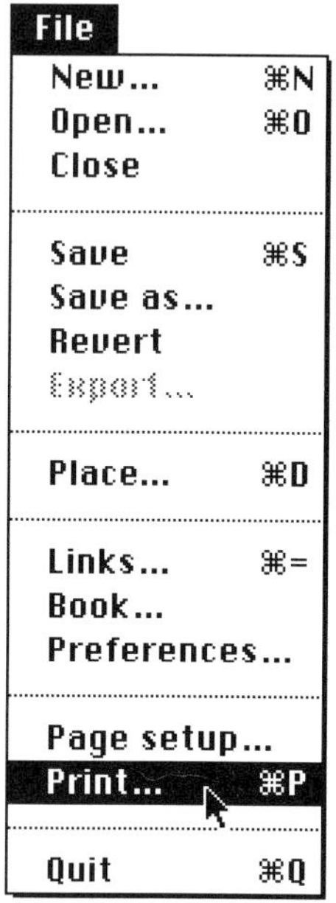

Preparing for print 46

File

New... ⌘N
Open... ⌘O
Close

Save ⌘S
Save as...
Revert
Export...

Place... ⌘D

Links... ⌘=
Book...
Preferences...

Page setup...
Print... ⌘P

Quit ⌘Q

In addition to the basic facilities described earlier, *Print...* on the *File* menu gives access to a variety of printing options.

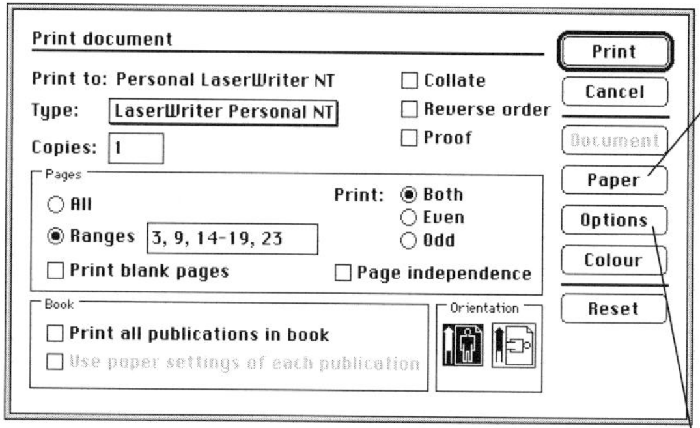

Print document

Print to: Personal LaserWriter NT

Type: `LaserWriter Personal NT`
Copies: `1`

☐ Collate
☐ Reverse order
☐ Proof

Pages
○ All
◉ Ranges `3, 9, 14-19, 23`
☐ Print blank pages

Print: ◉ Both
○ Even
○ Odd
☐ Page independence

Book
☐ Print all publications in book
☐ Use paper settings of each publication

Orientation

[Print] [Cancel] [Document] [Paper] [Options] [Colour] [Reset]

Paper

Paper
Size: `A4` 209.9 x 297.04 mm
Source: `Paper Cassette`
Print area: 198.97 x 289.63 mm
☐ Centre page in print area
☐ Tile: ○ Manual
○ Auto: overlap `20` mm

Scale
◉ `100` %
○ Reduce to fit
○ Thumbnails: `16` per page

Duplex
◉ None
○ Short edge
○ Long edge

[Print] [Cancel] [Document] [Paper] [Options] [Colour] [Reset]

Type page numbers to be printed (which need not be contiguous) separated by commas. A range of pages can be printed by putting a hyphen between two numbers in ascending order (e.g. 3–29). Several ranges can be specified, separated by commas.

Reverse order changes the order in which pages are usually printed on your printer.

For a fast print, with graphics printed as simple rectangles to show their position, check Proof.

Check Printer's marks if your commercial printer wants them. Speed up printing times by checking Optimised graphics (data the printer can't use is discarded).

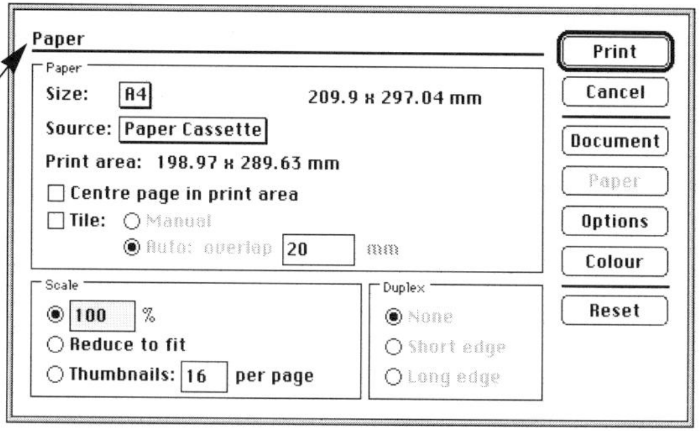

The Paper button provides further controls (above). You can choose a paper size and source (bin) available on your printer from the drop-down menus. Tile will print oversize pages in sections (tiles). To view an overall layout as miniature pages, check Thumbnails.

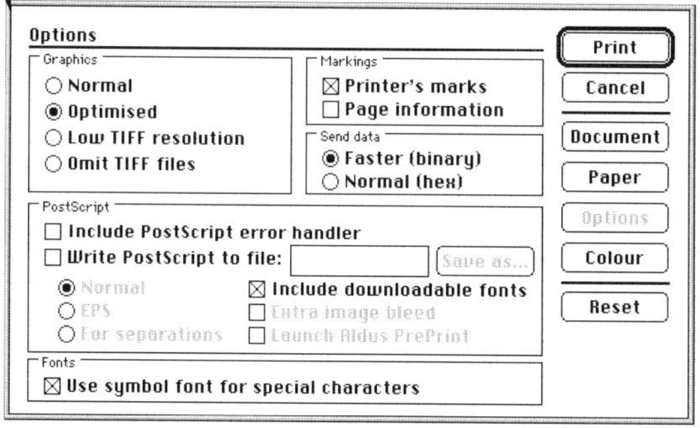

Options

Graphics
○ Normal
◉ Optimised
○ Low TIFF resolution
○ Omit TIFF files

Markings
☒ Printer's marks
☐ Page information

Send data
◉ Faster (binary)
○ Normal (hex)

PostScript
☐ Include PostScript error handler
☐ Write PostScript to file: `Save as...`
◉ Normal ☒ Include downloadable fonts
○ EPS ☐ Extra image bleed
○ For separations ☐ Launch Aldus PrePrint

Fonts
☒ Use symbol font for special characters

[Print] [Cancel] [Document] [Paper] [Options] [Colour] [Reset]

At various stages during production you will need to print your publication, to check it or to discuss it with someone else. Usually a straightforward print, as described earlier, is sufficient. However, there comes a time when you need to produce a master for volume printing.

If you are going to photocopy a laser-printed copy, or supply your printers with laser output, you need a clean final master with everything correct and in its place (called camera-ready copy, or CRC, in the printing trade). For higher quality masters you will need to print on an imagesetter. Your printers might have one, or you can use an imagesetting service to do it for you—but you need to tell them what your printers want.

Recommendation. Whatever you do, don't charge ahead and produce your finished publication without talking to your printers. They will advise you on the form of output they would prefer (paper, bromide or film) and on what you might be able to do to save costs. Try to involve them at an early stage in the process and run a few trial pages right through to CRC. Doing so will not only give you confidence but it can also highlight flaws in the production process before it is too late—fonts not being available somewhere down the line, or tints that can't be resolved by the printing plate maker. Don't make production decisions based on assumptions—ask questions!

Printing. Choose *Print…* from the *File* menu and set the options you require in the Paper, Options and Colour boxes in turn. Then click Print.

Document. Choose the name of the printer from the pop-up menu provided.

A Proof print is useful when you have graphics on a page which take an age to print. On proofs, graphics print as empty boxes so pages print faster.

Copies and page Ranges will be already familiar. The Paper, Options and Colour buttons give you to access to further printing controls.

Paper. The Printer chosen in the Document box, determines the paper sizes in the Size pop-up menu—'A4extra' on an imagesetter, for example.

For an overall view, check Thumbnails to put several miniature pages on single sheets of paper.

Tile allows you to print a page larger than the paper size as overlapping sections (tiles).

Options. If your printer asks for them, check Printer's marks to add marks to the edge of pages which they can use to trim the printed publication down to finished size.

Page information is an easy way of putting the date, time and file name on pages to keep track of them, but it only works when you print on paper larger than the page size.

• The Colour button is described earlier under Colour separation.

• Don't use the printer to collate multiple copies unless you have no choice. Each page is repeatedly constructed for each copy so printing is slower.

• Page independence stores font information with each page and is used only when pages need to be passed to another program.

• Turn background printing off (in the Chooser) if you are running out of disk space for printing.

• The Options available for different printers (notably non-PostScript printers) differ from some of those described here.

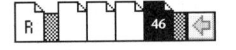

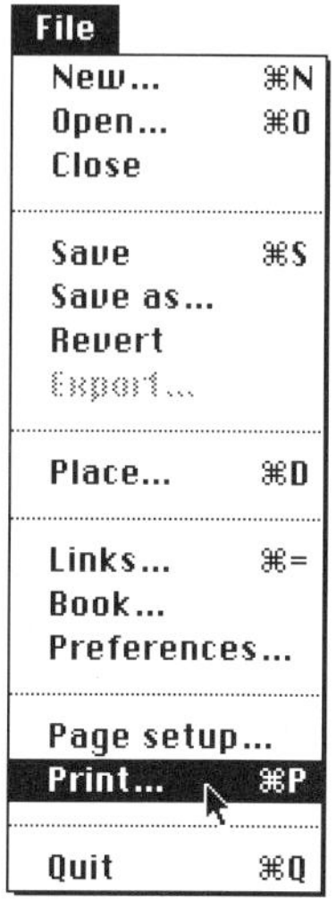

Using an imagesetter 47

File

New...	⌘N
Open...	⌘O
Close	
Save	⌘S
Save as...	
Revert	
Export...	
Place...	⌘D
Links...	⌘=
Book...	
Preferences...	
Page setup...	
Print...	⌘P
Quit	⌘Q

If you need to prepare a publication for printing on an imagesetter, choose *Print...* from the *File* menu.

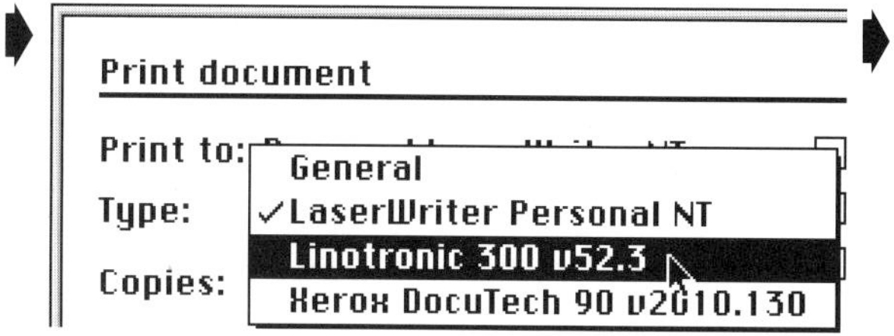

Print document

Print to:

Type:

Copies:

General
✓LaserWriter Personal NT
Linotronic 300 v52.3
Xerox DocuTech 90 v2010.130

In the Print document box, choose the final destination printer from the Type drop-down menu. PageMaker uses an installed PPD (printer description) file to make the options appropriate to that particular type of printer available, even though you are not connected to it. The Linotronic (above) is a high-resolution imagesetter.

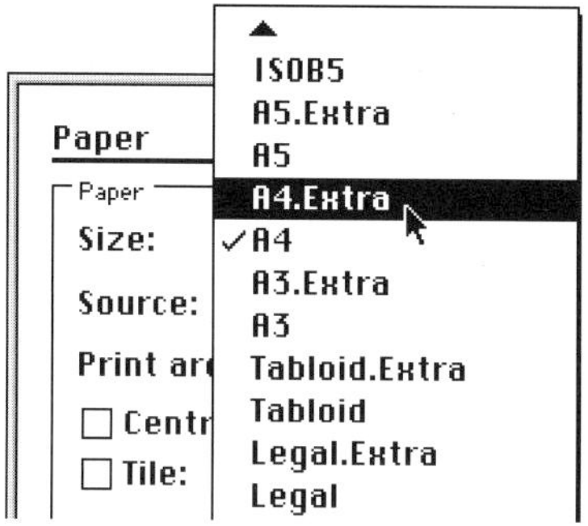

Paper

Paper

Size:

Source:

Print are

☐ Centr

☐ Tile:

▲
ISOB5
A5.Extra
A5
A4.Extra
✓A4
A3.Extra
A3
Tabloid.Extra
Tabloid
Legal.Extra
Legal

Depending on the printer chosen, additional paper sizes become available in the Paper dialog box (above). A4.extra (available on a Linotronic 300 imagesetter, for example) is slightly larger than A4 and will allow you to print printer's marks (or page information) just outside A4 page boundaries.

Click the Options button if you want to write PostScript to disk. Set the options you want (right) and type a name for the file. Use the Save as... button to put the file in a particular place on disk.

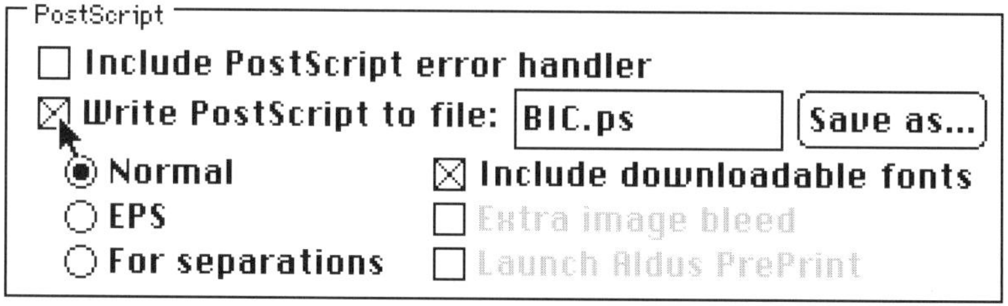

PostScript

☐ **Include PostScript error handler**

☒ **Write PostScript to file:** BIC.ps Save as...

● **Normal** ☒ **Include downloadable fonts**

○ **EPS** ☐ Extra image bleed

○ **For separations** ☐ Launch Aldus PrePrint

Once you have proofed your publication on a laser printer and you are satisfied with its content and appearance, there is very little extra effort involved in having it printed on an imagesetter. Taking advantage of the finer resolution that is the hallmark of these printers will ensure that you have masters of the highest quality for use in volume printing.

Imagesetters. Take a disk with your publication and original graphic files included (so they can be re-linked) to an imagesetting service bureau and they will print it for you on photographic paper (bromide) or on film. The better ones will ask you a series of questions or invite you to complete a form outlining your requirements; they will also do most of the extra work for you—checking the relevant options and buttons required to get the best results. Commercial printers, too, now have imagesetters and can take work on disk.

Printing options. The bureau will make a copy of your documents on their computer and will issue a *Print...* command in the same way you do. Since they are using an imagesetter, other options are available to them. You can access these options, too, by selecting that printer in the *Print...* box—PageMaker uses a special PPD file as a means of 'communicating' with the printer as though it is directly connected.

PostScript. To use some bureaux, and increasingly on-demand printers and in-house networked imagesetters, you will need to produce your publications in PostScript format. Since this is the language that most programs use to communicate with laser printers, all that is required is to print your publication to disk.

Do this by clicking the Options button in the *Print...* box and check the Write PostScript to file box. Give the file a name of your choice and click the Save as... button. When you click Print your publication will be printed to disk in PostScript format (open it in a word processing program if you are curious to see what PostScript looks like). You can then take this file to your bureau or printer (but only if they ask for it in that format—most will want original PageMaker documents) or send it across a network to an imagesetter if you have access to one.

Set the Normal button, too, in the PostScript box—EPS (for Encapsulated PostScript) is used only when you want to save a page image as a graphic to *Place...* in a document.

Check the Include downloadable fonts option to include fonts in the file that your printers do not have. Another reason for running a test job.

• Use the buttons provided in the *Save as...* box to copy linked graphics to disk when taking publications to a bureau.

• Ask the bureau to run a test job first to make sure that you are both using the same fonts—otherwise Courier will make its appearance to say you've got it wrong!

• When using imagesetters it is important to screen images at an appropriate frequency if you want to take advantage of the increased definition provided on these devices, but ask your printers first.

• Keep PostScript file sizes down by including fonts only when they are not available on the imagesetter.

• If you regularly use more than one printer, the *Printer styles...* addition will save you effort.

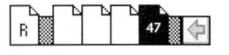

Working faster | 48

Edit

Cannot undo ⌘Z

Cut ⌘X
Copy ⌘C
Paste ⌘V
Clear

Multiple paste...
Select all ⌘A

Editions ▶

Paste link
Paste special...
Insert object...

Edit story ⌘E
Edit original

When you *Cut* or *Copy* something to the clipboard, *Multiple paste...* on the *Edit* menu will save you time if you need to *Paste* several copies on to a page.

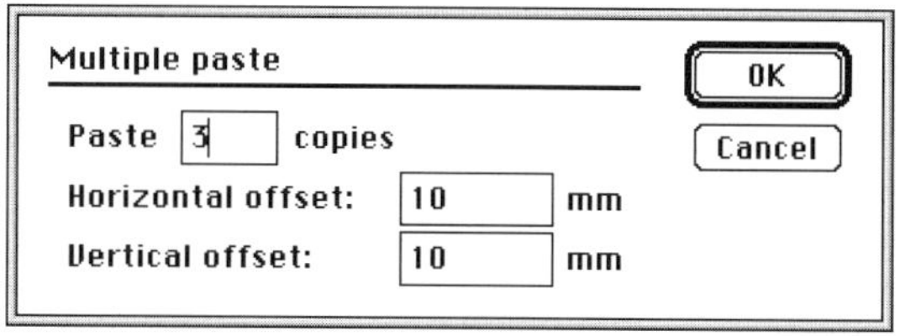

Multiple paste

Paste [3] copies

Horizontal offset: [10] mm

Vertical offset: [10] mm

[OK]
[Cancel]

In the multiple paste box (above), specify the number of copies you want to *Paste* and how you want them to be arranged relative to one another. This feature is particularly useful, for example, when you are constructing forms. You can construct a single box and *Paste* copies horizontally. Then select these and paste copies vertically.

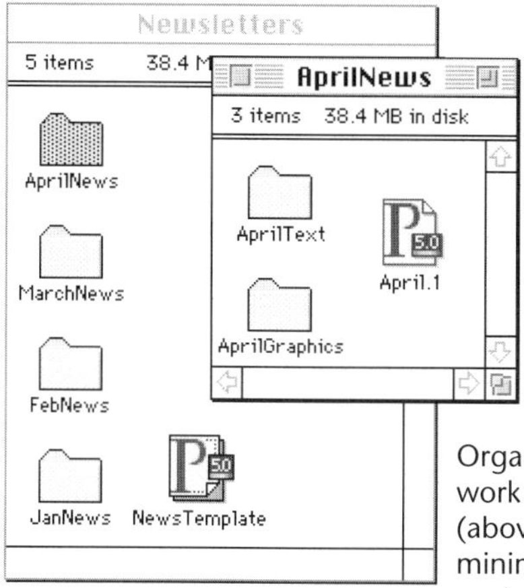

Newsletters
5 items   38.4 M

AprilNews

MarchNews

FebNews

JanNews   NewsTemplate

AprilNews
3 items   38.4 MB in disk

AprilText   April.1 (P 5.0)

AprilGraphics

Organising your work into folders (above) will minimise hard disk navigation and will save time and effort.

Preferences

[OK]
[Cancel]
[Other...]
[Map fonts...]

Layout
Measurement system: [Millimetres]
Vertical ruler: [Custom] [12] points

Layout problems
☐ Show loose/tight lines
☐ Show "keeps" violations

Graphics
○ Grey out
● Normal
○ High resolution

Guides
● Front
○ Back

Save option
● Faster
○ Smaller

Control palette
Horizontal nudge: [1] [Millimetres]
Vertical nudge: [0p1] [Picas]
☐ Use "Snap to" constraints

Use the *Preferences...* dialog box (*File* menu) to adapt program settings to suit you. Click Other... to reach a further set of preferences (far right).

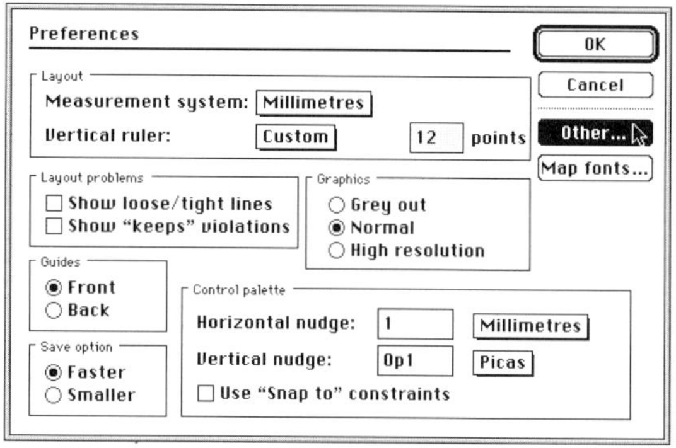

You can change Story Editor settings here, too.

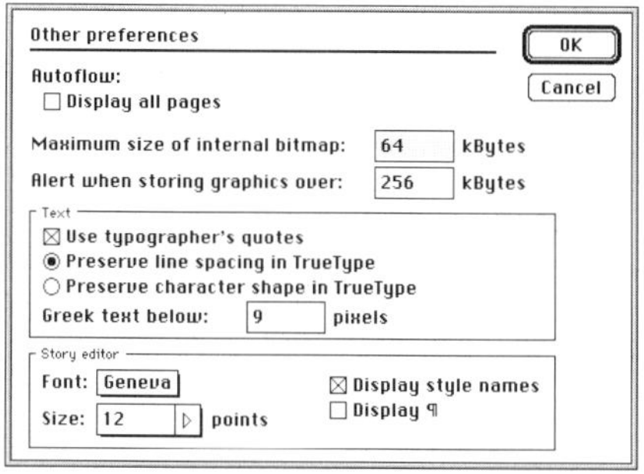

Other preferences

[OK]
[Cancel]

Autoflow:
☐ Display all pages

Maximum size of internal bitmap: [64] kBytes
Alert when storing graphics over: [256] kBytes

Text
☒ Use typographer's quotes
● Preserve line spacing in TrueType
○ Preserve character shape in TrueType
Greek text below: [9] pixels

Story editor
Font: [Geneva]   ☒ Display style names
Size: [12] points   ☐ Display ¶

You will know that you are getting to grips with the program when you find yourself waiting for PageMaker to finish what it is doing for you so that you can get on with your work. Once you accept the program as a tool, albeit a very sophisticated one, impatience begins to set in and you will want the program to work faster for you—particularly when production deadlines are approaching. There are steps you can take to get better performance.

Menu shortcuts. Use the keyboard shortcuts on the menus, particularly to access features you use regularly—you will remember them more easily with regular use and they do save time. They have not been stressed in this book because they are there on every menu for all to see. Try to develop the habit of using them.

Interrupting the screen. On pages with complex graphics or a variety of typefaces, you can become agitated waiting for the screen to redraw every time you make changes (unless you have a very fast computer). But you need not wait. Simply use the mouse or keyboard without waiting for the screen to redraw and you will be given priority.

Autoflow display. When you *Place…* text that is to flow across several pages using *Autoflow*, make sure that Autoflow: Display all pages is not checked in the Other… preferences box. If it is checked, each page is displayed as text flows, slowing down the process. When Display all pages is not checked, PageMaker displays the final page only.

Grey graphics. Display grey boxes instead of graphics (*Preferences…*) for faster screen scrolling.

Publication size. Make life easier for yourself by keeping your documents to a manageable size. This might mean dividing long publications into several smaller ones but you can use *Book…* on the *File* menu to combine them for printing, etc.

Plan. Get into the habit of creating a *New folder* (on the Finder's *File* menu) for each new project. This will encourage you to organise your work by keeping your publication and its associated text and graphics documents in one place, and will save needless navigation of the hard disk when you use *Place…* or *Save as…* (on the *File* menu).

Save regularly. Apart from the obvious reasons (guarding against power failure, etc.), if you *Save* before you do something complex, and it goes horribly wrong, you can choose *Revert* from the *File* menu to re-instate the saved document.

Printing. Use background printing and you can continue working while documents are printing.

• COMMAND-SPACE is a useful shortcut to select the pointer tool.

• It has to be said (and few listen!) but do get into the habit of taking a backup copy of your publications at regular intervals. It is soul-destroying (and unnecessary) to have to redo a lost publication from scratch.

• The Smaller save option reorganises the document to keep its size down, and is therefore slower. Use the Faster option as you work on a document but use Smaller when you finish.

• Set the vertical ruler to match text leading and make alignment across columns easier.

• Re-zero the ruler origins (or use Control palette) to save having to do the sums when positioning or resizing items on the page.

• Don't forget *Undo*!

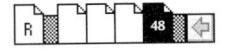

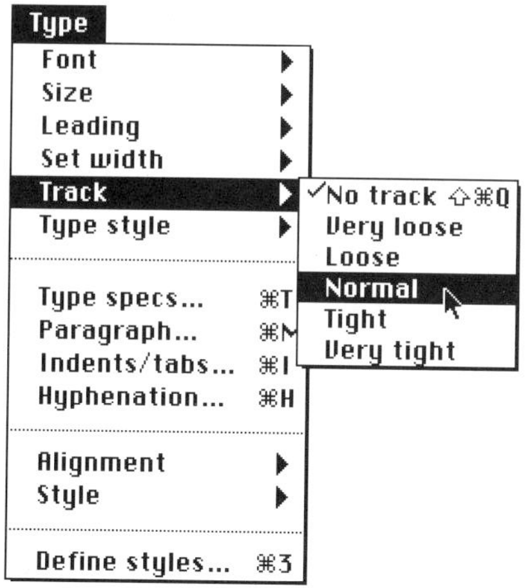

Gaining in confidence 49

Type

Font	▶
Size	▶
Leading	▶
Set width	▶
Track	▶
Type style	▶
Type specs...	⌘T
Paragraph...	⌘M
Indents/tabs...	⌘I
Hyphenation...	⌘H
Alignment	▶
Style	▶
Define styles...	⌘3

✓No track ⇧⌘Q
Very loose
Loose
Normal
Tight
Very tight

To improve the look of type, try varying the tracking—the space between characters. Tracking can also be set in the *Type specs...* box and should be specified as part of a paragraph style.

WAVE
WAVE

Pair kerning: ☒ Auto above [4] points

It is particularly important to adjust the spacing between individual characters in large type (left). Do this by putting the text cursor between characters and use COMMAND-DELETE to tighten the space—a process called kerning. A degree of automatic kerning can be set in the box (left) provided by the Spacing... button in the *Paragraph...* (*Type* menu) box. You can also use the *Expert kerning...* addition.

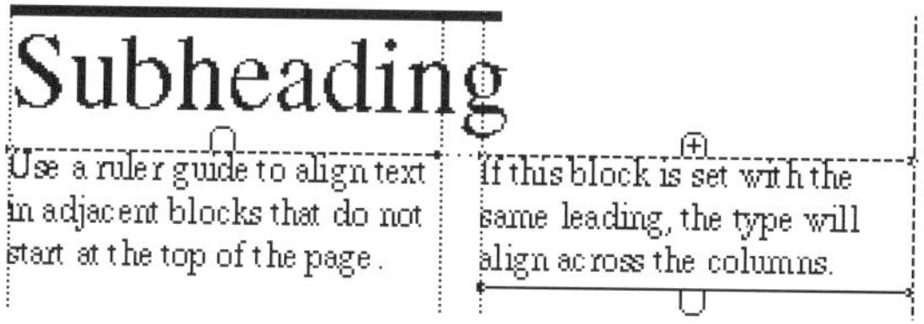

Subheading

Use a ruler guide to align text in adjacent blocks that do not start at the top of the page.

If this block is set with the same leading, the type will align across the columns.

Use ruler guides to align individual text blocks (left). Setting the vertical ruler to match the text leading (*Preferences...*) also helps.

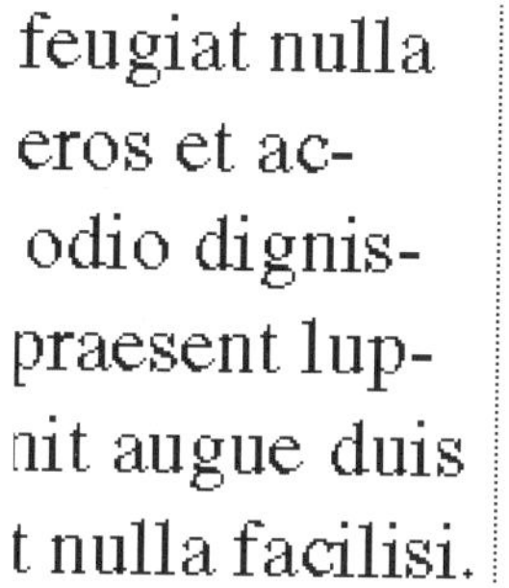

feugiat nulla eros et ac-odio dignis-praesent lup-nit augue duis t nulla facilisi.

Take control of hyphens. Avoid too many in a row (left) by limiting consecutive hyphens in the *Hyphenation...* box (right), reached via the *Type* menu. Use COMMAND-HYPHEN to insert a hyphen manually (but hyphenation must be on before you can insert manual hyphens).

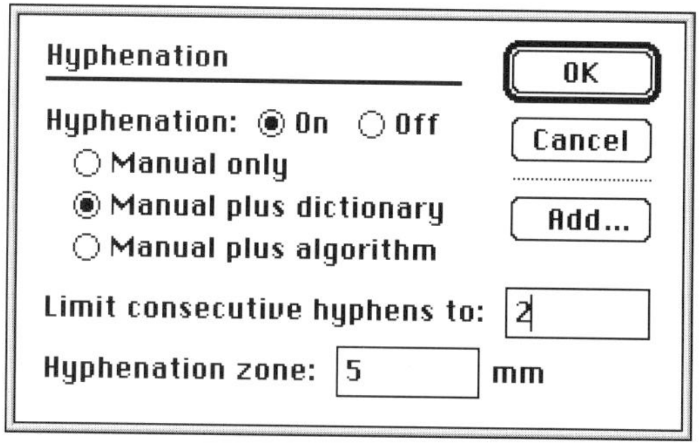

Hyphenation

[OK]
[Cancel]
[Add...]

Hyphenation: ◉ On   ○ Off
○ Manual only
◉ Manual plus dictionary
○ Manual plus algorithm

Limit consecutive hyphens to: [2]

Hyphenation zone: [5] mm

Once you have learned how to use PageMaker, unless you have a design or publishing background your biggest problem is going to be your lack of knowledge of the design and production process itself. While you can be confident that PageMaker has features to match your future requirements (even if you don't know what they are yet!), how can you improve your publications? Don't be intimidated by your lack of knowledge—there are steps you can take.

Planning. When you produce a publication yourself you are constantly faced with decisions. Paper size? Margin sizes? How many columns? Which typefaces? What type sizes? Where should graphics be placed? How should elements align with one another? This sequence of decisions is what determines the design of a publication. The more thought you can give to the way you want your publication to look, *before you start producing it*, the better. Look at other publications, particularly those whose appearance (design) you like, and see if you can learn from them—columns per page, master page items, type variation, etc.

Make the major decisions before you start, and produce a few test pages to try on friends and colleagues for their opinions. Use master pages and paragraph styles to ensure consistency within a publication and use templates to retain that consistency from publication to publication. Above all, *keep it simple* until you become more experienced.

If you feel that you need the services of a designer, because the budget or prestige of a publication warrants it, use a designer who is familiar with PageMaker and who is prepared to work with you.

Form vs content. DTP hides traps for the unwary. One is that page layout work, although satisfying, is labour intensive and can be very time consuming—it is often difficult to *stop* working on a publication. The other, is that you can pay too much attention to the appearance of a publication and not enough to the content.

Don't underestimate your readers. No matter how attractive a publication looks, if the content is weak they will simply ignore it. On the other hand, anything you can do to make your publications more attractive to potential readers and easier to read, is effort well spent. Let common sense be your guide to striking a balance.

Detail. Avoid the tell-tale signs that are the hallmark of work produced by the inexperienced (see right-hand column) and learn how to use the features provided by PageMaker to improve the quality of the type and of the layout.

• Don't use underlining (it doesn't look good) or **bold** (it shouts) for emphasis within paragraphs—use *italic* instead. Italic is more subtle and is only noticed when the text is read.

• Use TAB not SPACE to align columns of text or they won't align properly.

• Don't put two spaces after full stops. They are not needed with type.

• Use proper quotation symbols. Set this as you place text (click the button in the *Place…* dialog box). You can also set this as a preference for text typed on the page (*Preferences…* from the *File* menu) but it can then be difficult to get straight quote marks if you need them (for inches and feet, for example). When typing on a page use:

OPTION-[for "
OPTION-SHIFT-[for "

OPTION-] for '
OPTION-SHIFT-] for '

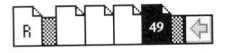

Where next? 50

Learning PageMaker 5.0

Look for the Learning PageMaker icon and double-click to start it.

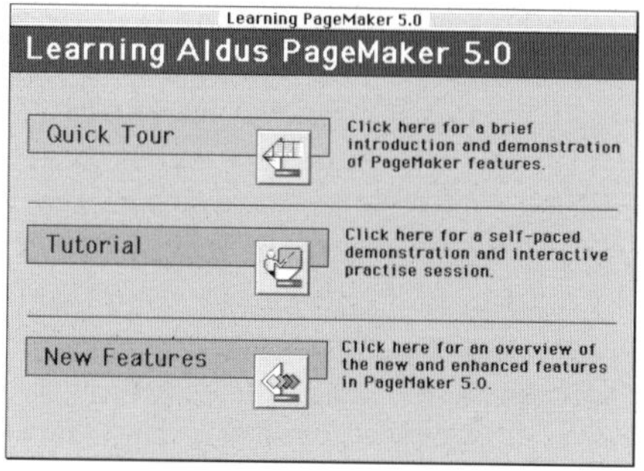

Learning Aldus PageMaker 5.0

Quick Tour — Click here for a brief introduction and demonstration of PageMaker features.

Tutorial — Click here for a self-paced demonstration and interactive practise session.

New Features — Click here for an overview of the new and enhanced features in PageMaker 5.0.

Click on a button to see a tour of the program, an overview of new features, or for tutorial and practice sessions.

The text and graphics files used in the Getting Started manual lessons are installed in a separate tutorial folder by the installer. If you can't find them you will need to install them from the PageMaker disks.

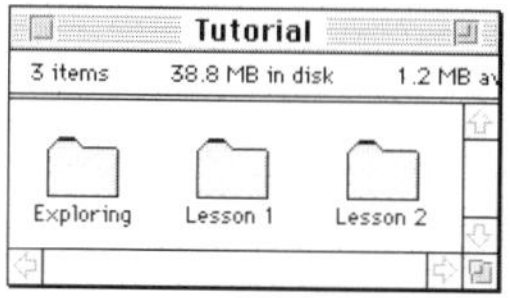

Tutorial

3 items   38.8 MB in disk   1.2 MB av

Exploring   Lesson 1   Lesson 2

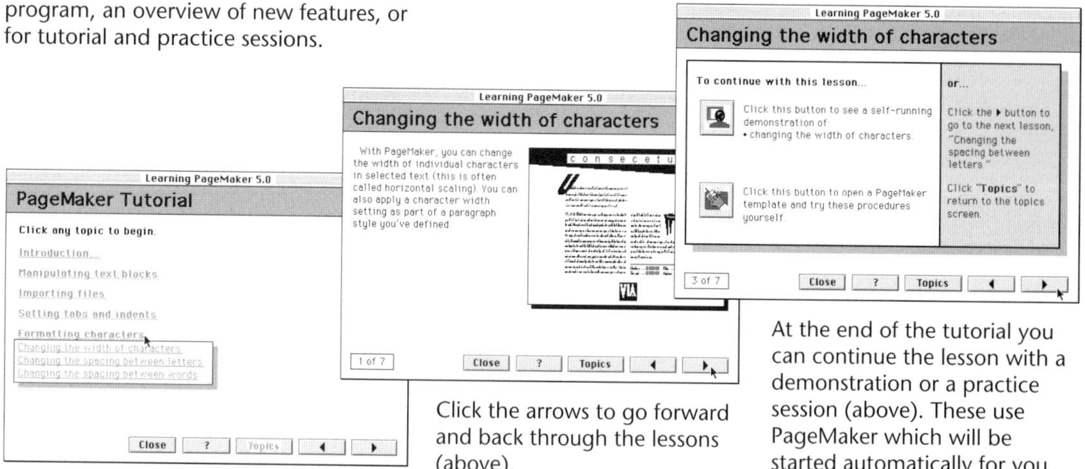

The tutorial button takes you to the topics screen. Click on the topic you want to learn more about and then on a particular lesson under that topic (right).

PageMaker Tutorial

Click any topic to begin.

Introduction
Manipulating text blocks
Importing files
Setting tabs and indents
Formatting characters
Changing the width of characters
Changing the spacing between letters
Changing the spacing between words

Changing the width of characters

With PageMaker, you can change the width of individual characters in selected text (this is often called horizontal scaling). You can also apply a character width setting as part of a paragraph style you've defined.

1 of 7

Click the arrows to go forward and back through the lessons (above).

Changing the width of characters

To continue with this lesson...

Click this button to see a self-running demonstration of
• changing the width of characters.

Click this button to open a PageMaker template and try these procedures yourself.

or...

Click the ▶ button to go to the next lesson, "Changing the spacing between letters."

Click "Topics" to return to the topics screen.

3 of 7   Close   ?   Topics   ◀   ▶

At the end of the tutorial you can continue the lesson with a demonstration or a practice session (above). These use PageMaker which will be started automatically for you.

There is no substitute for experience. The only way to get to grips with PageMaker is to start using the program in earnest. This book will have taken you through the initial learning phase but you now need to use the features of the program for yourself.

If you already have a 'real' publication that you want to produce, so much the better—you won't need further motivation. If not, work through the lessons described in the Getting Started manual supplied with the program. These take you, in stages, first through an exploration of program features, and then onto constructing a letterhead and a simple brochure. You should find that most of what is described in the manual has a familiar ring to it by now. The lessons are also a good way for you to consolidate what you have learned from this book.

Aldus manuals. Besides the Getting Started manual mentioned above, an excellent User Manual is also supplied with PageMaker. This contains not only an alphabetic and detailed description of each command, but also has useful sections describing the production process and the way PageMaker features can be used at different stages. Layout techniques are also described in a step by step manner.

By now, you should be in a much better position to pick and choose from the User Manual to study specific topics in detail. You need no longer be faced with the daunting task of reading it all!

Learning. A separate Learning program is supplied with PageMaker. This is a useful way of showing you some of the features which are difficult to describe in words. The program also uses PageMaker, so you will need sufficient RAM for both to run. Double-click the Learning icon to start the program.

Tech support. Occasionally, as with any program, you will hit snags. Something that does not quite work or that you don't understand. Aldus provide technical support to registered users at their office in Edinburgh (031-458 3366). They will need to know what version of the program you are using and will also ask for your serial number, so you need to have that information to hand (or be sitting at your computer) when you call.

They might also ask for version numbers of additions, import and export filters, etc. Hold down the COMMAND and OPTION keys and select *About PageMaker...* from the Apple menu. A window giving these details will be displayed.

Share. Don't work in a vacuum. Share what you learn with others and don't be afraid to ask others for help when you need it. Enjoy PageMaker!

- Return the PageMaker registration card to register for technical support and update information.

- Some of the items mentioned here might not have been installed. You will need to install them from the PageMaker discs.

- Don't forget to quit PageMaker, too, after a Learning session.

- Did you enjoy this book and find it useful? Are there topics you would have liked covered in more detail? Would you like information on new titles in the Essential series as they are published? We would like to hear from you. Drop us a line or contact us by email at

wysiwyg@iol.ie

on the Internet.

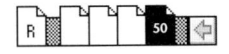

What's what? A1

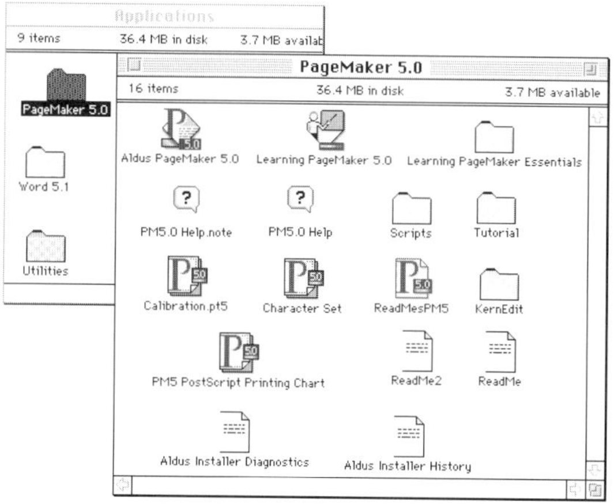

The Aldus folder (right) is installed in the System folder. Note, in particular, the Aldus Filters folder which contains the filters PageMaker needs to import and export files.

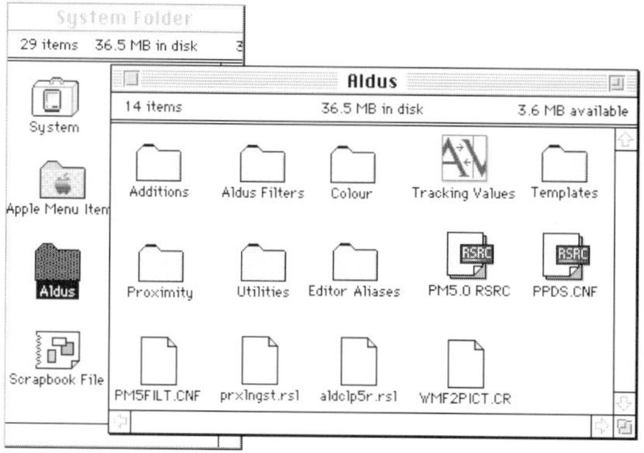

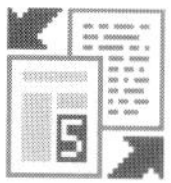

In the PageMaker folder *(above)* you will find the PageMaker program and a separate program on learning how to use it. The folder also contains the tutorial and script folders and important ReadMe and installation documents (in TeachText format).

DropCap.add

Photo CD Import.flt

Icons associated with PageMaker. Additions and filters (above), preset defaults (left) and printer driver (right).

PM5.0 Defaults

LaserWriter 8.0

You can increase the memory (RAM) available to PageMaker in the *Get Info...* box (below).

On the Macintosh, there are two important folders associated with PageMaker—the PageMaker folder and the Aldus folder. These contain most of the documents, resources and utilities used by PageMaker.

Apart from finding the PageMaker icon itself to double-click it and start the program, your use of the associated files is handled from within the program. However, it does no harm to be aware of their existence and to know where they are located.

PageMaker folder. This is where the PageMaker program itself is installed, together with the Learning PageMaker program and its essential files.

The folder also contains the Help files and sample scripts (in their own folder).

The documents used for the tutorial in the Getting Started manual are also located here—you will find them in a separate tutorial folder. Even if you decide not to follow the tutorial you will find the text and graphics useful as you explore the program and its features.

The Installer history and diagnostics documents are a record of the way PageMaker was installed on the computer. Double-click them if you need to check back or if Aldus Technical Support need the information to resolve a problem for you.

Read me. Two very important Read Me files are installed along with PageMaker. These contain information on last-minute changes to the program itself and to the documentation. They also contain useful hints and tips information. If you have not already done so, print these out and keep them with your PageMaker manuals.

Although very useful, the information is presented in an unimaginative way in these documents. If you want some PageMaker practice you could try placing the texts into a new PageMaker publication (call it something like ReadMesPM as in the screen example above) and then organise the information in a more useful and meaningful way before you print it.

Aldus folder. Here you will find separate folders containing Additions, filters for importing and exporting files to and from other programs, and a selection of pre-designed PageMaker documents (called templates) which you can use as starting points for your own publications.

Other folders contain dictionaries used for spell checking and hyphenation (proximity), colour libraries, and utilities such as the dictionary editor and installer (which allows you to insert any of the installation disks and double-click separate items rather than go through a complete installation again solely to install missing filters, etc.).

- PageMaker's resources under Windows are organised in a different way to those on the Macintosh. They are, however, organised in a way that will be familiar to you if you already use Windows.

- If you need but can't find any of the files mentioned here you should install them from the PageMaker installation disks.

- A separate Table Editor program is provided under Windows which is useful if you need to present material as complex tables.

- PostScript Printer Description (PPD) files used in the Print… dialog box are located in the Extensions folder.

- Copy Fit (in the Utilities folder) is a very useful text file for working out type sizes and word counts at the design stage.

Index to PageMaker   A2

This index will help you to find options within PageMaker. Each option is listed in alphabetic order together with the path you need to take through the menus to reach it.

For example if you want to change text to capital letters, look up All caps and you will see that to find that particular option you need to select the *Type* menu first, then *Type specs...* (on the *Type* menu) and finally the Case option (in the dialog box that appears).

Menu names and menu items are shown in *italic*; dialog box options are shown in normal type.

25% size (*Layout ➡ View*)
50% size (*Layout ➡ View*)
75% size (*Layout ➡ View*)
200% size (*Layout ➡ View*)
400% size (*Layout ➡ View*)
Acquire image... (*Utilities ➡ Aldus Additions*)
Actual size (*Layout ➡ View*)
Add cont'd line... (*Utilities ➡ Aldus Additions*)
Add hyphenation (*Type ➡ Hyphenation...* ➡ Add...)
Add word to user dictionary (*Utilities ➡ Spelling...* ➡ Add...)
Aldus Additions (*Utilities*)
Alert before updating (*File ➡ Links...* ➡ Options)
Alert storing graphics over (*File ➡ Preferences...* ➡ Other...)
Align centre (*Type ➡ Alignment*)
Align left (*Type ➡ Alignment*)

Align right (*Type ➡ Alignment*)
Align to grid (Control palette)
Align to grid (*Type ➡ Paragraph...* ➡ Rules... ➡ Options...)
Alignment (Control palette)
Alignment (*Type ➡ Paragraph...*)
Alignment (*Type*)
All caps (*Type ➡ Type specs...* ➡ Case)
All to process (*File ➡ Print...* ➡ Colour)
Angle (*Element ➡ Image control...*)
Apply (Control palette)
Autoflow (*Layout*)
Autoflow display all pages (*File ➡ Preferences...* ➡ Other...)
Autoleading (*Type ➡ Paragraph...* ➡ Spacing...)
Balance columns... (*Utilities ➡ Aldus Additions*)
Baseline offset (Control palette)
Baseline shift (Control palette)
Baseline shift (*Type ➡ Type specs...* ➡ Options...)
Book... (*File*)
Break (*Type ➡ Type specs...*)
Bring to front (*Element*)
Build booklet... (*Utilities ➡ Aldus Additions*)
Bullets and numbering... (*Utilities ➡ Aldus Additions*)
Cascade (*Window*)
Case (Control palette)
Case (*Type ➡ Type specs...*)
Centre page in print area (*File ➡ Print...* ➡ Paper)

Change… (*Utilities*) in Story editor
Clear (*Edit*)
Close (*File*)
Close story (*Story*) in Story editor
Collate (*File* ➡ *Print…*)
Colour (*File* ➡ *Print…*)
Colour (*Type* ➡ *Type specs…*)
Colour libraries (*Element* ➡ *Define colours…* ➡ *Edit/New…*)
Colour model (*Element* ➡ *Define colours…* ➡ *Edit/New…*)
Colour palette (*Window*)
Colour type (*Element* ➡ *Define colours…* ➡ *Edit/New…*)
Column break before (*Type* ➡ *Paragraph…*)
Column guides… (*Layout*)
Compose to printer (*File* ➡ *Page setup…/New…*)
Composite print (*File* ➡ *Print…* ➡ *Colour*)
Contrast (*Element* ➡ *Image control…*)
Control palette (*Window*)
Control palette nudge (*File* ➡ *Preferences…*)
Convert quotes (*File* ➡ *Place…*)
Copies (*File* ➡ *Print…*)
Copy (*Edit*)
Copy all linked files (*File* ➡ *Save as…*)
Copy colours (*Element* ➡ *Define colours…* ➡ *Copy…*)
Copy files for remote printing (*File* ➡ *Save as…*)
Copy master guides (*Layout*)
Create colour library… (*Utilities* ➡ *Aldus Additions*)
Create index… (*Utilities*)
Create keyline… (*Utilities* ➡ *Aldus Additions*)
Create new library (*Window* ➡ *Library palette* ➡ *New library*)

Create TOC… (*Utilities*)
Crop (*Control palette*)
Cursor position (*Control palette*)
Cut (*Edit*)
Define colours… (*Element*)
Define styles (*Type*)
Dictionary (*Type* ➡ *Paragraph…*)
Display 'paragraph marks' (*Story*) in Story editor
Display images (*Window* ➡ *Library palette* ➡ *Options*)
Display master items (*Layout*)
Display names (*Window* ➡ *Library palette* ➡ *Options*)
Display pub info… (*Utilities* ➡ *Aldus Additions*)
Display story info… (*Utilities* ➡ *Aldus Additions*)
Display style names (*Story*) in Story editor
Display textblock info… (*Utilities* ➡ *Aldus Additions*)
Double-sided (*File* ➡ *Page setup…/New…*)
Drop cap… (*Utilities* ➡ *Aldus Additions*)
Duplex (*File* ➡ *Print…* ➡ *Paper*)
Edit colour (*Element* ➡ *Define colours…* ➡ *Edit/New…*)
Edit original (*Edit*)
Edit story (*Edit*)
Edit tracks… (*Utilities* ➡ *Aldus Additions*)
Editions(*Edit*)
EPS (*File* ➡ *Print…* ➡ *Options*)
Expert kerning… (*Utilities* ➡ *Aldus Additions*)
Export… (*File*)
Facing pages (*File* ➡ *Page setup…/New…*)
Fill (*Element*)
Fill and line… (*Element*)

Find next (*Utilities*) in Story editor
Find overset text (*Utilities* ➧ *Aldus Additions*)
Find... (*Utilities*) in Story editor
Fit in window (*Layout* ➧ *View*)
Font (Control palette)
Font (*Type* ➧ *Type specs...*)
Font (*Type*)
Force justify (*Type* ➧ *Alignment*)
Go to page... (*Layout*)
Graphic (*File* ➧ *Place...*)
Graphic detail (*File* ➧ *Preferences...*)
Graphics optimised (*File* ➧ *Print...* ➧ Options)
Greek text below (*File* ➧ *Preferences...* ➧ *Other...*)
Grey levels (*Element* ➧ *Image control...*)
Grey out graphics (*File* ➧ *Preferences...*)
Greyscale (*File* ➧ *Print...* ➧ Colour)
Grid size (Control palette)
Grid size (*Type* ➧ *Paragraph...* ➧ Rules... ➧ Options...)
Guides (*Layout* ➧ *Guides and rulers*)
Guides and rulers (*Layout*)
Guides to front/back (*File* ➧ *Preferences...*)
Help... (*Window*)
High-resolution graphics (*File* ➧ *Preferences...*)
Hyphenation zone (*Type* ➧ *Hyphenation...*)
Hyphenation... (*Type*)
Image control... (*Element*)

Import Fetch items (*Window* ➧ *Library palette* ➧ Options)
In-line graphic (*File* ➧ *Place...*)
Include book publications in TOC (*Utilities* ➧ *Create TOC...*)
Include in table of contents (*Type* ➧ *Paragraph...*)
Include PostScript error handler (*File* ➧ *Print...* ➧ Options)
Indent (Control palette)
Indents (*Type* ➧ *Paragraph...*)
Indents/tabs (*Type*)
Index entry... (*Utilities*)
Insert object (*Edit*)
Insert pages... (*Layout*)
Insert text (*File* ➧ *Place...*)
Justify (*Type* ➧ *Alignment*)
Keep lines together (*Type* ➧ *Paragraph...*)
Keep with next (*Type* ➧ *Paragraph...*)
Kern (Control palette)
Kerning (*Type* ➧ *Paragraph...* ➧ *Spacing...*)
Layout problems (*File* ➧ *Preferences...*)
Leading (Control palette)
Leading (*Type* ➧ *Type specs...*)
Leading (*Type*)
Leading method (*Type* ➧ *Paragraph...* ➧ *Spacing...*)
Left master page (*Layout* ➧ *Go to page...*)
Letter space (*Type* ➧ *Paragraph...* ➧ *Spacing...*)
Library palette (*Window*)
Lightness (*Element* ➧ *Image control...*)

Limit consecutive hyphens (*Type* ➡ *Hyphenation…*)
Line (*Element*)
Lines/in (*Element* ➡ *Image control…*)
Link info… (*Element*)
Link options (*File* ➡ *Links…*)
Link options… (*Element*)
Links… (*File*)
List styles used (*Utilities* ➡ *Aldus Additions*)
Lock guides (*Layout* ➡ *Guides and rulers*)
Low TIFF resolution (*File* ➡ *Print…* ➡ *Options*)
Manual hyphenation (*Type* ➡ *Hyphenation…*)
Map fonts… (*File* ➡ *Preferences…*)
Margins (*File* ➡ *Page setup…/New…*)
Max size of internal bitmap (*File* ➡ *Preferences…* ➡ *Other…*)
Measurement system (*File* ➡ *Preferences…*)
Mirror (*File* ➡ *Print…* ➡ *Colour*)
MM Fonts (*Type* ➡ *Type specs…*)
Multiple paste… (*Edit*)
Negative (*File* ➡ *Print…* ➡ *Colour*)
New library… (*Window* ➡ *Library palette* ➡ *Options*)
New story (*Story*) in Story editor
New… (*File*)
No break (*Type* ➡ *Type specs…*)
Nudge in Control palette (*File* ➡ *Preferences…*)
Number of columns (*Layout* ➡ *Column guides…*)
Number of pages (*File* ➡ *Page setup…/New…*)
Omit TIFF files (*File* ➡ *Print…* ➡ *Options*)
Open library… (*Window* ➡ *Library palette* ➡ *Options*)
Open stories (*Utilities* ➡ *Aldus Additions*)
Open template… (*Utilities* ➡ *Aldus Additions*)
Open… (*File*)
Optimised screen (*File* ➡ *Print…* ➡ *Colour*)
Orientation (*File* ➡ *Page setup…/New…*)
Orientation (*File* ➡ *Print…*)
Orphan control (*Type* ➡ *Paragraph…*)
Overprint (*Element* ➡ *Define colours…* ➡ *Edit/New…*)
Overprint (*Element* ➡ *Fill and line…*)
Page break before (*Type* ➡ *Paragraph…*)
Page dimensions (*File* ➡ *Page setup…/New…*)
Page independence (*File* ➡ *Print…*)
Page information (*File* ➡ *Print…* ➡ *Options*)
Page number format (*File* ➡ *Page setup…/New…* ➡ *Numbers…*)
Page ranges (*File* ➡ *Print…*)
Page setup… (*File*)
Page size (*File* ➡ *Page setup…/New…*)
Pair kerning (*Type* ➡ *Paragraph…* ➡ *Spacing…*)
Pantone… (*Element* ➡ *Define colours…* ➡ *New…*)
Paper (*File* ➡ *Print…*)
Paper size (*File* ➡ *Print…* ➡ *Paper*)
Paper source (*File* ➡ *Print…* ➡ *Paper*)
Paragraph rules (*Type* ➡ *Paragraph…* ➡ *Rules…* ➡ *Options…*)
Paragraph space (*Type* ➡ *Paragraph…*)
Paragraph style (Control palette)
Paragraph… (*Type*)
Paste (*Edit*)
Paste link (*Edit*)
Paste special (*Edit*)
Percent scale (Control palette)

Place… (*File*)

Position (Control palette)

Position (*Type* ➟ *Type specs…*)

Posterise (*Element* ➟ *Image control…*)

PostScript (*File* ➟ *Print…* ➟ Options)

Preferences… (*File*)

Preferences… (*Window* ➟ *Library palette* ➟ *Options*)

Preserve character shape in TrueType (*File* ➟ *Preferences…* ➟ Other…*)

Preserve EPS colours (*File* ➟ *Print…* ➟ Colour)

Preserve line spacing TrueType (*File* ➟ *Preferences…* ➟ Other…*)

Print all publications in book (*File* ➟ *Print…*)

Print area (*File* ➟ *Print…* ➟ Paper)

Print blank pages (*File* ➟ *Print…*)

Print colours in black (*File* ➟ *Print…* ➟ Colour)

Print inks (*File* ➟ *Print…* ➟ Colour)

Print to (*File* ➟ *Print…*)

Printer resolution scale (Control palette)

Printer styles… (*Utilities* ➟ *Aldus Additions*)

Printer type (*File* ➟ *Print…*)

Printer's marks (*File* ➟ *Print…* ➟ Options)

Print… (*File*)

Proof (*File* ➟ *Print…*)

Proportional scale (Control palette)

Proxy (Control palette)

PS Group it (*Utilities* ➟ *Aldus Additions*)

PS Ungroup it (*Utilities* ➟ *Aldus Additions*)

Quit (*File*)

Read tags (*File* ➟ *Place…*)

Reduce to fit (*File* ➟ *Print…* ➟ Paper)

Reflect horizontal/vertical (Control palette)

Remove colour (*Element* ➟ *Define colours…* ➟ Remove)

Remove item… (*Window* ➟ *Library palette* ➟ *Options*)

Remove pages… (*Layout*)

Remove transformation (*Element*)

Replace entire story (*File* ➟ *Place…*)

Replace existing TOC (*Utilities* ➟ *Create TOC…*)

Restart page numbering (*File* ➟ *Page setup…/New…*)

Restore original colour (*Element*)

Retain cropping data (*File* ➟ *Place…*)

Retain format (*File* ➟ *Place…*)

Reverse (*Type* ➟ *Type specs…*)

Reverse (*Type* ➟ *Type style*)

Reverse line (*Element* ➟ *Fill and line…*)

Reverse order (*File* ➟ *Print…*)

Revert (*File*)

Right master page (*Layout* ➟ *Go to page…*)

Rotate (Control palette)

Rounded corners… (*Element*)

Rule above paragraph (*Type* ➟ *Paragraph…* ➟ Rules…)

Rule below paragraph (*Type* ➟ *Paragraph…* ➟ Rules…)

Rulers (*Layout* ➟ *Guides and rulers*)

Rules… (*Type* ➡ *Paragraph…*)
Run script… (*Utilities* ➡ *Aldus Additions*)
Running headers\footers… (*Utilities* ➡ *Aldus Additions*)
Save (*File*)
Save as… (*File*)
Save faster/smaller (*File* ➡ *Preferences…*)
Save preview (*File* ➡ *Save as…*)
Scale (Control palette)
Scale (*File* ➡ *Print…* ➡ *Paper*)
Screen (*Element* ➡ *Image control…*)
Screen angle (*File* ➡ *Print…* ➡ *Colour*)
Screen ruling (*File* ➡ *Print…* ➡ *Colour*)
Scroll bars (*Layout* ➡ *Guides and rulers*)
Search library… (*Window* ➡ *Library palette* ➡ *Options*)
Select all (*Edit*)
Send data faster/hex (*File* ➡ *Print…* ➡ *Options*)
Send to back (*Element*)
Separations (*File* ➡ *Print…* ➡ *Colour*)
Set left/right pages separately (*Layout* ➡ *Column guides…*)
Set width (Control palette)
Set width (*Type* ➡ *Type specs…*)
Set width (*Type*)
Show all items (*Window* ➡ *Library palette* ➡ *Options*)
Show clipboard (*Window*)
Show index… (*Utilities*)
Show keeps violations (*File* ➡ *Preferences…*)
Show loose/tight lines (*File* ➡ *Preferences…*)
Show pasteboard (*Layout* ➡ *View*)

Size (Control palette)
Size (Control palette)
Size (*Type* ➡ *Type specs…*)
Size (*Type*)
Skew (Control palette)
Small caps (*Type* ➡ *Type specs…* ➡ Case)
Small caps size (*Type* ➡ *Type specs…* ➡ *Options…*)
Snap to constraints in Control palette (*File* ➡ *Preferences…*)
Snap to guides (*Layout* ➡ *Guides and rulers*)
Snap to rulers (*Layout* ➡ *Guides and rulers*)
Solarise (*Element* ➡ *Image control…*)
Sort pages… (*Utilities* ➡ *Aldus Additions*)
Space before/after (Control palette)
Space between columns (*Layout* ➡ *Column guides…*)
Spacing… (*Type* ➡ *Paragraph…*)
Spelling… (*Utilities*) in Story editor
Standoff (*Element* ➡ *Text wrap…*)
Start page # (*File* ➡ *Page setup…/New…*)
Stop all editions (*Edit* ➡ *Editions*)
Store copy in publication (*File* ➡ *Links…* ➡ *Options*)
Story editor display para marks (*File* ➡ *Preferences…* ➡ *Other…*)
Story editor display style names (*File* ➡ *Preferences…* ➡ *Other…*)
Story editor font (*File* ➡ *Preferences…* ➡ *Other…*)
Style (Control palette)
Style (*Type*)
Style palette (*Window*)
Sub/superscript (Control palette)
Subscribe to… (*Edit* ➡ *Editions*)

Subscriber options… (*Edit* ➡ *Editions*)
Subscript (*Type* ➡ *Type specs…* ➡ Position)
Subscript position (*Type* ➡ *Type specs…* ➡ Options…)
Super/subscript size (*Type* ➡ *Type specs…* ➡ Options…)
Superscript (*Type* ➡ *Type specs…* ➡ Position)
Superscript position (*Type* ➡ *Type specs…* ➡ Options…)
Tab leader (*Type* ➡ *Indents/tabs…*)
Tab position (*Type* ➡ *Indents/tabs…*)
Target printer resolution (*File* ➡ *Page setup…/New…*)
Template (*File* ➡ *Save as…*)
Text flow (*Element* ➡ *Text wrap…*)
Text wrap… (*Element*)
Thumbnails (*File* ➡ *Print…* ➡ Paper)
Tile (*File* ➡ *Print…* ➡ Paper)
Tile (*Window*)
TOC and index prefix (*File* ➡ *Page setup…*)
Tool palette (*Window*)
Tool palette (*Window*)
Track (Control palette)
Track (*Type* ➡ *Type specs…*)
Track (*Type*)
Transparent background (*Element* ➡ *Fill and line…*)
Traverse textblocks… (*Utilities* ➡ *Aldus Additions*)
TrueType options (*File* ➡ *Preferences…* ➡ Other…)
Type specs… (*Type*)
Type style (Control palette)

Type style (*Type* ➡ *Type specs…*)
Type style (*Type*)
Undo (*Edit*)
Unlink (*File* ➡ *Links…*)
Update automatically (*File* ➡ *Links…* ➡ Options)
Update PPD… (*Utilities* ➡ *Aldus Additions*)
Use paper settings of each publication (*File* ➡ *Print…*)
Use snap to in Control palette (*File* ➡ *Preferences…*)
Use Symbol font (*File* ➡ *Print…* ➡ Options)
Use typographer's quotes (*File* ➡ *Preferences…* ➡ *Other…*)
Vertical ruler (*File* ➡ *Preferences…*)
View (*Layout*)
Widow control (*Type* ➡ *Paragraph…*)
Word space (*Type* ➡ *Paragraph…* ➡ Spacing…)
Wrap option (*Element* ➡ *Text wrap…*)
Write PostScript to file (*File* ➡ *Print…* ➡ Options)
Zero lock (*Layout* ➡ *Guides and rulers*)

Acknowledgements

I am very grateful to all those who took the time and trouble to send me comments on my previous PageMaker 4 book. The book owes much to them for their helpful suggestions and constructive criticisms, most of which have been taken into account during the production of this PageMaker 5 version of the book.

*A special thanks to my wife, Adelaide,
for her encouragement and support, and to my children
Mark, Paul and Lisa for their patience—yes, I have now finished the
book! Which direction is the beach?*

Index

800% view 6

A

A5 publications 44
About PageMaker... 1, 50
Active
   publication 39
   reference point 29
Actual size 6
Add
   tab 25
Add cont'd line... 42
Adding
   images to a library 35
   pages 40
Aldus Additions 36, 40, 41, 42, 43, 44
Aldus folder 41
Aldus manuals 50
Alias to PageMaker 1
Align to grid 20
Aligning
   columns of text 25, 49
Alignment 12, 15, 18
All capitals 15
Alternate between character and
     paragraph views 20
Anchor a graphic 33
Apply button 20, 29

B

Applying
   colours 37
   fonts 20
   styles 20, 22
Ask your printers 47
Asymmetric column guides 7
ATM 27
Attaching a line to a paragraph 18
Autoflow 5, 17
Autoflow display 48
Automatic kerning 49
Automatic leading 19

Back-to-back printing 2
Background printing 46
Backup copies 11
Balance columns... 42
Based on: 21
Baseline leading 19
Baseline offset 33
Baseline shift 20
Before you begin 1
Big files 36
Binding 44
Bit-map fonts 27
Bit-mapped
   images 2, 32
Book list 23, 45
Book... 45
Booklet 44

Bookmarks
   in Help 14
Break words
   at the end of a line 26
Bring to front 7
Build booklet... 44
Bullet 25
Bullets and numbering... 41

C

Camera-ready copy 46
Cascade 39
Change... 16, 24
Changing
   defaults 13
   presets 28
   styles 22
   text 15
Changing the position of a tab 25
Character count 41
Character view 20
Check a particular block of text 24
Choosing a tool 3
Circles 28
Close all 39
Close story 16
Close-up zoom 6
CMYK 38
Co-ordinates 29
Collating multiple copies 46

Colour 37, 46
  in imported graphics 38
  printing 38
  proofing 38
  separation 38
Colour of text 19
Colour palette 37
Column guides… 4
  moving 7
  stretching text blocks 8
Columns 4, 7
Commercial Printing Guide 31
Composite 38
Configuration 1
Connecting documents
  in a book list 45
Consistency 4, 23, 49
Consistency in design 40, 45
Consistent use of colours 43
Continuation lines 42
Contrast 32
Control palette 3, 13, 20, 21, 22, 29, 30, 33
Copy 10
Copy an item from a library 35
Copying
  a book list 45
  items between publications 39
  style definitions 22
Correct page sequence 44
Courier 47
Create colour library… 37, 43
Create index… 45
Create keyline… 43

Create TOC… 23, 45
Creating
  a library 35
  columns 4
Cropping graphics 7, 9
Cropping tool 3, 9
Cross-hair cursor 3
Cursor position 20
Custom lines 28
Customising
  rulers 13
  text wrap 34
  the program 13
Cut 8, 9

D
Date/time
  stamping 46
Defaults 13
Define colours… 37, 43
Define styles… 21, 22
Deleting
  a text wrap diamond 34
  an item from a library 35
  graphics 9
  tabs 25
Deselecting 7
  graphics 9
Design 1, 49
  considerations 4, 12
  decisions 21
Diagonal line 3
Dictionary 24
Differentiating between text blocks 5

Dimensions 2
Discretionary hyphen 26
Display master items 4
Display pub info… 36, 43
Display story/textblock info… 41
Display style names (in Story editor) 16
Dotted lines 28
Double-sided publications 2, 4, 11
Downloadable fonts 47
Downward arrow 5
Drag and drop copying 39
Drag place 17
Drawing
  box around text 28
  lines 3, 28
  squares and circles 3
Drawing tools 28
Drop cap… 41

E
Edit a style quickly 22
Edit original 36
Edit story 16, 24
Edit tracks… 41
Editing
  library details 35
  styles 22
  values 29
Editing tools 16
Emphasis 49
Enlarged first letter 41
EPS 42
EPS (Encapsulated PostScript) 47
EPS colours 37

Expert kerning... 41, 49
External graphics 36

F
Facing pages 2
Fill 28
Fill and line... 28
Filter 5
Find and change 24
Find next 16
Find overset text 41
Find... 16
Fine movement 29
Fit in window 6
Flip 29, 30
Flowing text 17
Font 15, 20, 26
    formats 27
    matching 27
    resolution 27
Fonts
    used in a publication 43
Force justify 18
Form vs content 49
Formatting
    paragraphs 18, 22
    retained 15
    several paragraphs 18
    text 3, 8, 15, 20
Four-colour printing 38

G
Get info 1
Getting Started manual 50
Go to page... 40
Grabber hand 6
Graphic
    behind text 34
    customised text wrap 34
    moving text wrap handle 34
    text wrap 34
Graphics 9
    embedded in text 33
    format 9
    from paint programs 32
    grey 48
    in a word processor 33
    in-line 9
    retain proportions 9
Grey shades 31
Greys 32
Grid size 20
Grouping objects 42
Guides 12, 13
Guides and rulers
    snap to 5

H
Handles 8
Hanging indent 25
Hard disk
    navigation 48

Headers and footers 10
Help 38
    shortcuts 14
Hot-spot 14
Hyphenation 24
    control 49
Hyphenation... 26

I
Image control... 31, 32
Image effects 32
Imagesetters 31, 47
Import filters 17
Importing
    graphics 9
    styles 22
In-line graphics 9
Inches 2
Include in table of contents 23
Indent markers 25
Indents 18, 20
Indents/Tabs... 25
Indexing 44
    viewing markers 45
Inline boxes 33
Inline graphic 33
    back to independent graphic 33
Insert pages... 5, 40
Insertion point 16
Installation 1
Internal help 14

Internet
    email contact 50
Interrupting the screen 48

J
Justifying text 26

K
Keep document sizes down 48
Keep text together 15
Kerning 20, 49
Keyboard control 20
Keyline 43
Keywords
    in help 14
Knockout 37

L
Landscape 2
Launch 1
Layers 7, 13
Layout grid 12
Layout problems 26
Layout view 16
Leader 25
Leading 15, 20
    methods 19
Learning more about PageMaker 14, 50
Letter spacing 26
Libraries
    colour 37
Library palette 35
Licence 2
Limiting a search 24

Line art 32
Line drawings 31
Line screen 31
Lines 28. *See also* Rules
Link
    management 36
    preferences 36
List styles used 43
Loaded
    graphic icon 9, 35
    text icon 5, 17
Local formatting 15
Locating words 16
Lock guides 7, 12
Loose/tight lines 26

M
Maintaining ratio 9
Manipulating objects 20, 29
Manipulating tabs 25
Manual flow 17
Manual rotation 30
Manuals 50
Margin guides 3
Margins 2
Master pages 3, 4, 10, 49
    headers and footers 42
    icons 3, 40
    page number markers 44
Meaningful style names 21
Measurement
    cycling 29
    preferences 13
    units 2

Menu options
    presets 13
Menu shortcuts 48
Millimetres 2
Mirror graphics 30
Mirror printing 38
Modifying
    an object 28
    images 32
    text 7
Move objects 20
Moving 29
    column guides 7
    from field to field 2
    from page to page 3, 40
    from textblock to textblock 41
    graphics 9
    page numbers 10
    text blocks 8
    through layers 7
    to another page 4
Moving pages
    in a booklet 44
Multiple paste... 48
Multiple windows 39

N
Navigating 40
Navigation
    of hard disk 48
Negative 32
Negative masters 38
Network Copy Detection 2
New library 35

New publication 2, 6
New... 2
No Break 15
Notes
    in Help 14
Nudge
    buttons 20, 29, 30
    icons 33
    values 13
Number paragraphs 41
Numbers... 2
    format 10

O

Object size 29
On-screen preview 32
Open stories 16, 41
Open template... 42
Open... 36
Options
    for printing 46
Organising work 48
Outline fonts 27
Oval tool 3
Overprint 28, 37
Overriding master settings 4
Oversize pages 46
Overview of PageMaker features 50

P

Page
    icons 3
    information 46
    size 2
    views 6
Page independence 46
Page number markers 10, 45
Page numbers 3, 12
    formatting 2, 10
Page ranges
    printing 11
Page setup... 2, 13, 45
Page slide show 40
Page sorter addition 40
Page structure
    defining 2
Page view
    change all 40
PageMaker
    icon 1
    window 3
Pages
    adding 40
PANOSE 27
Pantone® colours 37
Paper 46
Para... 21

Paragraph
    additional space 18
    emphasis 49
    indents 25
    rules 23
    styles 20, 43, 49
    view 20
Paragraph... 18, 19, 23, 25, 26
Paste 8, 10, 33
Pasteboard 3, 6
Pasting several copies 48
Perfect binding 44
Perpendicular line 3
Photographs 32
Picas 2
Place... 5, 9, 17, 31, 33, 36, 48, 49
    and drag 17
Placing text 5, 17
Planning 48
    decisions 49
    your publication 22
Pointer 3
Pointer tool 48
Points 15, 19
Portrait 2
Position indicator 20
Position objects 20, 29
Position only 36
Position guides 12
Posterise 32
PostScript 47

PostScript files 43
PostScript fonts 27
PPD files 47
Practice sessions 50
Pre-set screen ruling 31
Preferences… 2, 13, 16, 26, 29, 35, 36, 48, 49
Preparation 4
Preset values 13, 20, 26, 32
Print planning 44
Print… 11, 36, 38, 46, 47
Printer 31
Printer fonts 27
Printer styles… 43, 47
Printer's advice 31, 32
Printer's marks 46
Printing 11
   a book list 45
   all inks 38
   back to back 2
   colours 37
   in the background 48
   on an imagesetter 47
   page ranges 11
   print options 11
   queue 43
   to disk 43
Printing options 43
Printing press 31
Production 27
Program preferences 13
Proof 43
   printing 46
Proofread 16

Proportional leading 19
Proportional scaling 29
Proxy 30
PS Group/Ungroup it 42
Publication names 11
Publish 36

Q
Quotation symbols 49

R
Re-establishing links 36
Recommended configuration 1
Rectangle tool 3
Reference point 29, 30
Reflecting 30
Registration card 50
Registration marks 37
Remove item… 35
Remove pages… 40
Remove transformation 30
Removing
   styles 21
   text wrap 34
Repel text from a graphic 34
Resetting ruler origins 3, 12
Resizing
   bit-mapped graphics 2
   graphics 9
   inline graphics 33
   objects 29
   text blocks 8

Resolution 31
   target printer 2
Resolution on screen 36
Retain format option 5
Reverse line 28
Revert 48
RGB 38
Rotating 29
   objects 30
   restricting 30
   text blocks and graphics 3
Rotation tool 3
Rough images 31
Rough work 3
Rounded corners… 28
Ruler guides 12
Ruler origin 3, 48
Rulers 3
   customising 13
Rules (lines) 3, 18, 23, 28
Run script… 42
Running headers\footers… 42

S
Saddle-stitch binding 44
Sample pages 27
Save 4, 11
Save all 39
Save as… 11, 48
   buttons 47
Save regularly 4, 48
Saving effort 10, 43
Scale 29
Scanned photographs 32

Scanner 31
Scans
    high-resolution 36
Screen 31
    dot size 38
    frequency 32
    images 47
    presets 32
Screen font 27
Screen redrawing 13, 34, 48
Script Language Guide 42
Scroll bars 3
Scrolling the window 6
Search and replace 24
Search criteria 35
Search library... 35
Searching through Help 14
Select all 7, 8, 22
Selecting
    a text block 16
    graphics 9
    objects 7
    paragraphs 18
    text 7, 15
    text blocks and graphics 3
Selection 7
Send to back 7
Serial number 1, 50
Series of publications 23
Series of tabs 25
Set width 15

Setting tabs 25
Several publications open at once 39
Shortcuts
    Help 14
Show pasteboard 6
Showing links 36
Simple grid 17
Single-sided publications 3, 4
Size 15
Skewing 29, 30
Slide show 40
Slug 19
Small capitals 15
Snap to guides 5
Snap to rulers 12
Software versions 1
Solarise 32
Sort pages... 40
Space
    before and after paragraphs 18, 20
Space available 1
Spacing
    for justified text 26
Spacing... 19, 26
Speak to your printers 37
Specifications 18
Specifying
    leading 19
    type 15
Spelling... 16, 24
Spot colour 37

Spread 2
Squares 28
Standoff level 34
Starting PageMaker 1, 2
Status
    of linked objects 43
    of links 36
Stop autoflow 17
Story 5, 8
Story editor 15, 16, 24, 30, 33, 39, 41, 45, 48
Stretching a text block 8
Style 20, 26
    benefits 22, 23
    definition 23
    precedence 23
    tabs and indents 25
Style names 16, 43
    typing 20
Style palette 22
Styles 11, 15, 18, 21, 49
    editing 21
Sub/super scripts 15
Subscribe 36

T
Tab icons 25
Tab leaders 25
Table of contents 23, 44
    spanning publications 45
Tabs 25

Talk to your printers 43, 46
Target printer 2
Technical support 1, 50
Tell-tale signs
   of inexperience 49
Templates 11, 42
Test job 47
Text
   colour 19
   convert to capital letters 15
   convert to small capitals 15
   editing 16
   flow 4, 8
   flowing 17
   internal copy 36
   not yet placed 41
   printed over a graphic 32
Text blocks 5, 8
   aligning 42
Text cursor 8, 17
Text icon
   loaded 5
Text patterns
   in headers\footers 42
Text tool 3, 15, 18, 29
Text wrap… 34
Thumbnail view 40
Thumbnails 46
TIFF 32
Tile 39
Titles and captions 5
Tool palette 3
Toolbox 3, 28, 30
Tools 3

Top of caps leading 19
Tour of PageMaker features 50
Track 15
Tracking 20, 49
Transformation 33
Transparent background 28
Trapping colours 43
Traps for the unwary 49
Traverse textblocks… 41
Trimming graphics 3, 9
TrueType fonts 27
Type 13
Type size 20
Type specs… 15, 19, 33, 49
   colour 37
Type style 15
Type width 20
Type… 21
Typeface 26. *See also* Font
Typing mistakes 24
Typing text
   directly onto a page 5

U
Unauthorised use 2
Undo 8, 9, 48
Units 13
Unloading the cursor 5, 8
User Manual 14, 50

V
Versions
   of PageMaker 1, 50
Vertical ruler 48, 49

Vertical space 15, 19
View
   800% 6
   shortcuts 6
View by Icon 1
Viewing a page 6
Visual impact 30, 34, 37

W
Wildcard 24
Windows
   tile/cascade 39
Windowshade handles 8
Word processing
   filters 5, 17
Word processor
   formatting 15
   styles 22
Word spacing 26
Wraparound 34
Write PostScript to file 47
Wysiwyg@iol.ie 50

Z
Zero ruler origins 3
Zoom with accuracy 6

If you would like information on other WYSiWYG Books as they are published or would like a copy of our newsletter, feel free to drop us a line. Faxes and Internet email are also welcome.

Please let us know if you find any errors or omissions. We would also like your comments and suggestions on how this book could be improved.

Special discounts rates are available to those who want to use this book as a core text for teaching.

WYSiWYG Books
Galway Technology Centre
Mervue
Galway
Ireland

Fax: +353 (0)91–755635

Internet email to: wysiwyg@iol.ie